The Greatness Revolution

*Intentionally Living
the Transformed Life of Your Dream*

———————

Brad Thomas

The Greatness Revolution

Copyright 2021 by Brad Thomas, Grand Junction, CO 81504

No part of this publication may be reproduced or transmitted in any form or by any means, electronic or mechanical, including photocopying, recording, or any information storage or retrieval system, without prior permission in writing from the publisher.

ISBN (978-0-578-24873-8)

Printed in USA by 48HrBooks (www.48HrBooks.com)

Thank you Father for all the blessings in my life.

Thank you Jack Schlatter, a true teacher and an amazing storyteller.
Rest in peace. I'll see you again, brother. "God Love Ya!"

Thank you, Margaret. You are my world and my best friend.
Thank you Hannah and Benjamin.
I love watching you both walk in your Greatness!

Table of Contents

Foreword 6

1 The Problem 9

2 Believing is Seeing 15

3 The Shift 28

4 The Stories We Tell 41

5 The Why is Your Dream 55

6 The First Step Toward Your Dream 63

7 The How is Your Plan 76

8 Goals 91

9 The What 99

10 Spirals: The Listen and Learn Technique 109

11 Choice 122

12 C.A.R.: The Vehicle of Your Dream 133

13 Time Flow 156

14 The Three R's of Self-Destruction 168

15 Forgiveness and the Greatest Gift 184

16 The Six F's of a Great Life 202

Table of Contents (continued)

17 Mentors 232

18 A Journey 239

19 Time: Your Best Friend or Your Worst Enemy? 248

20 Transformation 260

21 Faith 268

22 The Greatness Revolution 285

Chapter Notes 305

Foreword

"No man can reveal to you aught but that which lies half asleep in the dawning of your knowledge."
-Kahlil Gibran

Dear Reader,

I am so excited for you . . . You are about to embark on a great adventure that will lead to Greatness, YOUR Greatness.

Thomas Jefferson wrote our 'political' Declaration of Independence. Ralph Waldo Emerson wrote our 'intellectual' Declaration of Independence. And now Brad Thomas has written our 'educational' Declaration of Independence. Brad is truly a Renaissance man: a fantastic teacher of literature, a very talented composer and musician, a successful businessman, and a most inspirational pastor. He has also become very knowledgeable in the fields of philosophy, mythology, history, biology, government, chemistry, and astronomy as you will see as you read these pages.

As I read this masterpiece, I was astounded to see how he blended all of these disciplines into a magnificent symphony of self-discovery. The Greek philosopher Plato observed that most of humanity was chained in a cave of ignorance. Brad has created a path out of that cave that leads to enlightened, self-confidence and the blossoming of the inner genius that lies within all of us.

In *Acres of Diamonds*, Russell Cromwell tells of a farmer named Ali Hafed who owned a prosperous farm, and had a loving family. He sold his farm and left his family in the care of a trusted friend to search for diamonds, which he never found. However, it was later discovered that his farm was the location for the richest diamond mine on Earth. He was sitting on his own "acres of diamonds" and left them in search for treasures outside of himself.

The Greatness Revolution leads one to discover the great

wealth that lies within. Most people go through life totally unaware of the genius and power that lies within their souls. I have read many books that proclaim this truth, but Brad has given us a step-by-step map to reach this gift that was given us at birth. He will guide you in creating an inner lighthouse that will keep you on course to the kingdom of Greatness.

You will learn how to discipline your thoughts so that they become a tremendous force in realizing the life you have always wanted. Emerson said that every great institution is the lengthened shadow of one great person. Every method that Brad shares with you has been tested in his own life, family, classroom and other professions where he has excelled.

This book is filled with spiritual and mental vitamin tablets that will transform your life into the human dynamo your Creator envisioned when He created you. The thoughts and wisdom in these pages will cause you to 'wake up' so you can dream!

In the movie, *Joe Versus The Volcano*, Meg Ryan's character says, "My father says everyone you meet, everyone you see, everyone you talk to is asleep. Only a few very special people are awake, and those people live in a state of constant astonishment." Brad's guidance will inspire you to become one of those 'very special' awakened people.

I have witnessed Brad's magic in the classroom. His secret is that when he encounters a student, he does not see the student's 'problems,' he rejoices in the student's 'potential.' He does not sympathize with their 'pain,' but rather reveals their 'power' to overcome any and all struggles.

He has found diamonds in his three D's: Desire, Discipline, and Determination, which are the building blocks of a Dream. He sees messages and lessons in all of life. The message of the caterpillar that becomes a butterfly will give your soul 'wings.'

This book is a love letter, a gift to humanity, given by a soul who has proven everything he teaches. Page after page you will find yourself coming to love Brad Thomas, and then, in a moment, you will discover that you love the person with whom you are spending 24 hours a day. You will experience a revolution within, a revolution that will lead to Greatness.

From this day forth you will spell impossible, I'M possible!

Jack Schlatter
Published Posthumously
July 5, 1935 – December 19, 2014
Motivational Speaker and
Author of *Gifts by the Side of the Road*[1], *I Am a Teacher*[2], and contributing writer to *Chicken Soup for the Soul*[3]
www.giftsbythesideoftheroad.com

1

The Problem

I have been trying to live my dream for most of my life. The problem was that I didn't know it. For most of my life I have done the right thing. Don't think I am being arrogant here. Actually, I am really being ignorant. And this is one of the big problems. I think more often than not we mistake arrogance for ignorance.

When I say I did the right thing for most of my life, the real question is, "Right according to whom?" I used to think "according to God." Then I realized what I really meant was, "according to me." Then I realized I was calling myself God, in a way, which definitely sounds arrogant, even if I was actually being ignorant.

Doing the right thing, as far as I could tell, had to have something to do with truth. And see, this is where it gets tricky. I mean, what is truth? That's the million dollar question humanity's been asking from the beginning.

I used to think doing the right thing was truth, and maybe that's partially correct. But I realized that when I did the right thing, I was actually doing what I thought was right. It was my perception of what was right. It was my perception of what I thought was true. But then something happened I didn't see coming. I woke up! Not literally, mind you, but spiritually.

I realized that truth might not be what I thought it was. Or maybe truth was more than I thought it was. Or maybe truth was something I would never know completely as I walked this earth. I realized that what I thought was right may have much more to do with what others told me was right and with pleasing the people around me by doing what they said was right.

Don't get me wrong. I think that most of the time what my friends and family were telling me was right was actually probably right, or at least part of what was right, but I also realized I was doing and thinking things because it's what I had always assumed to be true. And at some point in my life, I thought, "Maybe what is true is not what I believe to be true." And that, my friend, is the problem.

I read *Siddhartha* by Herman Hesse in my early twenties and was deeply troubled because it blew up my perceptions of truth. I read *A Prayer for Owen Meany* by John Irving and *Life of Pi* by Yann Martell, and it further heightened my awareness that there may be more to truth than I thought. I delved into very thick books of philosophy and religion. Then, I went deep. Dostoevsky...just wow! I encountered Soren Kierkegaard, and he blew my mind...when I could understand what he was writing. I realized that the right thing might be very different than what I thought.

Don't get me wrong. I really do believe that truth is constant. There really is a right and a wrong. I, of course, am not arrogant enough to believe that I possess absolute truth completely. But the way I see it, if truth is not absolute and constant, then everything is relative, and a relativistic world is not only meaningless but incredibly dangerous. I would suggest that the dangers we face in this world today may stem in large measure from a dogma that truth is relative. This, of course, is not the topic of this book, but I wanted to mention it so you understand where I am coming from.

I ran across this drawing on the internet a few years back and thought it really helped to sum up my relationship with truth. Here it is:

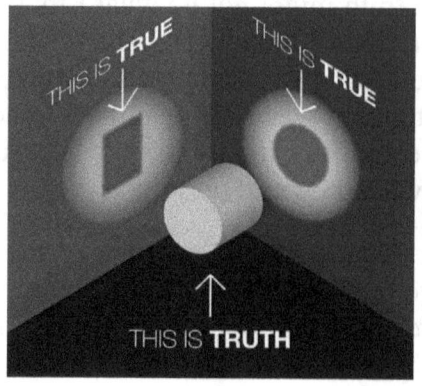

When the light shines on truth, it depends from what angle you view it. Perspective shapes perception, and perception shapes action, and action leads to one's way and quality of life. In Yann Martel's *Life of Pi* there are two stories. Is the first story true, or is the second story true? Maybe the answer is "Yes." It all depends on the angle. And this, my friend, once again, is the problem.

Awareness

Each of us has a conscious mind and a subconscious mind. I read somewhere that, according to some researchers, our conscious mind processes 2,000 bits of information per second while the subconscious mind processes 400 billion bits per second. That's a pretty drastic difference! The conscious mind is dependent on the five senses to prove our conscious thoughts, while the subconscious mind cannot necessarily distinguish between what is real or synthetic, or what is true or false. It basically accepts whatever the conscious mind feeds it. Our conscious mind serves to inform our subconscious mind based on the experiences and thoughts it is having.

What our parents or teachers or trusted people tell us in relationship to our experiences often goes a long way to form our perceptions of who we are and what we believe to be true about us, whether its actually true or not. For example, after failing a test or two in math as a ninth grader, my teacher said to me, "Well, maybe math isn't your thing. You just are not good at math." That was enough for me to believe it, even though up until that moment I had scored in the 95th percentile on all my standardized math tests. The conscious mind's experience of failing a math test, coupled with the words of a trusted adult and the feelings that followed, informed my subconscious to perceive I was a bad math student, even though there was much evidence to the contrary.

Negative Experience + Inaccurate Trusted Input + Negative Emotional Response
=
Negative Perception and Practice

By the same token, one's subconscious mind can also be introduced to a different way of thinking about something. This way of thinking could run contrary to what a person has believed consciously up to that moment, but the possibility of a different way of thinking "awakens" the person's subconscious mind to a new possibility. With the change in the person's level of awareness, coupled with experiences, and the feelings that follow, the possibility of a radically different way of behaving and seeing the world manifests. For example, after trying improvisational comedy in a class and being told by the director that I had a natural talent for comedy and improvisation, I went on to join an improvisation group and perform regularly. This led to doing stand up comedy for a time, which was a great experience. I would not have done any of those things or believed myself capable of those things if not for the experience of improvisational comedy and the words of an expert introducing me to the idea that I had a knack for that type of performance.

Positive Experience + Accurate Trusted Input + Positive Emotional Response
=
Positive Perception and Practice

Awareness is a crucial step to overcoming the obstacles hindering you from living your Dream. If you are ever to live your Dream, you will probably have to change your mind. That truth may be different than you thought is one of the steps to living your Dream, and it's something we will deal with in this book.

Action

Once a new idea sinks into one's subconscious mind, it becomes a belief, and once that belief is acted out, it becomes a reality. But getting to that place calls on one to step out of his or her comfort zone. When an idea moves from the conscious to the subconscious, this is what is most commonly called having a "change of heart." When one's heart changes, the Dream begins to be lived. But changing your mind alone will not empower you to live your Dream. You are going to have to *do* something.

There are four basic ways to make a new idea sink into one's subconscious mind: skills, study, awareness, and action. Of these four, one is more important than the others. You can study your Dream and know everything about it, and still it will not become a reality. You can develop the skills to live your Dream, and still nothing will come of it. You can be aware of your Dream and that it is possible, and still nothing will happen. The truth is that if you had to choose to practice just one of these four ways to get you to your Dream, *action supersedes awareness, skills, and study* because action jump starts the other three.

Once the idea of your Dream has broken into your subconscious mind, the most efficient and effective way to realize your Dream is to act on what you now know. *Study* as much as you can. Develop *skills* to the best of your ability. Be *aware* of your Dream. But more than any of those, *act*! Do something to get you to your Dream. Why? Because the more you act on that newly introduced idea, the more solid it becomes in your subconscious mind (your *heart* if you will), the stronger your belief builds, and the easier it is to recognize it as truth.

The Solution

I've been working on this book for quite a while now. My whole life in fact! We are going to tackle the problem of how to intentionally live the transformed life of your Dream. *Potential* is one of the greatest words in the English language. *Untapped potential* is one of the saddest word combinations in the English language. We are going to walk through the steps necessary to empower you to live your Dream, but even as we walk through them, you are going to have *to act* on these steps. And acting on these steps will be a struggle, sometimes with setbacks. As Paulo Coehlo writes, "[A]re defeats necessary? Well, necessary or not, they happen."[4] So brace yourself for the journey ahead. Know this: You are designed to live The Greatness Revolution. You are designed to live your Dream. You are designed to reach your full potential.

I encourage you to read each chapter. Do the *Your Turn* exercises at the end of each chapter before moving on to the next.

Then, put into practice the directives in this book on a daily basis. Also, check out the *Endnotes* on the diagrams at the beginning of chapters, beginning in *Chapter 3*. Many of the *Endnotes* not only explain the diagrams at the beginning of chapters but will add in-depth explanations to the concepts in the book. Keep your mind open to new ways of seeing yourself, the world, and truth. Keep your heart open to the concepts in this book. And, most importantly, *do something*!

The problem is within you. But so is the solution! (This should bring a smile to your face!) The rest of this book is about that solution. I want you to be who you truly are, living your full potential, bringing all of your gifts to your community and the world because we need you! The only way humanity will ever tackle the obstacles and opportunities before us is when all of us live the unique Dream placed in each of our hearts, a Dream that, I believe, is uniquely designed for each person and can only be lived by each person to the benefit of everyone in this world. Each Dream, in combination with every other, produces Greatness within, Greatness without, and Greatness all around. It's time to start. Are you ready? (This is where you say, "Yes!") Let's go!

2

Believing is Seeing

Danger: High Explosives

C.S. Lewis knew a woman who claimed to have seen a ghost. Despite this, she did not believe in an afterlife. Lewis said this just proves the point that seeing is not believing. Many people *believe* that seeing is believing, that what you see is what you get. We are going to blow that idea up right...now. BOOM! Are you ok? Dust yourself off, and let's proceed.

The Talmud tells us, "We do not see things the way they are; we see them the way we are."[5] In other words, our perception determines how we see the world and our place in it. Seeing is *not* believing. *Believing is seeing.*

Prentice Mulford writes that *thoughts are things*, and James Allen writes that *as a man thinks in his heart, so is he* (King Solomon should actually get credit for the quote. James Allen stole it from Solomon, and I am stealing it back). What we think about, we bring about, so *how we see the world* and our place in it *determines how we live.*

I can remember going to visit my grandparents in Oklahoma during the summers when I was growing up. They would greet me with a hug and then always say something like, "My, how big you are getting. You have changed so much!" I knew what they meant, but I soon realized that what they *meant* and what they *said* were not the same (seems like that goes on a lot in our world).

Many believe that people change and that in order to be great one must change. We are going to blow that idea up right...now. BOOM! Are you ok? I promise that's the last bombshell, for now. Let's keep going.

Did you know that you already possess everything you need within you to live the transformed life of your Dream? Seriously, it's true. You don't have to change. You must simply become more of who you truly are. Every one of us faces this choice: Do I become more and more who people say I am, or do I become more and more who I truly am? I want you to choose the second option. You definitely need to change, but what you may have to change is your thinking. Change the way you think, and you become more of who you truly are. But, it is going to take work, and it will be a struggle at times.

I don't want to burst your bubble or anything, but you need to know: You are not special. If it's any consolation, I am not special either. However, every one of us is *significant*, and that significance is what this book is all about! We are meant to bring our significance to this world we inhabit.

Sign-ificant. What does a sign do? It points to something else, something greater than the sign itself. An "exit" sign on the freeway points to your destination. A billboard sign by the road points to an idea or product that will (hopefully) make a positive impact on your life. You are the *sign* in significance. When you live your Dream, your transformed life, you point to something greater than just you. You are part of something greater, and this is a key to fulfillment.

So, first, *believing is seeing*, and secondly, *everyone is significant*. With these in mind, I'd like to tell you a story, and *you* are the main character.

Spelunking[6]

You find yourself deep in the bottom of a giant cave, seated on the ground, your hands and feet shackled, your head harnessed in such a way that you can only turn it about forty-five degrees in either direction. Looking to your right and left and before you, you see others shackled in the same fashion. You assume others are seated and shackled behind you as well because you hear voices and rattling chains at your back. Looking around, you see thousands of people, just like you, inhabiting the bottom of this cave.

All of you face the same direction, staring at a giant wall. Upon this wall dark shapes of all kinds move to and fro, colliding with each other. You hear all kinds of noises: voices yelling, mumbling, laughing, and crying. You hear strange noises coming from these dark shapes on the wall of the cave. Then suddenly, your shackles fall off!

You slowly stand up, looking at your feet and wrists in wonder. For the first time in your life, you turn your head and body one hundred and eighty degrees, making a complete about face. You see thousands, sitting on the ground, shackled just as you were a moment ago. Looking up, you see something in the distance. Uncertain, you walk toward it, weaving your way through rows of shackled people.

Some one hundred yards away you see an elevated walkway traversing the entire length of the giant cave. On the walkway all kinds of shapes move back and forth. As you approach the walkway, the shapes grow clearer, and you now see people dressed in all kinds of attire, walking, carrying all kinds of objects: animal figures carved out of wood, pieces of vibrant, colored cloth, books, garden tools, bags of groceries, and women carrying infants. Some people lead animals along the pathway.

You are overwhelmed. It's almost too much to take in. Then, your eye is drawn to a dancing light beyond the walkway. And for the first time in your life you see fire!

You climb onto the walkway, trying to stay out of the way of the bustling crowds, peering at the giant bonfire burning some fifty yards further up the cave. Your mind ignites! For the first time in your life you discover the answer to the mystery of your existence in the bottom of the cave.

Slowly, you turn around, look back from where you came, where you once sat, shackled. You see the thousands of chained people, their backs to you. You look beyond them to the giant wall at the base of the cave. You lift your arms in the air, waving them back and forth, and you see a black shape on the wall doing exactly the same thing. You realize all the shapes dancing on the wall, running into each other are but mere shadows of all those people, animals, and objects traversing the walkway in the cave, cast upon the wall by the giant bonfire that burns. You understand that the noises you've heard all your life are the echoing sounds made by those people and animals traversing the walkway.

Everything becomes clear. For most of your life, shackled at the base of the cave, facing the wall, what you considered real was only an illusion. Now you know the truth, what lies beyond your former existence, and you know your life will never be the same. You turn back toward the fire, taking in the light of knowledge. Your perception has radically shifted the way you see everything. You have awakened!

Then, out of the corner of your eye you see a tiny, round light, which, in comparison to the huge bonfire burning, shines much brighter. It is so small yet so intense, and it seems hundreds of yards away.

Suddenly, you find yourself surrounded by the brightest, purest, most intense light. To open your eyes brings piercing pain. But as time passes, your eyes grow accustomed to the light, and ever so slowly you begin to see.

Before you lay large, dazzling, green fields with grasses and cascades of flowers dancing in the slight, warm breeze. And in these fields large, green and blossoming trees sway in the breeze. Under these trees all sorts of animals rest and graze passively. A herd of horses gallop across the fields before you, jumping and whinnying. People drive horse-drawn carts with wagons brimming with fruits, vegetables, and wares of every kind. Children skip and play games together.

Beyond the fields lay houses and buildings with streets where people go about their day buying or selling. Beyond the town you see a huge, blue expanse that seems to go on forever, a deep, blue sea dotted with white sails and cutter ships. You turn around, to see what's behind you.

A large rocky mountain rises into the blue sky, and there, at its base opens a giant mouth to a cave. You've been transported from deep inside that giant mouth. Somehow you know that deep in that cave dwell thousands of people, shackled and bound, who have no idea that this beautiful world even exists.

You turn around again, taking in the beauty. You understand that while in the cave, the bright light you saw in the distance was the mouth you stand before now. Somehow you know that the people on the platform busily bustling to and fro in the cave have no idea what lies beyond.

Suddenly, you find yourself surrounded by deep darkness unable to see anything, but you recognize the noises you hear. It's the rattle of chains and the echoing sounds from the wall.

You reach down, and your hand rests on chains and flesh, and a man's voice yells, "Get off me! Leave me alone!" You look up, barely making out movements dancing on the wall of the cave. The beautiful light of the sun in which you were just immersed has left you blind in the darkness of your former dwelling place.

You stumble around, crying out to those shackled, "This is not real! Brothers and sisters, loose your chains! Rip them from your hands and feet and head! It's all just shadows! It's all illusion!"

As you stumble, yelling in desperation, scornful and mocking voices greet you: "Look at the blind fool! Leave us be!" Others gaze at you, horrified, a monster, an alien who has entered their world. And no matter how much you try to convince them that there is so much more to existence than this, your words fall on deaf ears. They will not see. They will not hear.

Sadly, you realize that all you can do is live what you have seen and heard. You resolve to begin immediately! Now! This very moment!

You've seen it. You've heard it. You've tasted it. You believe it. And so you begin. You turn away from the shadows on the wall, the illusions so many are content to live with, and you walk, beyond the shackled masses, beyond the crowds on the walkway, beyond the bonfire of human understanding, your eyes fixed on the light of the sun, of a world that awaits, of a vast universe, the truth of your existence, which has become your life-force. You walk one step at a time, ascending the steeps of the cave, the obstacles in your path, because you have tasted and seen, and for you, the journey is already done. Now, it is just a matter of walking it out!

Out of the Cave and Into the Light

Some scientists ran a test on a frog. They cut the frog's legs off and then yelled at the frog, "Jump!" The frog didn't jump. The scientists therefore concluded that when frogs lose their legs they become deaf.

It's all about perception. We can be seeing and never perceiving. We can be hearing but really not listening. The ancient proverb, "When the student is ready, the teacher appears" rings as true today as the first time it was spoken. So many of us are spelunking our way through life, shackled by our perceptions about what we see. Just like the scientists with the frog, perhaps we need to change the way we think about our world and our potential to become who we truly are. Perhaps there's more to this world than just meets the eye! Perhaps believing is seeing.

People Don't Change

Many years ago, psychologists studied a group of five-year-old children in New Zealand.[7] They performed personality profiles on the children. They returned ten years later and performed personality profiles once again, and guess what they discovered? The children's personalities remained the same.

When I heard about this study, I actually took the Meyers-Briggs[8] personality test again, the same test I had taken in high school some thirty years ago (give or take a few or many years. . .I admit nothing), and guess what? The outcome was exactly the same. What this New Zealand study led experts to determine was this: *People don't change. They become more fully who they already are.* And this leads us to...the butterfly (of course!).

Caterpillar to Butterfly

The metamorphosis from caterpillar to butterfly is one of the most astounding, surprising, and fascinating transformations in the natural world. Three things stand out about this incredible transformation.

First, *everything that makes the butterfly already exists within the caterpillar.* O.K., I know, I know, not the food it eats and all that stuff. All of the genetic material making the butterfly, all the DNA and all the parts, like the wings and the very different-looking body are all contained within the caterpillar.

If you did not know about metamorphosis, you might be inclined to say, "There is no way that 'slug' of a caterpillar will look and behave like a butterfly." You might believe they were two different creatures. And you would miss this very important lesson: *The butterfly already exists within the caterpillar*, which leads us to a second important idea.

The caterpillar must knit its own cocoon. It cannot waddle up to another butterfly just emerging from its cocoon and say, "Can I borrow your cocoon?" In fact, if the caterpillar does not knit its own cocoon, it will never become the butterfly. It must do its own work. The caterpillar determines whether it becomes what it was naturally intended to become. It is responsible for its destiny. This leads us to the third important idea.

The caterpillar must struggle if it is going to become the butterfly. If you were to see a caterpillar, now butterfly, in its cocoon just beginning to emerge, you would see it struggling to get out. If you had a little knife and said, "You know this butterfly needs some help getting out of this cocoon, so I'll just take my knife and cut open the cocoon just a little bit to make it easier," you would find the butterfly's wings would not correctly form. The actual struggle of the emerging butterfly serves to make the butterfly fully what it is intended to be and do what it is intended to do. Is struggle necessary? Well, necessary or not, it is a reality in a world of entropy. Anything of Greatness will entail struggle. Without the struggle, no butterfly. And without butterflies, beauty in this world is lost, not to mention all of the other organisms relying on the butterfly so they can thrive, becoming what they are intended to be.

You Are a Butterfly

You and I also experience transformation. You are *significant*. Within the word significant is the word *if* and *can't*, but those aren't important right now (I know, I am so funny!). As I mentioned a few pages back, within the word significant is the word *sign*. And what does a sign do? It points to something else. A road sign let's us know what's to come. Often, a sign gives us some information about something much bigger than the information the sign contains. We are each *SIGN*-ificant. We point to something much bigger than ourselves. Our Dreams (or our purpose or calling) always have to do with something bigger than ourselves. They are why we are here, right now. We were uniquely designed to weave our cocoon and become whom we are to bring this Dream to serve our community and world. Our Dream is not only fulfilling for each of us. It is also blessing others. If your Dream is only about you, then that's not a Dream. That's a nightmare!

Every one of us possesses a unique combination of gifts, strengths, or talents. No one else possesses this unique combination, and the world needs us to bring those gifts, strengths, or talents. Humanity is a body made up of many different parts, all different but unique, and each part has a specific role to play to make the body function at its best. If the human body was made up of all eyeballs, well, that would be frightening! That would be a monster. The diversity of the various parts of the body creates a whole person able to accomplish impossible things, things an eyeball or an elbow could not do on its own. The sum is greater than its parts. And it is the same with the community of humanity.

I am about to get all clairvoyant on you right now. Wherever you are reading this, look around you at the room you're in. How many walls are there in this room? Now, here comes the clairvoyant part. Ready? I am gong to tell you how many walls there are in the room, and I am going to be correct for every single person reading this right now! I know! Crazy, huh?

Here we go. The number of walls surrounding you are. . .one. They are just at angles to one another, but they are all connected. Boom! Another bomb! Sorry. I can't help all this shrapnellery (yep. . .I just made up that word. . . Boom! There I go again!). OK, if you are outside by the pool or on the porch, I realize my clairvoyance was severely lacking. Oh well, sometimes you win, sometimes you *learn*.

Now, take a look at your finger. I know, you're like, "What?!" Trust me. This is going to make sense in a minute. . .unless it doesn't. Look at your finger. Now, look at your elbow. Now, look at your kneecap. Let me ask you a simple question: Who is that finger? Who is that elbow? Who is that kneecap? (OK, that was three questions, but they were pretty simple, except for that part about *who* a part of your body was.). Is your finger you? (Hint: the answer is "Yes."). Is your elbow you? (Hint: I shouldn't have to give you a hint now). Is your kneecap you? (Hint: Really? You need a hint after the first two questions? You're killing me smalls!) Here's the *point* of your finger (see what I did there?), your elbow, and your kneecap. It's all you! It's all one. But each part is integral to you functioning at your highest level. Every part of your body is *significant*! Every part of the human body matters, just like all the walls in the room you're in matter and are, from a certain perspective, all one!

Just like the caterpillar, everything making us uniquely us already exists within. Our call is to bring those strengths to life by changing our minds about how we see ourselves based on the lessons of our experiences. We must knit our own cocoon. We are responsible for doing the work necessary to become fully who we truly are. We must not rely on others to do the work for us.

The only way for us to grow into our Greatness is to embrace the work before us and learn from that work. We must struggle if we are to be shaped and transformed. We must not let our struggles define us. Instead, we let our struggles refine us. It is the struggle that helps make us who we are. Just like the caterpillar, without responsibility, work, and struggle we cannot be transformed into who we are truly!

Greatness, What It Is

Your Greatness is who you truly are. It seems to me that all of the people we admire are incredibly comfortable in their own skin. They know who they are, why they are, and what they are called to do. They are focused. They're not perfect, just peaceful.

Take John Maxwell, for example. Here is a man who is the number one expert on Leadership, according to *Inc.* and the American Management Association. He has trained and spoken to millions of people throughout his life. He would be the first to admit he isn't perfect and has weaknesses, but he would also tell you he knows who he is, his strengths, his weaknesses, and most importantly *why* he is, his calling. He is focused.

John Maxwell is a great man. Why? Because he has several companies and is financially successful? No. Because he has been awarded many prestigious awards? No. He is great because he knows who he is and what he is called to do. There is a peace about John Maxwell. It is a peace that passes all understanding because he understands himself. Socrates said, "Know thyself." John Maxwell knows himself and his calling. He is an example of Greatness.

We're In This Together

John Donne writes, "No man is an island entire of itself. . .every man is a part of the main[land]. . .every man's death diminishes me" because I am a part of every man.[9] In other words, we are all connected, like a continent, not an island.

I recently had surgery to have a bone spur removed from my ankle from years of basketball. When I met with the surgeon, he said, "Well, you have one of the largest bone spurs I have ever seen, so we are going to have to cut off your foot and ankle." (gasp!)

Of course, he didn't say that! As I've touched on, when a part of your body, like an ankle, is not functioning, the body compensates for the injury until that part heals and can resume all of its functions within the body. Humanity is a body made up of various parts, all significant and integral to the body thriving, not just surviving.

Amputees often experience phantom pains. Long after a limb is removed, amputees will reach over to touch the leg or arm because it feels as if it is there, and they often experience excruciating pain. The body misses the significant part, and the body's existence is permanently altered.

A lost index finger means tying shoes will be more difficult. A lost big toe throws off the body's entire equilibrium. A lost eye creates difficulties with depth perception. Every part of the body is significant, and every part of humanity is significant, as well. This is why you must use the unique combination of strengths, gifts, or talents you possess. You are the only person who can bring your uniqueness and, in turn, your significance to your community and world.

And remember, those parts that are unseen are more significant than those that get all the attention. Washboard abs are great. If you got 'em, good for you! And a "beautiful face" is great! I highly recommend symmetry! But without a liver, you won't live very long! Without kidneys, you're not going to make it! Without a heart, it's over! Humanity needs a heart! If you're an eye, be an eye! If you're a toe, be a toe! If you're a lung, be a lung! Be who you are, and do what you were designed to do!

All too often we try to be someone we aren't. We try to be Michael Jordan or Lebron James. We try to be Johnny Depp or Tom Cruise. We try to be Steve Jobs or Bill Gates. We try to be Lady Gaga or Usher. We don't need another Lebron James, Johnny Depp, Steve Jobs, or Lady Gaga. We need you!

And let's be honest: you have weaknesses, and you need to know your weaknesses because they too are going to bless the body of humanity. What Brad? My weaknesses will bless humanity? Yes! I love this very famous statement: *When I am weak, I am strong.*[10] Here's the deal: When Socrates said, "Know Thyself," I'm pretty sure he didn't mean just what's good about you, or just what's bad about you. I think he meant know all of you, the good, the bad, the ugly, the beautiful, the strengths, and the weaknesses.

Your weaknesses make you an integral part of humanity as much as your strengths do. Think about it. If my eyesight is not so great, yes I might need glasses, but my body will compensate by making my other senses, like hearing and my sense of smell, more acute. That's what Marvel's *Daredevil* is all about! It's well-documented that people who are blind often have other heightened senses. Our weaknesses allow other parts of the body of humanity to rise to the occasion, to contribute their strengths just as your strengths contribute in areas of others' weakness. Know thyself! Every part of yourself!

Humanity is like a tapestry woven together to create a beautiful, diverse, multi-colored portrait, but when you try to be someone else (usually someone others are telling you to be), you are a missing thread from the tapestry, creating a gap, which leads to a tear in the fabric of humanity, growing larger and larger as humanity faces the difficult challenges of this world. You may think you are just a small thread with little strength, but the strength of your thread, combined with other threads creates the strength to endure and overcome the weight of the world. The loss of each person's unique gifts over time leads to the unraveling of humanity.

So be who you are, and if you don't know your unique combination of strengths, gifts, and talents, start searching and finding them, and bring them to your community and world. This book will get you headed in the right direction!

What Matters

From this chapter remember:

1. Believing is seeing. Your perceptions shape the way you see everything.

2. Everything you need to live a transformed life is already within you.

3. To live a transformed life you must "knit your own cocoon," do your own work. No one can do it for you.

4. To live a transformed life you must struggle. Necessary or not, struggle is a part of the process, and all transformed people embrace struggle.

5. You are a significant part of humanity, and you have a unique set of gifts or talents you are meant to bring to humanity and this world. Without you humanity is less.

So where does this transformation begin? With The Shift!

Your Turn

Step One: Write down at least two ideas from this chapter which impacted your thinking.

Step Two: Describe a moment in your life when what you thought was true about the moment was actually an illusion (like the shadows on the cave wall). What was really true about this moment? How did the experience make you feel? How do you feel about it now, looking back? What did you learn?

Step Three: Before reading the next chapter, what do you think The Shift means? Write down your thoughts.

STOP! DO NOT READ ON UNTIL YOU'VE COMPLETED THE *YOUR TURN* SECTION OF THIS CHAPTER.

3

The Shift

11

Making Waves

It is one of the largest, most powerful natural forces on the planet. It remains practically imperceptible until it reaches the shore. And where did it originate? Deep in the center of the ocean, the crust of the earth shifts a mere four inches and, out of that four-inch shift a wave begins, building momentum, crossing a thousand miles of ocean at six hundred miles per hour, towering one-hundred feet as it rapidly approaches the shore. From an imperceptible four-inch shift comes a massive, overwhelming force. A tsunami.

A Different Kind of Wave

So, I know, you're saying, "Brad a tsunami, tidal wave, a.k.a. massive wall of ocean racing toward those on the land, is destructive!" Yes, I get it. The point is that out of a small shift comes massive momentum and force. We are called to be a different kind of tsunami, by changing our minds about *who* we are, *why* we are, *when* we are. Just a slight shift in the way we see the world and our place in it creates momentum and a force for positive change in our lives and the lives of those with whom we have relationships.

When you make The Shift you change your mind about whom you are capable of being and what you are capable of accomplishing. When you make The Shift, you begin to value significance over success (We'll unpack that later.). When you make The Shift, you stop seeing with your eyes and start seeing with your heart. When you make The Shift, you stop seeing things as they are and start seeing things as they could be. When you make The Shift, you stop focusing on the probable, and you start focusing on the possible. When you make The Shift you turn your *maybe* into *will be*.

Super Computer

It is the most powerful processor, working a trillion computations in any given second. No super computer comes close to its potential computations. What is this super computer? Your brain! And, like the shift of the crust of the earth deep in the center of the ocean that brings massive momentum and overwhelming force in the form of a tsunami, the time has come to make The Shift in your mind!

Remember that Cave from the last chapter? It's time to break free of the shackles holding you in the bottom of the cave of illusion, to make an about face, to see and hear the truth with new eyes and ears. Remember the metamorphosis of the caterpillar to butterfly from the last chapter? It's time to begin to knit your own cocoon and be transformed into the person you truly are. It's time to make The Shift.

Change your mind, and realize who you truly are! Access your untapped potential and unlock your Greatness! Become a tsunami of positivity, impacting your future and the future of others in your life. Become a gift and a blessing to the community and world you inhabit by seeing the blessing in every situation.

Decide Now!

So, what is The Shift? It is changing your mind! And guess what? You can do that in an instant! Right now! I'm not kidding. You can do it right now! You don't have to be like those scientists seeing legless, deaf frogs.

When you look at your life, what do you think? What thoughts do you replay every day about *who* you are, *why* you are, *when* you are? Are they positive or negative? Do they tell you, "Impossible!" Or do they tell you, "I'm possible"? Do they keep you from manifesting your Dream? Or do they spur you on to living *who* you are? Because the truth is *you control your mind*.

You decide what you think. You get to choose how you see yourself and the world around you.

When my son, Ben, was in tenth grade, he struggled with seeing the world, his situation, and his schooling from middle school on positively, so much so that my wife and I had to have several talks with him about what was going on. We were deeply concerned and expressed that to him, saying we were willing to do whatever it took to help him with shifting his perspective. Then, what seemed overnight, our bright, happy, positive Benjamin showed up one day! When I asked him what changed, he said, "I was tired of being negative, so I decided to be happy." And that was it. He simply made a decision and acted upon it.

A little four-inch Shift in your mind is all it takes to walk in your Greatness. Just a simple change in thinking. It moves us from a seeing-is-believing to a believing-is-seeing mind set, from a fixed mind-set to a growth mind-set (We'll talk more about this later in the book.). The Shift that needs to take place differs for everyone.

The Accuser

OK, so you know that voice? The one you wake up with, and who stays with you all day? The one that tries to get you down and keep you there? The one that never relents? Ya, that one. I like to call him The Accuser because that's what he is. He's that voice that points out everything you've done wrong, you're doing wrong, or you're going to mess up because of what you've done wrong in the past. He's the one who tells you that you weren't good enough, you aren't good enough, and you'll never be good enough. He's the one who comes to steal your day, kill your Dream, and rob your joy. Ya, that voice!

And here's the thing: he doesn't show up in the big things. He shows up in the little things. You know what I mean? The big stuff I'm prepared for. It's in those little moments when I'm not suspecting his accusations that he does most of his work.

One of the Accuser's major weapons is fear. It's been said that we are born with only two fears: the fear of falling and the fear of loud noises. But very quickly the Accuser works his way into our minds and starts rattling off more fears until we find ourselves paralyzed by those fears. Ever struggled with any of these: Fear of failure? Loss? Losing control? Not fitting in? Rejection? Being uncomfortable? Vulnerability? Judgment? Not being accepted? What others think of you? Pain? Illness? Death? Inadequacy? Loneliness? Powerlessness? Being exposed as a poser, a hypocrite, or a pretender?

A second weapon the Accuser uses on us is shame. In his book, *Crash the Chatterbox*, Steven Furtick explains that shame shows up and practices The Three P's on us. Shame is personal, pervasive, and permanent. The Accuser's use of shame shows up in my life far more than I'd like to admit, but I'm going to admit it to you right now. Let me tell you about a time where the Accuser showed up in one of those small moments to wreak big havoc in my mind and, consequently, my life.

One day my wife was having an open house at our home for our business. She asked me to set up the coffeemaker, so that when people began to arrive she could start it, and we could have fresh coffee. So, I set up the coffeemaker and pressed the button to turn it on. About halfway through the brewing of the coffee I realized what I had done: turned on the coffeemaker instead of just getting it prepared. And that's when the Accuser showed up:

> *You are so stupid!* [personal] *You never listen!* [permanent] *Why can't you do **anything** right?* [pervasive] *Even with the simple things you do, you are a screw up!* [pervasive] *You think you're a good example?* [personal] *You think you can speak into people's lives?* [pervasive] *What a hypocrite!* [personal] *You are so arrogant!* [personal] *You are full of pride!* [personal] *What makes you think you can share any wisdom?* [pervasive] *Nobody wants to listen to you!* [pervasive].

Here's the process when I submit to the power of the Accuser: A mistake becomes guilt, and guilt becomes condemnation, and condemnation becomes shame, and shame renders me powerless. Have you been there before? Maybe these resonate with you:

- *You'll never be good enough.* [pervasive]
- *You'll never be successful.* [pervasive]
- *You're a failure.* [personal]
- *Everyone thinks you're a loser.* [pervasive]
- *You're no mathematician.* [personal]
- *You can't make, let alone, save money.* [personal]
- *Your marriage is a failure, and so are you!* [permanent]
- *You have no friends.* [pervasive]
- *You are unlovable.* [personal]
- *Everyone judges you all the time.* [pervasive]
- *You're not lucky.* [personal]
- *You can't trust your feelings.* [pervasive]
- *You can't trust anyone.* [pervasive]
- *You're weak.* [personal]
- *You're not capable.* [personal]
- *You're so stupid!* [personal]
- *What makes you think you can be happy?* [permanent]
- *You don't deserve happiness!* [personal]
- *You have no talents.* [personal]
- *You are not gifted.* [personal]
- *Everyone else has strengths except for you!* [permanent]
- *You have nothing new to offer.* [personal]
- *You're not a business person.* [permanent]
- *No one likes you.* [pervasive]
- *You are average.* [personal]
- *You are mediocre.* [personal]

Do any of those examples resonate with you? Some of them do for me. But here's the deal: these are lies! The Accuser is a liar! Don't you dare believe him or her (If you are a woman, he sounds like a woman I've been told by women. In fact, in my head he sounds a lot like me, and this is common also I've been told. I just have to remember that he sounds a lot like me, but he is **NOT,** I repeat, **NOT** me or you!) So how do we overcome what I call the head trash that seems to plague every human in some way or another? How do we stop listening to the Accuser and change these stories?

The Advocate

Well, there's this other voice. This one we must practice listening for and to because our natural default is the Accuser. In Judaism this other voice is called the "still small voice" (the literal Hebrew translation is *a voice without sound*). In *The New Testament* it's called the Holy Spirit. In much of wisdom literature it is the voice that speaks Truth. This voice of Truth *reminds* you - literally gives you a *new mind* - of whom you truly are.

When the Accuser showed up at the coffeemaker, the Advocate swooped in and said, "Brad, it's just coffee." And in that moment the Accuser was vanquished. If my mind is the courtroom, the Accuser prosecutes me using every little piece of the circumstances to get me down and keep me there. But circumstantial evidence in the court of my mind is never enough proof to render me guilty unless I allow it. So listen, listen, listen: My circumstances do not define me. **Where** I am **IS NOT who** I am! The Advocate shows up and defends me against the false charges, and in **TRUTH**, tells me who I am. The case of trumped up charges is thrown out!

Here's the process when I listen to the Advocate: A mistake leads to grace, and grace leads to conviction, and conviction leads to a change of mind, and a change of mind leads to a transformed way of life, and a transformed way of life renders me powerful.

"So Brad, how do I listen to the Advocate and not the Accuser?" Great question. Let's look at something you can *do*.

Positive Affirmations

When the Accuser shows up, and you are thinking negatively about yourself or a circumstance in which you find yourself, one of the most important skills you can develop is to let the Advocate change your negative thinking to positive thinking regarding yourself or the circumstances.

The good news: It really is that simple. The bad news: It isn't easy at first because the Accuser is going to show up every day. The good news: It is a choice to practice listening to the Advocate. The bad news: You will have to do this every day for the rest of your life. The good news: Just like anything in life, it will get easier as you practice it more and more.

Now, this is going to blow your mind: When it comes to practicing this, think of it this way: You are already choosing to believe the negative things the Accuser is telling you. You are already choosing that defeatist attitude. So why couldn't you choose a victorious attitude by listening to the Advocate?

Your subconscious mind is just going to process what you feed it. So if you feed it negative morsels, it's going to grow into a big nasty monster, but if you feed it positive morsels, it's going to grow into a young, svelte, capable, victorious Adonis[12]. Now, what would you rather be? (Hint: Greek gods are cool!)

I may not know you, but I already know some things about you because you are human, and so am I. . .most of the time. Let me tell you three things I already know about you:

You Are Amazing![13]

From a purely biological standpoint you are amazing! The visual cortex in your brain is connected to the retina of your eye, which consists of some one hundred ten million cones, seven million rods, with over a million nerve fibers, and that is why you can read this right now. You have several one hundred billion brain cells with trillions of neural connections. Not one of your brain cells is exactly the same. And that's why you can process this information right now.

Every cell in you contains about six feet of DNA. Taking the DNA of all the cells in your body and laying them end to end produces eighty billion miles of genetic code, enough to go from the earth to the sun and back four hundred times! Your body is hard-wired to be you and no one else! You are amazing!

You Have a Calling![14]

"Thank God it's Friday!" We've heard it. We've said it. We've lived it. Not many people scream with joyful exuberance, "Thank God it's Monday!" Why? Because most people are waiting . . . waiting for something better . . . waiting for the weekend when they are free! Free to do what they want: spend time with their family, go to the party, or cheer at the football game. They're free. . .for two out of seven days. Most people spend about seventy percent of their life doing something they don't love, living a victim's life, "trapped" in a job they simply tolerate. This is not how it has to be.

You have a calling! Soren Kierkegaard writes that every person has a calling, a vocation. The word vocation has the same root from which we get the word vocal. Metaphorically, it is your voice, your unique song to sing. A vocation differs from a job in that a vocation comes from your heart (in wisdom literature the word mind and heart are synonymous). Your vocation entails the use of the unique combination of your strengths or gifts. A job is simply a way to make money and pay the bills. You've probably heard the old joke, "What does JOB stand for? Just Over Broke!"

So, what if you could find your calling, your vocation, your purpose, your passion, and live it seven days a week? What if you lived what you were uniquely called to do, what you were meant to bring to your community and world? What if you awakened every morning, and when your feet hit the floor, you could say with conviction, "TGIT! Thank God it's today!" Is it possible for your job to also be your vocation? Absolutely. But for many people, your job is a vehicle to living your calling. As a high school English teacher, my job is to teach reading and writing skills, but my calling is to help students see themes in literature that can open up their eyes to who they are and what they are passionate about. I'm called to empower others to discover who they are and bring that to their community and world. Job: teacher. Vocation: mentor.

We must find our calling and pursue it with *passion*. The Latin root definition of the word passion means *pain and suffering*. In other words, you would follow your calling even if it was uncomfortable and a struggle, just like the caterpillar, because you know it is why you're here, for this time and this place. It's who you are. Your calling is part of your Greatness! You have a calling!

You Have Today!

Spencer Johnson's *The Precious Present*[15] tells the story of a man who searches his whole life to find the precious present, a gift that could make him completely happy and whole. He crosses the world searching for the precious present. He climbs mountains, treks through jungles and explores the depths of the sea but cannot find the precious present. Eventually, he becomes ill from his fruitless search until he stops trying.

Then, it happens! He realizes that the precious present is just that: the present. The man stops feeling guilt about his past or worrying about his future and learns to live now!

You must not allow yourself to be trapped or paralyzed by the glory, guilt or failure of your past. Yesterday is dead and over. You must see those past events simply as moments from which to learn, helping you live fully now!

Yesterday was today, but it is gone. All it gives are the lessons learned if you choose to learn. Tomorrow has not arrived, so plan for it with proper vision. Tomorrow becomes today. All we really have is today. Today is the only reality we ever experience.

I love this statement: "This is the day that the Lord has made! I will rejoice and be glad in it!"[16] If your eyes open in the morning, your feet hit the floor, and you are walking upright, then that is a blessing in itself! If you have indoor plumbing, running hot and cold water, a roof over your head, food to eat, and a steady income, that is more than most people in the world. I heard recently that if you make $35,000 per year, you are in the top one percent for wealth in the world. Gratitude today in the little things leads to a big heart of gratitude. The little things are actually huge! In medical circles, an enlarged heart is not healthy, but in spiritual circles, an enlarged heart is absolutely necessary! Gratitude is a habit of mind. Speak gratitude for the little things every morning, and feel your heart getting bigger over time.

If you live your calling today, which is every day, then you wake up and live your Dream daily, and you experience an inexpressible joy welling up in a very enlarged heart!

What I Know About You

So, here's what I know about you: You are amazing! You have a calling! You have today! These are three statements the Advocate will speak to you every morning when you wake up if you will allow him. When the Accuser accuses you of being mediocre, you're not! You are amazing! When the Accuser says you have nothing significant to bring to life, it's a lie! You have a calling! When the Accuser haunts you every day with your past and tells you your future's going to suck, he's full of it! You have today!

These statements by the Advocate are called positive affirmations. They are promises for a better life that you can practice and live every day, and if you don't already speak truth over your life daily, start with these easy to remember statements. You can add, change, and adjust more as you go. If you say these every day with belief (even when you don't *feel* like it), you will change the way you think, feel, and act. You will be making The Shift! What you think about, you bring about! What you focus on grows! Here's what I highly recommend: Every day before you get out of bed, with belief, speak the following:

- THANK YOU. THANK YOU. THANK YOU.
- I AM AMAZING!
- I HAVE A CALLING!
- I HAVE TODAY!

- IT'S GOING TO BE A GREAT DAY!

"Ya, Brad, but I don't think I'm amazing." Don't worry, you will! (This book is going to help you with that.) "Ya, Brad, but I don't know my calling." Don't worry, you will! (This book is going to help you with that.) "Ya, Brad, but, as Freddy Mercury sings, bad mistakes, I've made a few. . .in my past." And you're going to make more (I make them all the time and so does everyone else.), but you have today to learn from them and grow in your Greatness! (This book is going to. . .well, you know.) You have to start somewhere, and that starting place is The Shift, now! Change your mind today and every day, listening to the Advocate and speaking positive affirmations!

Part of the purpose of this book is to help you replace the negative stories paralyzing you with the positive stories that serve you and help you walk methodically in your Greatness and live your Dream.

Here's a second recommendation: Whatever head trash the Accuser has been filling your mind with, whatever negative stories are keeping you from your Dream and your Greatness, listen to the Advocate and his truth, and write a one sentence positive affirmation that refutes those totally bogus thoughts!

"But Brad, How do I do this?"

I'm glad you asked! You're going to do that in the *Your Turn* section, and in our next chapter we'll look at the stories we tell, why we tell them, and how to change them.

What Matters

From this chapter remember:

1. You must make The Shift, changing your mind about who you are and the possibilities before you.

2. The Accuser is that voice in your **head** that tries to put you down and keep you there. Don't listen to him or her

(remember, he or she sounds like you). Listen to the Advocate.

3. The Advocate is the voice of truth in your **heart** that speaks life, positivity, and possibility in you. Speak out loud the words of the Advocate! Develop positive affirmations about yourself and speak them out daily.

4. You are amazing! You have a calling! You have today!

Your Turn

Step One: What is something negative you think about yourself? These begin with things like, "Well, I'm not as _____ as so and so." They sound like comparisons a lot of the time. They may sound like this: "I'm not very good at _____." They may occur when you are paid a compliment, and you poo-poo the compliment. For example: "You are such a gifted singer." And you respond, "Well I'm no _____," instead of just saying , "Thank you." So, what Shift do you want to make in your mind? Write down what it is. Begin your sentence, "The Shift I want to make is. . ."

Example: "Well, I'm not as smart as those I work with. The Shift I'd like to make is that I see myself as a smart person who has good ideas and thoughts to bring to my co-workers and company."

Step Two: Create three positive statements about you around The Shift you said you wanted to make in Step One. Write them down. The first will begin, "I am amazing because. . ." The second will begin, "I have a calling to. . ." The third will begin, "I have today to. . ."

Example:

"I am amazing because I am intelligent."

"I have a calling to inspire my co-workers and company with innovative ideas."

"I have today to change my co-workers lives and my company for the better."

Step Three: If you were a tsunami of positivity, what kind of things would you want to bring to the world and the people you encountered? Make a list – just scribble as quick as you can without too much thinking.

Step Four: What will you do today to be a tsunami of positivity, bringing that positive wave? What small, simple action(s) will you enact *today*, and continue doing daily?

Step Five: Do them! Today! And every day!

STOP! DO NOT READ ON UNTIL YOU'VE COMPLETED THE *YOUR TURN* SECTION OF THIS CHAPTER.

4

The Stories We Tell

The   17

―――――――――――――――――――――――►

Shift

How do you think the unthinkable? With an itheberg! Ha! Sorry, gotta throw in one "Dad joke" as my kids call them. Here's a Titanic story with a Titanic lesson:

> *As he stood on the deck of the Titanic, the man's friends and family begged him to get in the lifeboat. He replied, "Never! This is the Titanic! It's unsinkable!"*
>
> *As the ship sank lower and lower into the water, his friends and family implored him to get in the lifeboat, but he clung to what he knew to be right. "The Titanic is unsinkable!" he responded time and time again. He was so set on being right that he was eventually dead right!*

Some people care more about being right than being successful. The two most common stories we tell ourselves are about being right and looking good. These stories originate from what we think others think of us. We care more about the voices outside of us than the voice inside. Please underline the next sentence. *Don't let the voices outside override the voice inside.* That true voice inside is the Advocate from the last chapter. What stories have you written about your life?

Stories That Serve

Henry David Thoreau writes, "The mass of men lead lives of quiet desperation. . .What is called resignation is confirmed desperation. . .despair is concealed [] under [] the games and amusements of mankind."[18] Thoreau's "quiet desperation" is one of my favorite paradoxes of all time. We think of desperation as anything but quiet, right? When someone is desperate, he tends to make all kinds of noise, right? But Thoreau taps into a deep truth of human nature.

Has your life become a vacuum? Are you caught in the vortex of a life that has sucked you into chaos, busyness, putting out fires, working paycheck to paycheck, paying the bills? A vacuum sucks! Don't let your life be a vacuum! The events of life lead most of us to resign ourselves to an unfulfilling life because we never sing our song and live our calling, our Dream.

Instead, we cover over the despair of unfulfilled potential with the "games" or "amusements" Thoreau writes about. There is nothing wrong with television, movies, and sporting events in moderation, but when television, movies, and sporting events keep us distracted from examining **who** we are, **why** we are, **when** we are, we may have a problem. As I recently read, when Americans spend 41% of their time in front of a screen, most of which is designed to avoid the realities of life, we may have a problem. Often it seems that hectic schedules, debt, and obligations keep us from pursuing our Dream with passion, even desperation. Instead, our desperation turns quiet. We go through life slowly fading away, anesthetized by games, amusements, and pleasure, by television, cell phones, and social media because we think this will salve our sore hearts longing for significance when all it really does is numb the pain of disappointment and let-downs. Sometimes it seems that the events in our lives are just too disappointing and painful to deal with. If we can avoid thinking about the pain of a life that is not going the way we dreamed, we can pretend everything is just fine. And once we are sufficiently numb, we don't even recognize that this resignation is actually the despair of an unfulfilling life.

So here's the deal. Events happen in our lives. It is our human nature to attach meaning to every event. Psychology and neuroscience confirm that every time an event occurs in our lives, within the synapses of the brain we create a super-highway between the event and the story we choose to believe about that event. Every time we think of the event, the synapses fire, and we travel that super-highway between the story and the event. We do this continually, unconsciously. You are actually doing this right now. If the stories are positive and serve us, then, no problem! We can walk in our Greatness. But if the stories we write don't serve us, they can potentially paralyze us or ruin our ability to walk in our Greatness, leading to our self-destruction.

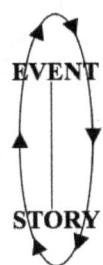

Once we've written and attached the story to the event, we will either consciously or subconsciously look for other events in our lives proving the story we've written. Sometimes we even create events proving the story we've written.

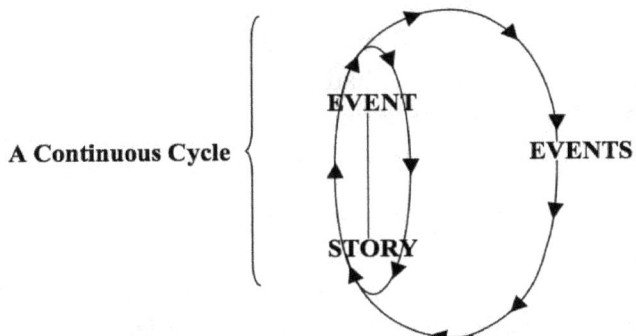

The stories we tell matter. We are always writing our stories, and eventually those stories rest in our hearts. When this happens, it is very difficult to edit or rewrite the story, but it can be done with The Shift, a mind change.

Psychologist Carl Jung writes, "Until you make the unconscious conscious it will rule your life, and you will call it fate."[19] All the stories we write can propel us into the great life we are meant to live. But the trick is to pay attention to the stories we are writing, to make the unconscious stories we have been telling most of our lives conscious, and, if they do not serve us, change the stories. This is absolutely possible.

Good or Bad Coach?

As a high school basketball coach for fourteen years, I experienced some pretty rough moments: cutting kids from the team (always heart-breaking), politics with parents, administration, and mistakes I made in judgment. When I decided to stop coaching, I realized I had attached the following story to coaching: "You will never be good enough. You will never measure up. You are a failure." The Accuser had me in his grasp! I knew I could not walk away from coaching with this story attached to my experience.

If left ungoverned, our thoughts will always tend toward the negative. When this happens, most of us ask, "What's wrong with me?" and we resign ourselves to Thoreau's life of "quiet desperation."[20] But here's the better question to ask: "Is this story serving me?" In my case the story, "You are not perfect. You made many mistakes. You will never be good enough. You are a failure," was not serving me. I had to exchange the story for one that served me. I needed to practice listening to the Advocate, and here's what the Advocate reminded me:

Ten of my fourteen years coaching, my teams had winning seasons; four of those seasons we took first place in league. Two of my years as a Varsity coach we won league titles. We advanced into the playoffs those two years. I was awarded Coach of the Year twice. Most importantly, I continue to hear from players about the births of their children, important family events, and "thank you's" for the lessons they learned and the fun they had. I exchanged my story:

You are a successful coach.
Yes, you made mistakes, but you learned from them.
You have influenced others for the better
and made a difference in many people's lives.

Will that story serve me? Yes!

Jake: A Success Story!

So let's get real here. This journey to writing stories that serve you is not easy, but is absolutely possible for anyone. My good friend Jake, a man I greatly admire, exemplifies how The Shift and the stories we choose to believe can overcome great adversity.

Wake Up Call

Jake was thirty years old, sitting in a bar, and he thought, "I never thought I'd live past thirty." Five years later, he was sitting in a jail cell.

It's quiet in a jail cell. There's time to reflect, and he examined his life. His uncle came to visit him in jail, and for the first time in his life he heard the Advocate, the *voice within,* through the voice of his uncle.

"How's this working for you, Jake?" his uncle asked.

Silence.

Then his uncle asked, "Who are you Jake? What do you want to do with your life?"

"I want to be a writer or a teacher." It was the first time he had really ever answered that question. It was his first brush with his Greatness. It was the beginning of The Shift, a shift that would take many more years to manifest.

He was out of jail, living in Phoenix, attending Junior College, but he wasn't *really* attending Junior College. He was totally strung out on drugs. He was hanging out with a twenty-four year old kid. They were robbing homes and businesses to feed their drug habits. The kid invited him to travel to Bristol, Tennessee to run guns for a guy. Once again, he heard the Advocate and his second brush with his Greatness.

"You are using to escape the events from your childhood. It doesn't have to be this way."

Childhood

When Jake was four years old, his parents divorced, something scandalous in 1955. His Father disappeared completely from his life. He blamed himself, and he wrote the first story that didn't serve him.

Story #1: I am unlovable.

His mom raised him, working long hours to provide. They lived with his loving and kind Grandparents who created a wonderful environment for their grandson.

One day at the age of eight, he told Grandad, "I hate my Father."

"You can't hate your Father," Grandad responded. To an eight year old suffering from abandonment Grandad's response sounded like condemnation, and this little eight-year old boy, filled with shame, listened to the Accuser a second time, and wrote the second story that didn't serve him.

Story #2: My feelings are wrong.

When he was twelve years old, Jake befriended a young man, a neighbor, a very natural thing to do for a little boy searching for a father figure. The young man seduced him. He never told anyone. The Accuser tightened his grip, and Jake wrote the third story that didn't serve him.

Story #3: I can't trust anyone.

That year, he started using "dope," skipping school, going to the local pool hall, and hanging out with the "losers," reinforcing the Accuser's stories. By age seventeen he had so reinforced these stories with other events, he became a loner.

Jake joined the military. It was an easy way to keep running from his problems.

Lost

In Germany, Jake was scheduled to be released from the military. He was to fly back to the U.S. and into civilian life. Instead, he attended a Deep Purple and Black Sabbath concert, reconnecting with a guy from Florida he'd known. They downed some barbituates, and after a drug-induced evening of revelry, he returned to the States. Eight months later he moved to Florida where he reconnected with the same guy from the concert.

Jake's friend had "gotten saved" in a Pentecostal church, so he accepted Christ and hung out with his friend for about eight months. But one day, a carload of junkies from Illinois showed up, and he was gone. He took off with them across the country, "wandering in the wilderness" for the next nineteen years, until he found himself on his way to Tennessee to be a gun runner.

Return to the Present

Here Jake was, on his way to Tennessee to run guns. On the way he got into a fight with the kid, and he had his third brush with his Greatness. In the middle of the fight, the Advocate gave him a vision. He saw himself going away to jail for a very long time. It frightened him so badly that Jake walked away.

Awakening

Jake was driving down I-40 and saw the sign: To Telluride. It was the next brush with his Greatness. He took the road to Telluride, Colorado.

A year later he was delivering baked goods from Telluride to Grand Junction, Colorado, one of his many duties as a handyman for the place he worked. He'd driven the road many times, but on one particular delivery run, Jake came around a corner and saw a mountainside covered with aspen. In the middle of the aspen grove was one lone blue spruce, and he heard the Advocate again: "You are a spruce among aspens."

In that moment he had another vision. He saw himself fixing toilets, painting, and delivering for the rest of his life. Then, as clear as the day he'd experienced it, he remembered the conversation with his Uncle. *Who are you Jake? What do you want to do with your life?* In that moment he decided: "I want to be a teacher!"

As soon as he committed, everything began to line up. He found an affordable place to live in Grand Junction, Colorado. The Advocate showed up in the form of the Education Department chair at the college who took him under her wing. She helped him every step of the way through his coursework and student teacher placement. She hand delivered his transcripts and teacher certification application to the Colorado Department of Education.

When he asked her why she was helping him, she said, "You have more to give than most people." He listened to the Advocate and began rewriting the stories from his childhood. He graduated Magna Cum Laude from his University and got a position teaching High School English.

Relationships and Relapse

Jake had met her in Telluride. They were good friends. Their relationship blossomed, and they decided to head to Vegas to get married. They had a son. Both were recovering addicts, and they had been clean for ten years. But that all changed.

He took a hit on a joint that led to more drugs and a seven-year descent into the lowest and darkest hell of his life. His marriage ended, a result of the demon of addiction. He reached his lowest spiritual point. He was on the verge of it all unraveling. His newly established teaching career and his fatherhood were on tenuous footing.

Yet, through it all he had held unwavering to this one story: "My son will never feel like I felt as a child. I will tell him, 'I love you.' every day." He resolved to give his son the healthiest childhood he could by focusing on how he could best love and serve his son, even as he fought the greatest battle of his life with addiction. His love for his son was the glimmer of light that sustained him in this darkest of times. And once again, Jake had a brush with his Greatness!

Reawakening

His sponsor told him, "Jake, You will never be rid of your addiction until you surrender to the disease of addiction." He knew he was trying to control it. He let go, accepted who he was, his strengths, weaknesses, and his brokenness, and asked the Advocate to help him rewrite his stories.

On that day he changed his stories:

Story #1: I love myself as I am, and I am loved. I will love others.

Story #2: My feelings are one part of me that I do not deny. My feelings may be real, but feelings can either agree or disagree with Truth. My thoughts and feelings will serve me.

Story #3: I choose to trust others, giving them the benefit of the doubt, knowing most people are people of good will who sometimes make mistakes.

He vowed to remember all the signs, visions, and the voice within throughout his life that led him into his Greatness. He committed to love himself and others, trust in his circumstances, recognize truth, and write the stories that served him.

Today

Jake confronted and changed the stories from his past that were not serving him. He recently retired from teaching. His son is now in college, and Jake recently finalized his Dream to open a transitional house for recovering addicts who have just been released from prison. He is a Narcotics Anonymous sponsor at two local prisons.

Jake could have let his childhood stories paralyze him forever, and though his journey had set backs and obstacles, he never gave up. He made The Shift, rewrote stories that would serve him, and today he is living daily to serve others and walk in his Greatness.

A Mixed Bag of Tricks

Jake's story and my experience coaching proves one thing: we are all a mixed bag of tricks. Yes, we make mistakes and do things we wish we hadn't, but we also do beautiful things that bless the lives of others. Grace is the one indispensible component the Advocate provides when we rewrite our stories. When we make mistakes, we don't beat ourselves up again and again. Under the influence of grace, we learn from our mistakes, and our mistakes lead to conviction, and conviction leads to a change of mind with stories that serve us, and a transformed way of life, empowering us to press on toward our Greatness.

Quite often it is those very mistakes and struggles that serve us in serving others. Jake is a Narcotics Anonymous sponsor not in spite of his struggles with addiction but because of them. Because of his experiences, his compassion for and understanding of those in the throes of addiction are gifts he uniquely possesses and has been given to bless and serve others with. When we bless others by living our calling, we embrace our Greatness because our Greatness is always about using our gifts and talents to serve our community and world.

It's Never Too Late

So you might be thinking, Brad, can I really change my stories or is this just psychological mumbo jumbo? The answer is definitely, Yes You Can! (And no, it's not PMJ!)

Recent studies in neuroscience are changing the way we understand the brain.[21] In the past most psychiatrists believed for all human beings anywhere from seventy to eighty percent of our behavior in our adulthood stemmed from early childhood experiences and development. And while that actually tends to be the case, it is not because the stories we attach to experiences in childhood are unalterable. It is because most people accept those stories. They let the Accuser hold sway!

When an event occurs in their lives, people often revert to that story they wrote when they were five, eight, or sixteen years old. They become children all over again, paralyzed by moments so long ago, unable to overcome them simply because they have accepted that what has always been will always be. They unconsciously accept the stories that don't serve them, and instead of making the unconscious conscious, they accept these stories and call their negative situation in life "fate." But neuroscience is discovering this is simply fiction.

Here are the facts! As I mentioned at the beginning of this chapter, in our brains are pathways between the event and the story we attach to the event. Think of them as super-highways. The more similar events occur, the more the super-highway is used and strengthened. This super-highway never goes away. It always exists in our brain. But neuroscience has discovered we have the absolute ability to create new super-highways between the event and an alternate story.[22] In other words, we were created with the ability to change the story we attach to an event, by creating an entirely new super-highway.

Telling an alternate story is not acting like an event did not occur or denying the negativity of the event. It's changing the story to serve you to move on from the event in a way that keeps you from being a victim of the event, paralyzed by it.

When we choose to tell ourselves the alternative story that serves us, that super-highway strengthens while the highway of the story that doesn't serve us atrophies as we tell that old story less and less. Thus, the story that serves us grows stronger and the story that doesn't serve us grows weaker within our minds. We replace the Accuser's stories with the Advocate's stories.

This is good news! We are super-highway engineers within our own minds! We have it within our own minds to change stories, even stories decades old, and thus change our minds, the way we see ourselves, and the way we see the world we inhabit. This leads to changing what we do in our lives! What begins in the mind travels to the heart, and what rests in the heart determines who we are and what we do.

The Why

If you were paying careful attention to Jake's story, you will have noticed two very important things that led to Jake discovering his Greatness. First, Jake found his calling to teach when he was quite young, but it took a while for him to manifest his Dream. Second, and more importantly, although Jake changed his stories, and continued on his journey, the one overwhelming motivation that propelled him to move beyond addiction and live a whole life was his love and devotion to his son.

Jake's son was his Why, his motivation. The love of his uncle, the love of his friends, and the love of his wife were significant (**SIGN**-*ificant*) to Jake's life, signs pointing to something greater than Jake, something to which Jake was connected. But Jake's love for his son, born in part from Jake himself, was not only Jake's love for another, but Jake's love for himself. This is the golden rule. And the golden rule is not a rule. It is a reality! Jake shows that how we love others is how we love ourselves. Jake's Why, his love for his son, rooted in his decision to love himself, was the motivation to Jake breaking his addictions and realizing his Greatness. In a very real sense, Jake's son was Jake's heart.

All of us have a Why, and in the next chapter we find it!

What Matters

From this chapter remember:

1. Most people would rather be right in other's eyes than successful, and that's why so few people ever take the risk to live their Dream.

2. The two stories most people live by are being right and looking good because most people care more about what others think of them than about who they truly are.

3. Don't let the voices outside override the voice inside. (Listen to the Advocate.)

4. Events happen in your life, and you write and attach the stories to them.

5. If you have written a negative story that doesn't serve you, and attach it to an event, you can Shift your mind, change the story, writing and attaching a different   story that will serve you to walk in our Greatness. Write stories that serve you.

Your Turn

Step One: **Identify the event(s).** Write down events in your past that have impacted you negatively and have stayed with you on a difficult emotional level. Look for other events that have happened that bring up the same difficult emotions.

Step Two: **Identify the stories you've attached to the event(s).** Next to the event(s) still having negative emotional impacts on you, write down the negative story or stories you have been telling yourself.

OR

Maybe you believe something about yourself that is negative. Write that story down and ask, "Why do I think this about myself? What happened in my life to make me think that?"

Step Three: **Ask, "Is this story serving me?"** If the story is having a negative emotional impact on you and it is keeping you from trying new things around similar events, then it is not serving you. After you've asked the question and the answer is, "No," then, move to **Step Four**.

Step Four: **Write a story that serves you.** See the event(s) in a new way by asking, "What can this difficult event teach me about myself? How can I grow from this experience? How will I make this event serve me to become the person I truly am?" Write a story that will serve you from this day forward.

Step Five: **Exchange stories.** Tear up the old stories that were not serving you. Literally! Take the paper and rip it up! Then throw them away in the trash! Burn them! And throw away the negative emotion you have been carrying with the old story. Let that old story waste away, and let that new story grow stronger by reading aloud the new story daily!

Step Six: **Attach the new story to the event.** Look at the new story you have written and memorize it. Whenever you think of the event that took place, repeat this new story aloud. When similar events come along in your life, tell yourself the new story, and make your new story **THE** story!

Step Seven: **Repeat daily the stories that serve you.** Put these new stories to heart and repeat them every morning and evening (and throughout the day for good measure) with positive emotions.

Step Eight: **Attach these stories to the events transpiring in your life daily.** Watch your beliefs turn into actions and actions turn into Greatness, *The Greatness Revolution* within you.

STOP! DO NOT READ ON UNTIL YOU'VE COMPLETED THE *YOUR TURN* SECTION OF THIS CHAPTER.

5

The Why is Your Dream

The	**Your**[23]
Shift	**Why**

William Barclay writes, "There are two great days in a person's life – the day we are born and the day we discover why." Hanging on one of my walls is the following statement: "The question is not, 'What do I want to do with my life?' The question is 'Why?'" If you don't know why, you'll never really try.

In his book *Start with Why: How Great Leaders Inspire Everyone to Take Action*[24], Simon Sinek explains the three layers of Greatness using what he calls *The Golden Circle*.

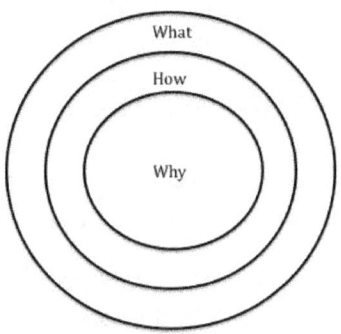

The Golden Circle

Sinek's *Golden Circle* consists of three concentric circles. The inside circle is one's Why. The next outer circle is one's How, and the third outer circle is one's What. The key to one's Greatness lies in the interwoven implementation of the three circles, but the core is the Why.

Sinek uses Steve Jobs, the Wright brothers, and Martin Luther King, Jr. as three examples of The Golden Circle. Each of these figures exemplifies the power and influence of one's Why. As we briefly examine the three layers of Greatness in The Golden Circle and these three case studies, open your mind and ask yourself, "What is my Why, my Dream?"

Steve Jobs

What made Steve Jobs an influential human being was his relentless attention to make the most attractive, sleekest, easy to use, accessible technological devices on the planet. And it all comes back to his Why. Jobs connected his Why to those working for Apple. Apple engineers weren't necessarily brighter than engineers at other companies. Apple had a CEO who was deeply committed to his Why. It drove everything Jobs did, and consequently everything his employees did.

The Wright Brothers

If God had wanted man to fly,
He would have given him wings.
-Bishop Milton Wright
(Father of Orville and Wilbur Wright)

The Wright brothers will forever be remembered for inventing manned flight. But most significantly, the Wright brothers' Why was to make a better world and improve the lives of all humanity. It was not simply to invent manned flight.

The Wright brothers had a contemporary who wanted to invent manned flight. This man had everything going for him. He was a professor at a major university with funding and connections with the press and government. He had all the advantages. But he lacked one thing the broke, untrained, poorly connected, evidently unsupported by their father, cow-pasture-for-an-airfield, bicycle-making Wright brothers possessed: a powerful Why. The professor's Why was to become rich and famous.

When the Wright brothers flew for the first time, this professor simply quit. He didn't even entertain trying to improve flight. The difference between the Wright brothers and the professor was their Whys. A Why solely focused on you will not last. That kind of Why is not a dream. It's a nightmare!

Martin Luther King Jr.

What made Martin Luther King Jr. an influential leader of the Civil Rights Movement? King spoke to the nation from a different place than most: his heart. King's most famous words deviated from his originally planned speech for that day on the steps of the Lincoln Memorial. Instead, King shared his Why. King's most famous speech was not I Have a Plan or I Have a Great Activity We Can Do. It was I Have a Dream, that his children would live in a world where every human being was judged by the content of his character and not the color of his skin. A Dream connecting with others is the most powerful force on earth.

It All Depends on Why

Steve Jobs, the Wright brothers, and Martin Luther King Jr. all possessed the one component essential to living one's calling: a Why. Everyone has a Why. Everyone! But not everyone discovers it or uncovers it because many struggle to see beyond themselves. A Why is always caught up in service to something bigger than one's self. The greatest leaders see themselves in service to a higher authority. A Why rests in your heart. It is the most important component to finding your Greatness. Your Why:

- always engages your imagination.
- always concerns serving others.
- is your vision for your life.

A famous book of wisdom reads, "Where there is no vision, the people perish."[25] A Dream brings life!

Warning: Dreams, Zombies, and Sheep

Winston Churchill said, "When you're twenty you care what everyone thinks. When you're forty you stop caring what everyone thinks. When you're 60 you realize no one was ever thinking about you in the first place." It's likely your Why or Dream will not be appreciated, understood, nor necessarily valued by those around you. Why? Most people are too busy thinking about themselves to appreciate someone else's Why.

Another reason others may not appreciate your Why? Jealousy. Most people have locked away their Dreams, their imaginations, and their creativity in quiet desperation. They have traded the spirit of adventure for the spirit of safety and security. They have resigned themselves to their fates. They are walking dead. Zombies! It's one of the reasons I think we are fascinated with the zombie apocalypse. Most of us are living it already!

Friederich Nietzsche called this the herd mentality.[26] According to Nietzsche we are sheep, seeking security and safety in the herd over true, vibrant life! When a Martin Luther King Jr. comes along, someone who says "think different," we don't like that. We want ease, comfort, and safety. We don't want to change. We don't want to be vulnerable. We want to avoid pain, even if who we truly are and our Why is on the other side of struggle, vulnerability, and pain.

In the English Department copy room where I teach there is an old Apple advertisement. It depicts an old Mac Computer, and below the picture is one of Apple's old slogans: "Think Different!" In red pen, written between the *t* and the exclamation point is an *ly*. Obviously, some English teacher felt compelled to correct Apple's advertisement to reflect the proper form of the modifier after the word *think*.

Besides making all English teachers look like completely uptight, unhappy, nerds, ironically, the corrector of said advertisement completely missed the irony, and, instead, became part of the joke! Why, because most people would rather be right than be successful. Most people would rather be safe and secure in the way things have always been than take risks, think outside the box, or see things from a different point of view. Most people would rather remain the same rather than grow.

The herd. In most of public education, people move from pen to pen when the bell rings and the shepherd (teacher) lets them go. At our J.O.B. (just over broke, but comfortable) we punch in, get our fifteen-minute break, one-hour lunch, and punch out. We know what's coming. It's our lot in life. It may not be a lot, but it's a life.

Then someone comes along and completely blows up all our preconceived notions, all our traditions, all our community ethics, all we've come to know and expect, and we don't like it one bit. Who are these people? Ancient Aliens? No! They are people like Gandhi, Martin Luther King Jr., Mother Theresa, Steve Jobs, Jesus of Nazareth, Henry David Thoreau, Teddy Roosevelt, Lao Tzu, Henry Ford, the list goes on and on. (Come to think of it, maybe they are aliens. They seem so foreign to most of us!) You know them because they transform humanity and society.

Arthur Schopenhauer writes, "All truth passes through three stages. First, it is ridiculed. Second, it is violently opposed. Third, it is accepted as being self-evident."[27] We struggle to understand that the Dreams of others serve us even though we may not know we are being served until much later. However, if we make The Shift, we see that change is inevitable but growth is optional. We discover that our own Dream will serve those we love, even if they don't understand it at first.

This is what happened in the U.S. in the 1950's and 60's. In the United States, even though we have a long way to go, as the evening news makes clear, many of us see racial equality as self-evident. But not long ago, large numbers of Americans were threatened by, troubled by, and resistant to racial equality. Those who lived to overcome racial injustice in the U.S. experienced the three stages of truth: ridicule, violent opposition, and self-evident acceptance. Thank God they were willing to lead in love, sticking with their Dream to transform a nation to truly practice its original creed that all people are created with unalienable rights, among those being life, liberty, and the pursuit of happiness.

Your Dream And No One Else's

Albert Camus writes, "The only way to deal with an unfree world is to become so absolutely free that your very existence is an act of rebellion."[28] Camus was not saying be a rebel. Like, "They say yes, so I say no. They say stop, so I say go!" That's just silly.

He was saying be unapologetically who you are. You are uniquely you for a reason. Jobs, the Wright brothers, and King all understood this. You have a Dream for a reason. That reason is grounded in love for yourself and others. As Arthur Schopenhauer suggests, your Dream, your reason, and your love are all found in Truth that is self-evident. It is integral to the world you inhabit, and, regardless of the voices around you, you must bring your Dream into the world, whether or not others understand, appreciate or value it. You must give it and continue to give it. This is the pathway to real life, abundance, and success. This is the path of walking in your Greatness.

to be nobody but yourself -- in a world that is doing its best, night and day, ***to make you everybody else*** *--*
means to fight the hardest battle any human being can fight;
and never stop fighting[29]

- e.e. cummings

Your Dream begins with your Why. So, what is your Why? Let's find out!

What Matters

From this chapter remember:

1. The two greatest days in a person's life are the day we are born and the day we discover why.

2. ***What*** you do and ***How*** you do it only bring complete fulfillment when they are interwoven with your ***Why.***

3. Your ***Why*** will make you uncomfortable because you must leave "the herd" to accomplish it, but it will also free your imagination and ignite your passion.

Your Turn

Step One: For the next few minutes set this book aside and reflect on your life. Where have you come from? Where are you now? Where are you headed? Write down your answer to the following question: What is your why, your Dream?

If Step One is Difficult:

Step .5: If you are having a hard time answering this make a list of the things you do that fill you up, the things that make you feel completely alive, alert, invigorated, and strong. List the things that flow so naturally from you that even if they are difficult at times, you still would do them because, well, quite frankly, they're just in you to do.

Step .75: Now, look at the list of things you wrote down, and look for what all of these things have in common. Do they all coalesce around music, sports, medicine, art, business, socializing, or service?

Step .80: Next, write down what about these things lights your fire. This should give you a good idea of what your why is. This is a starting point.

Note: If you just don't know what your Why is, don't sweat it. The important thing is to start living your life paying attention to your passions, the activities that fulfill you, activities you love that serve others and point to something beyond yourself. To intentionally heighten your awareness of your potential calling will bring you closer to knowing. Maybe a first step is to look at your life, what you are currently doing, and set some goals in different areas like relationships, finances, employment, education, or your spiritual life. Goals are a great place to start because you can focus on results in the relatively immediate future.

STOP! DO NOT READ ON UNTIL YOU'VE COMPLETED THE *YOUR TURN* SECTION OF THIS CHAPTER.

6

The First Steps Toward Your Dream

The   **Your**[30]

———————————————————————————→

Shift   **Dream**

Give and It Will Be Given To You

Thomas Jefferson said, "He who lights his [candle] at mine, receives light without darkening me."[31] Put another way, if you have ideas, share them; there are more where those came from! If you have money, give some away; there's more where that came from! If you have only one piece of bread, give it to someone who is hungry; you can bake more bread! Abundance thinkers believe, know, and live like there's always plenty to go around.

Some say that *the getting is in the giving*, but, truth be told, *give and it will be given to you.*[32] The difference between these two statements matters, so understand: whatever you give, will be given to you. I am not talking about karma. No, this principle, this truth, is different. In karma you get what you deserve. That is not the same as give and it will be given to you. This subtle difference between "the getting is in the giving" and "give and it will be given to you" lies in intention. What do I mean?

Well, it's like the mother who took her daughter shopping at the mall. The mother was frustrated with the parking lot being too full, the man who cut her off to steal the parking place she wanted, and the crowded corridors between stores, filled with obnoxious, thoughtless people. By the time they got to the department store it was evident by the mother's expression that she was quite resentful of the whole situation. After purchasing their clothing, the mother and daughter began to walk out of the store. The mother leaned over to her daughter and said, "Did you see the look that clerk behind the counter gave me?" The daughter turned to her mom and said, "Oh no Mom, you already had that look on your face when you came into the store."

Ouch! Give and it will be given to you.

If you approach your life with the principle that the getting is in the giving, then you will be giving so that you can get. Your intention is self-seeking, often based on punishment or reward. And this makes it really difficult to live your calling and your Dream, because your Dream is not just about your fulfillment but fulfilling a service to others by using your passions and gifts. In fact, giving freely from your heart of abundance your gifts, talents, possessions, money, or food with no expectation but to love, bless, and serve the receiver always moves you toward living your calling and Dream.

If you simply give of yourself to others, others will see your generosity, genuine heart, and transparency in your life. They will be more likely to reciprocate that same kind of genuine and transparent giving. But even if they do not reciprocate, that is ok because your intention was in the giving, not the getting, and it is the giving that brings joy and fulfillment.

If you have a hard time believing this, try this simple experiment. During your day, deliberately wear a smile on your face as you walk by people and greet them or simply make eye contact with them. Then keep track of how many people smile back at you and how many people do not change expression or pretend to ignore you, etc. In my experience most people reciprocate my smiling expression. But don't take my word for it. Try it. I think you'll be amazed at the number of smiles you receive. And even if someone doesn't smile at you, you'll still be smiling, and that's a good thing.

You see, when the getting is in the giving, people owe you. And when people owe you, they are not responding to you freely. That's called manipulation. But when someone gives to you, it is a gift of his or her own free will, no strings attached, no expectations involved. The gift flows from the heart and is given freely with love, good will, and as an expression of gratitude and kindness.

When we love others to get love, often we are disappointed. When we are kind so that others will be kind to us, many times we're let down. When we feign compassion and empathy out of obligation or just because it's the right thing to do, or so that others will like us and hopefully act the same way toward us, we often find ourselves on the short end of receiving, and we are unhappy.

But, when we genuinely love others, using our gifts or strengths, it is far more likely that love will be given freely to us. When we wholeheartedly practice acts of kindness, it is likely kindness will be given to us. When we fully show compassion and empathy for others, it is likely compassion and empathy will be given to us. These are all gifts given from intrinsic motivations, not extrinsic obligations. This is depth of soul.

Those who realize *it is better to give than to receive*[33] also understand that if you live in the realm of abundance and give your ideas, your time, your mind, your body, your soul, and your material goods to others, all of it will be given to you ten-fold in some way at some time. Yes, the gift you receive may be monetary or something material, but the gift you receive could equally be a sense of fulfillment within, a sense of gratitude to be able to give to someone and add value to someone in need. When you live imaginatively and creatively, expecting new opportunities and new ways to give and grow, you're free to give what you have because you know you'll always have more. This is depth of soul.

But those who believe it is better to receive than give live in the realm of scarcity. Driven by fear of loss, they often hold on to their ideas, use their time only for themselves, withholding their mind, body, soul, and material goods. They fear that opportunities are limited and tend to react to what is happening. Scarcity thinkers keep score of what they give and what they get back for that act of giving. This is life in the shallows.

The irony of scarcity thinking is that those who do it, don't realize that the scarcity lies within themselves. It has little to do with the world around them, and everything to do with the world within them. Emptiness lies within. Typically, scarcity thinking is driven from the outside in, the exact opposite of abundance thinkers who see the world and all circumstances from the inside out.

Margaret, my wife, is a Regional Vice President in her company. One of the perks she enjoys is the company car for achieving a certain level of success. The car is a white Mercedes Benz. It's a really nice car. What it represents is Margaret's decision to work every day toward adding value to others' lives. Because she has built her business and helped many others achieve success and personal growth by introducing them to great products, the company she works for says thank you by giving her a company car. The car represents Margaret's hard work and abundance mindset.

But here's the point: the car, or the paycheck, or the income that allows us to live well and give more, will never equal Margaret seeing the transformation and change in those she has served by simply introducing them to the products and opportunity her company offers. Margaret's service, love, and compassion for others far exceeds a piece of metal, even a nice piece of metal like a Mercedes. The car is a manifestation of the far deeper, richer, and rewarding experience of an abundant heart. At the end of the day, it's the relationships and the fulfillment of a heart grateful for the opportunity to give that matter more than things.

Abundance thinkers are candles giving away their light, losing nothing. On the contrary the light is passed on from candle to candle until the entire world they inhabit dispels the darkness. If you give light to those around you, you'll never be in darkness. Shine and share your light! In your business, at school, at church, in your family, with your spouse or partner, in every moment shine!

A Truth to Live For

Soren Kierkegaard writes, "I must find a truth that is true for me . . . an idea for which I can live or die."[34] We must find our unique calling residing within each of us, a significant purpose only we can bring to our community and world. This calling is part of truth, and truth is always caught up in love in some way. This is your Why.

My Why is why this book exists. One of my goals is to get in front of as many people as possible, as often as possible, and, through writing, speaking, teaching and coaching, help them find their Why, discover their Dream, unlock their Greatness and transform so the world is a better place. Every endeavor I am involved in from teaching, to business, to speaking and coaching is caught up in empowering people. I want to play to my strengths every day in everything I do and say, and it must be the same for you, your gifts and your Dream.

Money, You're Gonna Need It

Zig Ziglar once said, "Money isn't everything, but it ranks right up there with oxygen!"[35] Just as the body needs oxygen to survive, so, too, in this world we must have money. Of course, oxygen is a corrosive when there is too much of it. And money can become corrosive when we fail to see it with the proper perspective.

Really, money is not a corrosive. The love of money is corrosive. That's called greed. I don't recommend it (greed that is). But we can love the opportunities money gives to transform our community and world. We must make The Shift in the way we see and use money.

Money is a tool. If your Dreams are big, and they should be, then you are going to need a big toolkit. Money is a liberator of abundance thinkers driven to live their Dreams for the transformation of their community and world.

Have Fun!

"All work and no play makes Jack a dull boy." He types it over and over thousands of times, and soon Jack Nicholson is trying to kill his wife and child in *The Shining*. To this day it is one of the scariest films I have ever seen. And maybe this is overkill (pardon the pun), but have you ever been working and working and working, building up stress until you snapped? Maybe it was a friend you snapped at, maybe a family member. Or maybe it was the ghosts inhabiting the halls of the big creepy hotel you were supposed to be taking care of. The point is "all work and no play" does not a happy camper make!

I love trail running, road biking, singing, playing the guitar, and training for the occasional marathon or triathlon. I enjoy Disney World, the beach, the mountains, and travel. I like to play! And it must be the same for you!

Many studies find that playing is essential to brain development and greater social learning skills. Playing alleviates stress, keeps your mind healthy, and replenishes your ability to live your Dream imaginatively and affectively. Oh, and it keeps you from wanting to murder your family in the dead of winter in a creepy hotel in the middle of nowhere.

So what do you love to do? Find some healthy playtime and enjoy your lifetime. Schedule it and make it a consistent routine. The rest of your life (and your family) will thank you!

They're Always Watching

Parents, I am going to shoot straight with you right now. Have you given up on, locked away, or put aside your Why, your Dream, because you wanted your children to have the opportunity to live their Dream? Please consider that you are the most important mentor your child will ever have, and you have great influence in shaping the way your child sees him or herself, the world he or she inhabits, and his or her potential to live out his or her Greatness in this world.

I am speaking from experience now. I would like you to consider that your actions speak louder than words. If I say to my kids in words and deeds, "I chose to give up on my Dream so that you could live yours," the message I implicitly send my children is, "Give up on your Dreams because it's what I did." You may have to set a slower pace for your Dream working in the nooks and crannies of your days because of financial and family obligations, but you certainly don't have to give up on it.

Remember, your Dream is caught up in serving others, and one of the greatest ways you can serve your children is to live your

Dream because it sends them the message they can live their Dreams as well. The "pursuit of happiness"[36] is an unalienable right, and nothing brings more happiness (and, yes, struggle) than pursuing your Dream daily. You may be thinking one of the biggest lies many parents tell themselves, so here is the truth to that lie: It is never too late to live your Dream! You are your child's greatest mentor, and your children must believe, "If Mom and Dad pursue and live their Dreams, then so can I!"

What Am I Doing?

Finally, when it comes to your Dream, you've got to ask this question: Is what I am doing now ever going to get me to my Dream? Is it the vehicle that will take me there? Look five years into the future. Where will you be in five years if you keep doing what you are doing? Do you like what you see? Look at others who have done what you are doing for five years longer than you. Do you like what you see? If the answer to either of these scenarios is no, then consider making a change. The definition of insanity is doing the same thing and expecting different results, right?

Find the right vehicle to take you to your Dream. See your Dream morning and night. Live it every day, and you will begin to walk two inches taller. Your feet will never touch the ground because, as everyone knows, hope floats.

What Matters

From this chapter remember:

1. It is better to give than to receive.

2. Shift your mind to be an abundance thinker, and let go of any scarcity thinking.

3. Money is a tool. The more you have the greater your influence. Money is a liberator of abundance thinkers.

4. Have fun living your Dream. Play!

5. Parents, you are the single most important influence in your children's lives. Pursue your Dream, so your children know they can pursue their Dreams too!

6. It's never too late to live your Dream. A true Dream is not age dependent.

7. If what you are doing now is not moving you toward your Dream, change what you are doing.

Your Turn

Step One: Open your mind and heart, and clear them of any obstacles. To do this, close your eyes and empty your mind of every thought you are having. As thoughts arise, take each thought to the edge of your mind. Imagine there is a wastebasket there, and drop each thought into it until your head is completely empty. Do the same with obstacles you think may hold you back from achieving your Dream. Money is not an issue. Drop it in the wastebasket. Current circumstances have no bearing. Drop them in the wastebasket. Let your imagination take over. Have fun and listen to what's in your heart.

Step Two: Write one sentence, answering this question: If money is no obstacle and the world is your oyster, what is your Dream?

Step Three: Now, take that sentence, your Dream, and imagine five years from now your Dream is coming to pass. Write four to five sentences answering the following questions:

Where are you?

Who are you with?

What are you doing?

Who are you serving?

You now have a basic idea of your Dream and what it looks like. Now it is time to risk, to take the next step. To some it may feel silly. To others it may feel like a leap of faith. Are you ready? Will you commit? If yes, read on. If not, give this book to someone in your life who you know will live his or her Dream. Is your answer yes? Then take the next step.

Step Four: Sit down by yourself with your one paragraph Dream, more paper and a pen, or laptop, and imagine. See everything, all the details of that moment five years out. Write down that date. Look it up on a calendar.

Create the Scene: Take a half hour and write it all out, from what's out the window to what the room looks like, or perhaps you're outside, to whether it's day or night, to the type of computer you have, to what you are wearing, to the car you are driving, to the relationships you have in your life. Imagine it all. You can always revise your Dream, but, right now, simply see it, taste it, feel it, and write it down. Take yourself there. Do this now before taking the next step. I know you're going to want to look at the next step before you do this one, but I want to encourage you not to read the next step before you do this one. Go!

Step Five: Make a Dream Board. Cut out pictures from magazines or download pictures from the internet and create a collage featuring the many aspects of what your life looks like from your description in Step Four. Create an actual visual representation of your life when you accomplish your Dream.

Step Six: Live your Dream every day doing what you need to do to see it realized. It's been said that we vastly overestimate what we can accomplish in one year, and we vastly underestimate what we can accomplish in five years. See your Dream happening in five years! You can do it!

Step Seven: Read this Dream before you go to bed every night so you can dream about and see more details, and read this Dream every morning when you wake up so you can live it every day.

What if? ← This Question is Important!

You may say, "I wrote all this down, but what if I don't accomplish this in five years?" But what if you do? Remember, five years are going to pass regardless of what you do (or don't do).

For the sake of argument let's say you get five years down the line and only three quarters of your Dream is accomplished, or maybe just half is accomplished. That is far closer to your Dream than you were five years ago. Margaret and I had a five-year plan to be completely financially free with no debt, so we could do what we wanted, pursue our passions, and go wherever whenever. It took us six years, but we did it.

It's the 80/20 Rule, sometimes called The Pareto Principle, named after Vilfredo Pareto, an Italian economist. You've probably heard something like eighty percent of the work is done by twenty percent of the people. However, the 80/20 Rule applies to all kinds of situations, one of which is your vision. The key is to understand that consistent work toward a goal over time creates exponential returns to one's effort. When you begin, it takes a while to see any results, but eventually the returns begin flowing, and if you look back on the journey, you'll usually find that the last twenty percent of the time it took to accomplish a goal, the faster and greater the returns on your effort.

R.A.S.

Ever heard of the Reticular Activating System (RAS)? It's in your brain. It is the mechanism that brings relevant information to your attention, and it plays a major role in achieving your goals. You can deliberately program the RAS by choosing to send specific messages from your conscious mind like setting goals, saying positive affirmations, or visualizations to your subconscious mind. By consciously sending a positive message the RAS makes the subconscious and the conscious mind focus on and carry out the message. If the message is negative (like, "I could never do that.") it will carry out that message as well.

The RAS doesn't differentiate between positive and negative. It simply obeys what message you send it (This is why the stories we tell from chapter three are so profoundly important). The RAS cannot differentiate between a real and synthetic event. It believes whatever message you send it, even if the message has not taken place in the real world (as if our thoughts and visions aren't real, I guess!). Every person has experienced this phenomenon in his or her life. How does this work?

When I was a kid, my buddies and I used to play this game when we were in the car called "slug-a-bug." The object of the game was to be the first to spot a red Volkswagen bug. If you did, then you got to punch the other guys as hard as you could on the arm. When I played this game, I saw Volkswagen bugs everywhere. And I had a really sore arm! But even after the game was over, I would still see Volkswagen bugs when I thought about the game because I had fed my RAS the information to see red Volkswagen bugs.

But this isn't just a thing for kids. Have you ever decided that you are going to buy a certain type of car, and then that is the car you see everywhere you go? It's like all of a sudden everyone else in the world had the same brilliant idea to buy the car you want too! RAS! Of course, you realize that all those people driving the car you want didn't just go out and purchase the car the day before you decided you wanted that particular car. What's changed is your awareness of that particular car. The car you want to purchase has come to the forefront of your conscious mind.

Bill Russell, the great NBA player for the Boston Celtics who led his team to 11 NBA Championships, was a five-time NBA Most Valuable Player, and a twelve-time NBA All-Star, was also cut from his Junior High School basketball team, was nearly cut from his High School team at the age of fourteen, and was ignored by major university basketball programs across the country. He is the most storied player in NBA history, holding eleven, yes, **eleven** Championships in his thirteen-year playing career.

At the center position, Russell went up against players like Wilt Chamberlain who was five inches taller than Russell. When asked how he won so often and how he knew he would win, Russell replied that he knew he would win because he had already played **and won** the whole game in his mind the evening before. There it is! The Reticular Activating System! Through visualization, practice (goal-setting), and his belief in his ability to win (positive affirmations), Russell placed his championship mentality at the forefront of his conscious mind. In other words Russell had vision, a plan, and listened to the Advocate. It's the same with your Dream!

Write It Down and Do It

When it comes to accomplishing a Dream, when you write down your Dream, create a Dream Board to visually stimulate your mind, heart, and body, and focus on it every day, you not only consciously pursue it, but your subconscious also focuses on it as well. You have to create a vision and visualize it, positive affirmations and affirm them, goals and work them if you want to accomplish your Dream.

Here's why: The Reticular Activating System and the 80/20 Rule. Eighty percent of your Dream will be accomplished in the last twenty percent of the time set for your goals. The first eighty percent of your time builds the foundation for the exponential growth in the last twenty percent of your Dream timetable. All those visualizations, affirmations, and goal-setting compound over time, building momentum, like that tsunami from chapter three. If you have no vision, positive affirmations, and goals written down, then you are not dreaming! You are wishing. So, write it down, create a Dream Board, visualize it daily, speak your positive affirmations, and set and accomplish goals along the way. Your Reticular Activating System will obey you!

With the vision, positive affirmations, and goals you've written and spoken I guarantee, ninety-nine times out of a hundred, you will be closer to your Dream than if you had none because intention brings results. It may get messy and difficult. It may seem like two steps forward and one step back (Remember, that's a step forward!). It may not look exactly how you visualized it. In other words it may not be "perfect" (whatever that means to you). But here's the dealio. Let me speak freely: It's not about perfection. It's about progression.

What Matters

From the previous section remember:

1. Through visualization, practice, goal-setting, and positive affirmations you can influence your Reticular Activating System (RAS) to think differently about what is before you, and you can change outcomes.

2. Write down your Dream, and speak it daily.

3. Look at your Dream Board daily and visualize you living the life you see on the board before you.

4. It's not about perfection. It's about progression. Process, process, process.

STOP! DO NOT READ ON UNTIL YOU'VE COMPLETED THE *YOUR TURN* SECTION OF THIS CHAPTER.

7

The How is Your Plan

The — **A Plan** — **Your**[37]
Shift ⟶ **Dream**

What's a Dream?

How will you manifest your Dream? **Activity!** (Right here is where I wish there was swelling music like when Hobbits do something heroic, but you'll just have to pretend you hear it.) Vision alone will not serve. (Right here is where Vision cries amidst the swelling music: "I can't carry your Dream for you, but I can carry you!") You can visualize your Dream every evening and morning, but unless you actively do something to live your Dream, it will simply remain a wish. You are going to have to go through the *Dead Marshes* of your Dream or climb your own personal steps of *Cirith Ungol*. That's nerd-speak for "sometimes it's going to be tough." What's the difference between a Dream and a Wish?

A Dream...	A Wish...
...is proactive and constant.	...is reactive and fleeting.
...burns within your heart despite circumstances.	...flickers and fades as circumstances change.
...pierces your heart, like a wound that aches to be realized.	...misses the mark of the heart completely.
...is accompanied by passion, tears, and joy.	...begins with excitement and spontaneity but soon subsides as emotion fades.
...stays with you.	...strays from you.

Your Dream is your **Why**. Your activity is **How** you reach your Dream. But here's the million-dollar question: What mind-set must be in place to keep practicing the activity when *Dead Marshes* and *Steps of Cirith Ungol* block my path? I'm glad you asked! You've got to be transformed daily by renewing your mind[38] with The 3D's of a Dream: Desire, Determination, and Discipline.

Desire

The word desire originates from the Latin root *de sidere*, meaning from the stars. Desire is attached to your destiny. Most people think Destiny is something that comes from something "out there," from a distance. But destiny is not fate. Your destiny is written within your heart. It originates within you. Your destiny is the unique combination of gifts within that you are designed to give on this earth. Because of this, true desire can never steer you in the wrong direction.

Desire also comes from *de sire*, meaning from the Father. Desires are God-given, written into your very being. Desire is one of the essences of your soul that serves to transform you so you can bring your unique combination of gifts to the world.

A beautiful ancient poem reads, "Take delight in the Lord, and He will give you the desires of your heart."[39] And just so you know, the name of the Lord in this ancient poem is *I AM Who I AM*. It's a statement of each person's ultimate identity: I am who I am. Being who you are fully and living who you are is your destiny and just what this world needs! In other words, take delight in who you are, with the unique combination of gifts, talents, and strengths placed in you, and bring them to this time and place.

What is absent in so many people's lives is their heart. Listen to what is proactive and constant in your heart. Listen to what burns in your heart despite all circumstances. Listen to what pierces your heart, longing to be realized. Listen to your passion, a deep commitment to do something even if it brings pain and difficulty. Listen to those things that bring tears because they touch something deep in your heart. Listen to those things that bring great joy because all of your being is invested in it. Listen to these and follow your desire, and experience fulfillment. Rumi writes, "Everyone has been made for some particular work, and the desire for that work has been put in every heart."[40]

Written in the Stars

Do you remember Disney's *Pinocchio*? Jiminy Cricket's song was about wishing upon a star, but, really, if you know anything about Walt Disney, you know he had big Dreams and many setbacks, including bankruptcies. What made Disney continue? Disney had a desire to create the happiest place on earth where imagination was king and Dreams really did come true, a place where tomorrow was today, and a place that showed people the realm of possibility.

The song *When You Wish Upon a Star* tells Disney's life story. The essential element making Disney's Dream come true occurs in two lines from the famous song:

*Anything your heart **desires** will come to you. . .*
*When **your heart** is in your Dream, no request is too extreme.*

After spending considerable time studying people who lived their Dreams, the one common denominator, the difference-maker, the one essential component I found is the heart. I will spend more time later on the importance and power of the heart, but for now, know this: The desires of your heart draw your Dream to you. Feel your desire and begin activity. Your activity focuses on where you are, where you're headed and how and when you're going to get there. Your activity and desire are connected. You know your Dream. You know what you want. Your desire feeds your activity, which leads to the next essential component after desire.

Determination

Determination is resolve, willpower, strength of character, single-mindedness, purposefulness, and intentness. Someone who practices determination has integrity. He says yes when he means yes and no when he means no.[41] He follows through on his commitments regardless of his feelings or the circumstance. That's strength of character.

He is focused on and works toward his goals that will move him toward his Dream. He does not get distracted or drawn away from his Dream. He doesn't let his critics sideline him. He focuses on the race ahead as if to win it[42] and doesn't stop to address those in the stands criticizing because he knows who he is, where he is, when he is, and why he is. That's single-mindedness, purposefulness, intentness, willpower, and resolve.

Teddy Roosevelt captured Determination best:

It is not the critic who counts; not the man who points out how the strong man stumbles, or where the doer of deeds could have done them better. The credit belongs to the man who is actually in the arena, whose face is marred by dust and sweat and blood; who strives valiantly; who errs, who comes short again and again, because there is no effort without error and shortcoming; but who does actually strive to do the deeds; who knows great enthusiasms, the great devotions; who spends himself in a worthy cause; who at the best knows in the end the triumph of high achievement, and who at the worst, if he fails, at least fails while daring greatly, so that his place shall never be with those cold and timid souls who neither know victory nor defeat.[43]

Commit. Employ Determination. Choose a definite goal, moving you closer to your Dream. Invest all of you: mind, body, heart, and soul. When you commit, all heaven breaks loose; it just looks and feels like hell for a while.

Stay committed, and keep moving. Yes, achieving your Dream will be difficult. You will encounter Obstacle-Opportunities and struggles, but when you are struggling to live your Dream, your Desire to see your Dream come true can fuel your commitment.

Remember the caterpillar from chapter one? It must knit its own cocoon and struggle to emerge. The struggle is integral to its transformation. Like the caterpillar, we embrace struggle and learn and grow. Obstacles do not define us. They refine us. We keep our Dreams before us, and we know the difficult experiences are moving us closer to our Dreams.

Decide. The word *decide* has the same root as the words suicide, homicide, and genocide. The root *cis*, as in the word incision, means to cut or cut off. The form of *cis*, *cide* means to kill or to kill by cutting. When you decide, you are cutting out or killing off other choices in your current circumstance. Determination is a decision, a cutting off of choices, a commitment to go through the struggle because your Dream is number one in your heart. Determination means you overcome by adjusting to the obstacle, like water that finds its way down the river. Over time your decision to commit to your Dream will reap rewards.

Never Look Back

My wife Margaret began her new business many years ago. For the first few years she treated it like a hobby. Studies show that ninety-eight percent of the people who work the business she's a part of like a business become top income earners within ten years.

One day one of the consultants on Margaret's team asked her what the key to her success was. Margaret, who had reached financial success responded, "If you have experienced an obstacle in your business, I probably have experienced it too. If you have made mistakes in your business, I have probably made the same mistake as well. There is only one reason why I am successful: I decided to never give up! So Decide! Decide to never give up!" That's determination!

Napoleon Hill writes, "Burn your bridges."[44] When it comes to your Dream, give yourself no way out. Commit to never quit but to train daily at your pace. When desire is afire, adversity is simply another moment to grow stronger while you pursue your Dream. As Tim Redmond says, "Weak people look outward and make excuses. Strong people look inward and make adjustments."[45]

Discipline

Did you know that when it comes to exercise, whether walking, jogging or running, a person will burn just about the same amount of calories? The same distance is accomplished. The same calories are burned, but each person goes at his or her own pace. The runner will accomplish the task sooner, but if he does not run the next day, while the walker does, guess who goes farther and burns twice as many calories?

So, set your pace. Are you going to walk, jog, or run toward your Dream? Any pace is acceptable, just as long as you have one. A Chinese proverb reads, "Be not afraid of going slowly. Be afraid only of standing still."

Be consistent. A mile a day walking for one week is 700 calories burned; one mile a week running is just 100 calories burned. The same is true for your Dream. Achieving your Dream is about a consistent set of practical actions and a constant pace of those actions on a regular basis. In a word, discipline.

Doing small, simple tasks consistently over a period of time produces exponential results. When it comes to your Dream, or any goal in your life, remember it's a marathon and not a sprint. A steady pace finishes the race. Consistent training and practice over time means victory. As Jeff Olson points out, "Successful people do daily what unsuccessful people do occasionally."[46]

Ready. Fire! Aim.

How did the U.S. Apollo Program spacecrafts reach the moon? As they made the 238,900 mile journey, the spacecrafts constantly adjusted their direction using a gyroscope. The gyroscope calibrated the direction the craft had to go. Though the destination was known and the way was certain, the plan was constantly being adjusted as the craft flew through space and time. The craft headed toward the moon was off course ninety-seven percent of the time and on course only three percent of the time. The craft was constantly correcting its course on the journey. It's called Course Correction.

You and I are crafts traveling through space and time. We have a vision, create a plan based on our goals, and implement the plan. When we see the plan not working because we are thrown off course, we adjust the plan and act on the new plan to accomplish our Dreams. As John Maxwell says, we set our goals in concrete, but we set our plans in sand.[47] Plans change. Goals are fixed.

Many of us have a skewed sense of what success looks like. You may have seen this illustration before, but it captures that success looks very different from most people's perception:

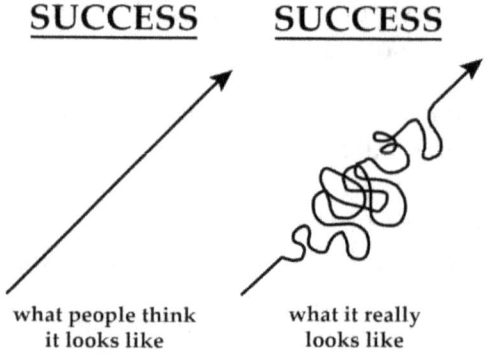

Success is typically not neat, clean, and perfect. Most of the time it is going to be messy. One of the major fallacies common in our world is that successful people have fewer problems than those who are not successful. The truth is that most successful people have more problems because they are working toward their goals and pressing up against greater adversity because of it. That's why creating a system of daily practices is essential to success. That's why creating plans and adjusting those plans to fit the circumstance is paramount. That's why setting goals in concrete and working to accomplish them matters.

Doesn't this just capture where we find ourselves sometimes? Plan definite ways and means to acquire the Dream and the abundant life you seek. Even if your plan seems short sighted or incomplete, write it down and start doing it. The gaps in your plan are the gaps in your knowledge and understanding of what you need to do to accomplish your Dream.

As you implement your plan, you will find the gaps in it. Experience is your gyroscope! You can revise your plan, and guess what? When all the gaps disappear, you'll find new gaps! This is great! We continually refine our plan as we discover new Obstacle-Opportunities to grow. Every moment brings new lessons to learn and new adjustments to make for the next moment.

Growth Mind-set versus Fixed Mind-set

Psychologist Carol Dweck from Stanford University performed a study regarding praise on four hundred fifth graders. In the first step of the study she gave all the kids an easy non-verbal I.Q. test. In the second step of the study all of the children were praised in one of two ways. Half the children were praised for intelligence, the other half for effort. The children praised for intelligence were told, "Wow! You must be smart at this!" The children praised for effort were told, "Wow! You must have worked hard." What Dweck wanted to measure was the impact of these two different types of praise on students.

In the third step of the study she gave kids options for their next test. Students were told there was a harder version of the next test, and, "This will be a great opportunity to learn and grow." Students were also told there was an easier version of the next test and, "You will surely do well on the test." The results? Sixty-seven percent of the students praised for intelligence chose the easier option of the test, but ninety-two percent of the students praised for effort chose the harder option of the test.

In the fourth and final step of the study all four hundred students were given one final test that was as easy as the first test they had taken. The students who were praised for intelligence performed twenty percent worse than on the first test they took. But the students who were praised for effort performed, significantly, thirty percent better than their first test. There was a fifty percent difference in performance between the students praised for intelligence and the students praised for effort. Dweck explains the difference between the two sets of students:

The child or adult hears: oh, you think I'm brilliant and talented. That's why you admire me – that's why you value me. I better not do anything that will disprove that evaluation. As a result they enter a **FIXED** *mindset. They play it safe in the future, and they limit the growth of their talents. Whereas focusing on the strategies they use, the way they are stretching themselves and taking on hard tasks, the intense practice they are doing, those are the kinds of things that say. . .it's about the* **PROCESS** *of growth. As a result they don't feel: oh, if I make a mistake you won't think I'm talented. They think: oh, if I don't take on hard things and stick to them, I'm not going to grow.*

For those praised for their intelligence, the desire to be right and look good is a temptress, leading to the fear of failure and paralysis. One must shift his or her way of thinking. Course Correction is not about intelligence. It's about diligence, the diligence to commit to a process over time to learn and grow. This is the difference between what Dweck calls a fixed mind-set and a growth mind-set.

A Person with a:	Fixed Mindset	Growth Mindset
Intelligence is:	Static	Developed
Challenges are:	Avoided	Embraced
In Setbacks:	Gives up	Persists
Sees Effort as:	Fruitless or worse	The Path to Mastery
When Criticized:	They Ignore it.	They Learn from it.
Others' Success:	They are Threatened.	They are Inspired.
Achievement:	They Plateau early.	Reach higher levels.
View of World:	Fate	Free Will

A pottery teacher decided to do an experiment. He broke his students into two groups. In group A he told the students that their entire semester grade would be based on one grade for the quality of one piece of pottery. In group B he told the students they would be graded on the sheer number of pieces they produced, regardless of those piece's quality. Without exception, the best pieces of pottery came from group B. Why? Because the students in group B had no fear of failure. They were free to focus on process, honing their skills, learning, with every iteration of pottery they produced, how to make a better piece of pottery. The students in group A made fewer pieces, and, as a result, had less experience in honing their skills. Group A had a fixed mind-set, and group B had a growth mind-set. Group A tried to be perfect. Group B practiced excellence. Group A tried to get it correct. Group B Course Corrected. It is the same for you and your plan to live your Dream!

There is no perfect plan, except the plan that gets you going! If you wait until you have the "perfect plan," you'll never shoot for the moon! So Ready. (plan) Fire! (do) Aim. (adjust). Have a growth mind-set focused on process, progress, and effort!

Always remember: Comfort is everyone's friend. He'll whisper sweet nothings into your ear. He'll tell you what you want to hear. But Discomfort is your best friend. He'll tell you what you need to hear if you'll listen, so embrace Discomfort and walk hand in hand through your plan with him. When you do, you'll grow into your Dream and your Greatness.

Persist

Never give up! Adjust as you practice your plan. Remember, your plan is attached to your desire to achieve your Dream. When you find yourself struggling alongside your friend Discomfort, remember your goal to manifest your Dream. Persistence is determination. Your Dream is the force behind desire, discipline and determination. If you care about your transformation and serving your community and world, you will employ your plan, set the pace by walking, jogging, or running, and adjust as you go.

The "Perfect Plan"

Here is the perfect plan for a multi-billion dollar company that has shaped world culture. First, create an animation company you must dissolve after a short time and become so broke you have to eat dog food for your meals. Next, create a mildly successful cartoon character that is a rabbit and lose the rights to it. Have the artists working for you stolen out from under you by the company owning the rights to the rabbit cartoon character.

Next, create another cartoon character that is a mouse and is rejected by MGM Studios for promotion because it would "scare women." Then, create an animated film based on the story of the three little pigs only to be rejected for distribution by major film companies. Next, create an animated film based on *Snow White and the Seven Dwarfs*. Show the film to college students only to have them walk out half way through the film. After this, create an animated film based on the children's story *Pinocchio*, and lose a million dollars in the first release.

Next, create an animated feature set to classical music and have it fail miserably in the theater upon its release. During this time go bankrupt and lose millions of dollars. Then have a feature motion picture entitled *Pollyanna* fail at the box office. After all of this, build an amusement park in an orange grove for seventeen million dollars partially funded by reluctant investors. And when the park opens have it panned by critics in newspapers as doomed to failure.

Now, doesn't that sound like the perfect plan to one of the largest media conglomerates in the world? But that is exactly what Walt Disney did. Talk about Course Correction! Disney is easily one of the most influential men of the 20th Century, but if one were to delve into his biography, he would find Disney suffered bankruptcy, severe depression, and a mental breakdown along the way of his "perfect plan."

To his credit, and to the blessing of millions, Disney never gave up. He had a vision, a plan, implementing constant Course Correction, and with desire, determination, and discipline he succeeded with his Dream to fire the imagination of humanity!

A Mouse

You might be thinking, "I am no Walt Disney." Disney said, "I hope that we never lose sight of one thing - that it all began with a mouse." Do you know who the mouse was? Think carefully. The mouse was...Walt Disney.

In his poem, *To A Mouse, On Turning Up Her Nest With a Plough,* Robert Burns writes, "The best laid plans of mice and men often go awry," and it's true. Plans do often go awry, but in Walt Disney's case, the man and the mouse made a decision to plan and plan again, to keep striving toward the Dream. No one would deny that Walt Disney has left a legacy that continues to grow even after he is gone. Whenever you feel overwhelmed, discouraged, small, and insignificant, remember Walt Disney. We all feel like a mouse sometimes, and when you feel like giving up, remember the difference between those who live their Dreams and those who don't: desire, discipline, and determination.

What Matters

From this chapter remember:

1. Practice the 3 Dimensions of a Dream: Desire, Discipline, and Determination.

2. Obstacles and struggles do not define you; Obstacles and struggles *refine* you!

3. Weak people look outward and make excuses; strong people look inward and make adjustments.

4. Jeff Olson: "Successful people do daily what unsuccessful people do occasionally."

5. Plans change. Goals are fixed. Set your goals in concrete, but set your plans in sand.

6. Course Correct. Embrace a Growth-mindset.

7. There's no perfect plan, except the plan that gets you going.

8. Discomfort is your best friend. He'll tell you what you need to hear to live your Dream.

Your Turn

Now it's your turn to create a plan for your Dream. Keep it simple. You will constantly be adjusting your plan, and it is safe to say the plan that gets you to your Dream will probably faintly resemble your first plan. But that's part of the adventure on this journey called life! So focus on the key components of the plan and execute it. Right now, take these steps to create your plan:

Step One: Write down your plan. Keep it simple; say, a few sentences. (We'll get more specific in chapter nine on goals). Include three things:
1. **What** – Explain simply what is your Dream.

2. **How** – Set goals. Work backward from one, three or five years out and write goals working backward. Explain what action(s) you will take, starting tomorrow and every day after that, to get you to your Dream.
3. **When** – Create a *lifeline* (Most people call them deadlines but I like life!) for accomplishing the action(s) in your plan. Five years? Three? Six months?

Step Two: Post your plan prominently so it is one of the first things you see in the morning and the last thing you see when you go to bed. Post it on your bathroom mirror, on your refrigerator door, on the dashboard of your car, on your desk at work, on your computer screen as a screensaver or wallpaper, or in your planner. The point is, keep it before you all the time.

Step Three: Every day practice "Ready. Fire! Aim." Pay attention to where you are spending your time: on things that move you toward your Dream or away from your Dream. Course Correct, using the gyroscope of experience. Revise your plan as often as necessary. Don't be afraid of little or big changes. Keep your focus on your Dream, letting every moment inform you and serve you to bring your Dream closer to manifesting.

Step Four: Remain open. Have fun in steps one through three. Enjoy the journey! Employ spontaneity, intuition, laughter, and a spirit of adventure as you walk out this journey. Avoid letting yourself get too frustrated, overwhelmed, or depressed because you are probably going to be off-course about ninety-seven percent of the time. So enjoy the adventure and just keep Course Correcting with a smile on your face!

A Word Regarding Course-Correcting Your Plan

While plans need Course Correcting, remember, results from the activity of your plan usually take a while. Sometimes we give up on our plan too quickly. Therefore, when you adjust your plan, typically those adjustments will be minor changes over time. Throwing out a plan entirely is not common and should probably be avoided. Many people overestimate what they can accomplish in a year and underestimate what they can accomplish in five years. People often give up after just a few weeks on a plan, but it is going to take a lot of small consistent activities over a long period of time to really see results. It's not how you start; it's how you finish. Stick with a plan and look for positive results. If after a prolonged period of time it doesn't seem to be working, you may consider drastically revising your plan.

STOP! DO NOT READ ON UNTIL YOU'VE COMPLETED THE *YOUR TURN* SECTION OF THIS CHAPTER.

8

Goals

The Plan	Goals	Commit	Set Pace	48 Your
Shift		The 3D's		Dream

What does your plan need to include? Goals. Goals are different from your Plan. A Plan is the broad brushstrokes on the canvass of your life. Goals are the smaller strokes, the details that incrementally bring the Dream into focus and, finally, completion. In the previous chapter you have already determined when you want to achieve your Dream (six months, a year, three years, five years, etc.). You have a Plan in place with general ideas of what you want to accomplish. Now it's time to be specific and detailed, to work your way backward on a calendar from when you want your Dream to be achieved with definite goals. You create a timeline on a calendar, prioritizing what you must accomplish first, second, third, and so on to complete the painting of your Dream. Before you write your Plan in the **Your Turn** portion of this chapter, here are the seven principles to keep in mind.

1. **Fix the Exact Amount**

    Fix your mind on the exact amount in these areas:

    - **Resources** – List the resources you need to accomplish your Dream. These may be material resources, such as computers, office space, etc., or these may be human resources, such as mentors, experts, workers, designers, etc. When will you accomplish having all of these resources in place and in what order?

    - **Skills** – List the skills you will need to accomplish your Dream. Is there training involved? Will you need to take a course? Do you need an internship? Do you need a mentor? When will you have each of these skills in your repertoire?

- **Funding** – Figure out how much money you need to fund your Dream and how you will accumulate the funding to work toward your Dream. How much will it cost to obtain the resources and skills necessary to accomplish your Dream. Figure out how much money you want to live on. Will you live below your means and save to fund your Dream? Figure out how you will fund your Dream and the lifestyle you desire.

2. **Give and It Will Be Given to You**

Over two thousand years ago a young man approached a great rabbi filled with wisdom. He asked, "Rabbi what must I do to truly live?" The rabbi responded, "Go and sell all that you have and come follow me." The young man went away sad because he possessed great material wealth. He was not willing to give it all for his Dream.[49]

Determine exactly what you are willing to give to accomplish your Dream. Write down what you are willing to do. . .and double it! You may never be required to do all of it, but you must be willing. A Dream will always cost us more in time, effort, resources, and struggle than we anticipate. But remember, "When your heart is in your Dream, no request is too extreme." Your Dream may ask you to give over some extremely difficult things at times. You decide if you are willing to give them. It helps in those moments to measure the short-term sacrifices for the long-term dividends.

Just a word regarding difficult choices and sacrifices. There seems to be a lot of talk about balance in life. Many life-coaches will talk to their clients about having a balanced life, but I would like to suggest that instead of thinking about balance in life, think about seasons of life. King Solomon said that to everything there is a season.

Summer, Fall, Winter, and Spring are very different seasons, and every one of them is necessary to a healthy and whole planet. When you pursue your Dream, you may have to spend more time on the road away from family, or longer days at work, or doing a lot of foundational work that seems mundane to establish the right conditions for your Dream to manifest. These difficult or mundane periods of time are just a season. While every season is necessary, another important thing to remember is that seasons end as well (unless you live in Hawaii, then obviously you are already living the Dream).

Seasons in life are the short-term sacrifices we give for the long-term benefits. Everything in life commands an exchange. The one most of us know is trading time for money (which actually doesn't have to be an exchange at all. We'll talk about that later in the book). As you pursue your Dream, you'll have to make some exchanges, some short-term sacrifices for long-term rewards. If you find yourself in a season for five years, then please, seek help!

3. **Set the Date**

I don't believe in deadlines. Instead, set lifelines! Remember you are planning and striving to truly live!

Establish exactly when you will achieve the amount of resources, skills, and wealth for your Dream. Write them down, maybe on a calendar, then work backward on the calendar, creating benchmarks of measurement. If your goal is to save $1000 four months from now, write down that goal on the calendar four months out. Then go back one month from that lifeline and write $750. Then go back two months and write $500. Then go back another month and write $250. Keep the $1000 goal in the back of your mind, and laser-focus on the $250 now for this month. When you achieve your $250 goal. Set your laser-focus on the $500 goal.

If you achieve your $250 goal early, don't coast until the month is over and begin the $500 goal. Begin immediately. If you want to challenge yourself, move the time-table up for your goals.

If it takes you five weeks instead of four to accumulate the first $250, then adjust your other lifelines to five-week increments. Make the plan and adjust accordingly. But definitely set lifelines and use your superhero laser focus (yes, you are a superhero, don't forget it!).

4. **Ready. Fire! Aim.**

Even superheroes plan, and guess what? Their plans never work out! How do I know? Because then we'd have no movies! Listen, even in all of your superhero-iness (yes, I made up that word!), your plans are going to make loud sucking noises sometimes. That's ok! We all do it! There is no perfect plan, except the plan that gets you going.

So, create a definite plan and practice it daily to manifest your Dream. Whether you are ready or not, the process will teach you.

And don't close your mind, Captain Laser-Focus! Keep your mind open Wonder Laser-Focus Woman! Keep your heart open. Listen to everything. Reflect on everything. Learn by taking in what serves you. Discard what doesn't serve you. Adjust your plan. Then, move on.

5. **Write It All Down**

As a review of 1 through 4, clearly and concisely write down:

- the amount of resources, skills, and funding you want

- Lifelines! (the time to accomplish your goals, working backward on a calendar from when you want to complete your Dream)

- what you are willing to exchange for the funding, skills, or resources you need, all the while thinking seasons

- a simple, clear, adjustable, daily plan to realize your Dream.

6. **Read It Aloud Morning and Night**

Read your written statement and plans in the morning before you start your day to keep it in the forefront of your conscious mind, so you can engage the Reticular Activating System (RAS) in your mind and evaluate your activity in the day, practicing the 80/20 Rule, spending eighty percent of your time doing activities that are moving you toward your Dream and twenty percent of time on necessary activities that must be done but aren't directly moving you toward your Dream. Spend eighty percent of your attention focused on the top twenty percent of activities that will move you toward your Dream. Always keep your Dream in the back of your mind, your goals in the front of your mind, planted in concrete, and your plans in your hands, planted in sand, able to be adjusted for course correction.

Read your written statement aloud before bed, so you can evaluate your day, asking, "Did I move closer to my Dream today with what I did?" If not, ask yourself what you can do differently tomorrow, and make a plan before you go to bed and rest well knowing you are being proactive with the life you want to lead, something ninety-five percent of the world population is not doing. If so, then celebrate your successes and rest well knowing you are moving toward your Dream.

Read your written statement aloud before bed, so you can dream about your Dream and how you will manifest it. As you sleep, your dreams will reveal new visions that will fill the gaps of your plan and move you forward.

7. Make S.M.A.R.T Goals

Use this acronym when making your goals so that they are very clear:

Specific: Ask these kinds of questions to make the goal specific: What do I want? Where? When? How? With Whom? What are the conditions and limitations? Why do I want to reach this goal? What are potential, alternative ways of reaching this goal?

Measureable: What is the concrete evidence you will see when you achieve your goal? Saying I feel better because I am eating healthier is not concrete, but saying, I have lost seven pounds in the last two weeks and 3 inches in my waist is concrete. Write down what you will see, hear, and feel when you achieve the goal.

Attainable: Investigate if the goal is realistic. You will have to give up to go up. In other words, when you set a goal, it needs to be attainable, but it will also cost you something: time, money, less relationship time with some people, etc. Count the cost. Also, if you don't have the time, resources, or skills to attain the goal, you will be discouraged. Sometimes the goal we have must be set after we have accomplished some other goals that prepare us to achieve our original goal. Set goals that are attainable and realistic. Make them incremental if necessary.

Relevant: Is the goal relevant to you? Is it what you want? Is it in your "wheel-house"? Will it advance you on the trajectory of your Dream, or will it take you down a path away from your true Dream? Is the goal relevant to your *Why*? What's the objective, and will this goal actually reach that objective?

Timely: Install *lifelines* (not deadlines) for when the goal will be accomplished. These can, of course, be adjusted, but having a time when the goal is accomplished matters to the daily, disciplined activity you must practice to accomplish the goal in a timely manner. Keep the *lifeline* realistic and flexible enough to keep you from getting down on yourself. Too strict of a lifeline becomes a deadline, and discouragement, leading to self-criticism, never empowers you to continue the path to accomplish your goals.

In the Middle of the Night, Write It Down

Keep a pen and paper by your bed, so when you awaken with visions filling the gaps of plans and goals, you can write them down. I've found if I don't do this, I either forget the visions or the visions keep me up all night as I mull them over again and again. You've got to get some sleep if you are going to live your Dream!

What Matters:

From this chapter remember:

1. Set goals.

2. Fix the exact amount of resources, skills, and funding you need to get started on living your Dream.

3. Determine what you're willing *to give up to go up* for your Dream. (You may not have to give them all up, but you must be prepared.)

4. Set lifelines for goal accomplishments and adjust accordingly.

5. Keep an open mind, and Course Correct.

6. Write down your goals.

7. Read aloud your goals, night and morning.

8. Make your goals S.M.A.R.T.: Specific, Measureable, Attainable, Relevant, and Timely.

Your Turn

Step One: Write down the exact amount of resources, skills, and funding you will need to accomplish your Dream.

Step Two: List everything you are willing to give up to achieve your Dream. (Remember, you may never have to give it up, but you must be willing to if the time comes).

Step Three: Write down your lifelines. Set the date when you will accomplish your Dream. Place that date in your planner or calendar. Next, work backward. Establish dates to achieve specific goals that mark a step toward your Dream.

Step Four: Write a daily activity plan moving you toward your first goal(s) you have set. Periodically re-evaluate your activities for efficacy. Are you accomplishing marked and measureable benchmarks? Can you see them? Can you see the effect of your actions? If so, continue. If not, adjust your daily activity.

Step Five: Write a simple, succinct statement you can use as your mantra every morning and evening. For example, "I will spend fifteen minutes a day making three phone calls with potential clients," or "I will read ten pages per day of a book on healthy relationships and apply what I read to my relationships with others in my life," or "I will spend thirty minutes a day studying others who have been successful in my field."

Step Six: Do it.

STOP! DO NOT READ ON UNTIL YOU'VE COMPLETED THE *YOUR TURN* SECTION OF THIS CHAPTER.

9

The What

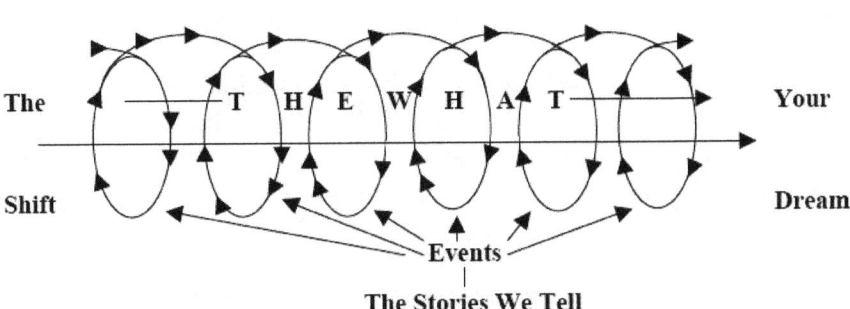

What do you want? What you do has a lot to do with what you want. If what you do is not moving you toward what you want, then you need to change what you do. If you want your Dream to manifest, ask, "Is what I'm doing now ever going to get me there?" Remember, the definition of insanity is doing the same thing and expecting different results.

Give yourself permission to Dream. Open your mind and imagine what that Dream looks like. Remember: Where there is no vision, the people perish.[51] So, have a vision!

Most people coming out of high school or college, regardless of their interests, majors, and, dare I say, Dreams, are content to simply get a job in order to pay the bills. And it is good to get a job and be responsible for yourself, paying your bills. However, often, many don't have a plan and don't know or have forgotten about their Whys and Hows. But here's the thing, if you don't know where you're going, any road will take you there.

Money is not *the* most important reason to get a job, though making enough to support yourself and your family if you are married is good and appropriate. Coming out of college, John Maxwell, leadership expert and pastor, had the choice of a big, well-established church with a good salary, or a small, country church in Indiana with very little salary. Guess which job he took. The small, country church in Indiana. Why? Because he knew it would get him closer to his Dream to influence others to live a life of significance through leadership. He realized the small country church provided opportunities for growth in leadership that the well-established church would never stretch him to experience. He realized that there were other things more important than money.

Money is a tool, just like ideas, resources, skills and time. If you want to pay the bills, any job will do, but if you want to manifest your Dream, be selective how you spend your greatest capital: your mind, heart, strengths, and time.

With that said, we must start somewhere. Often, our employment experiences teach us one of two things:

1. The skill sets we do and don't possess, helping us build on our strengths and manage our weaknesses

2. New skills or strengths we didn't know we possessed, serving us for the future.

These jobs train us to distinguish between what it means to work hard, smart, and strong versus soft, lazy, and weak. Any experience teaches us to grow in our Dream and our Greatness if we choose to learn.

Good reasons exist to work in a job that will not monetarily advance you. Here are some of those reasons:

- it's all you want in life professionally
- to learn a specialized skill set
- to climb the ladder in a specific organization which is a part of your Dream
- to maintain a cost of living while you work in the nooks and crannies of your day on activities helping you accomplish your Dream.

However, the best scenario is to research opportunities that:

- will increase your monetary toolkit, giving you freedom to pursue your Dream.

- will increase or improve your character and skill sets necessary for accomplishing your Dream.

- will play to your strengths so you are happy, approaching your daily activity with eagerness and a positive attitude, knowing you are serving others and pursuing your Dream daily.

Desire + Discipline + Determination = Your Dream

Desire fuels Dreams. Desire ignites Discipline and Determination. This is focus. Once you Dream, the real battle begins: the battle within. If you truly surrender it all to your Dream, Desire wells up in you. That Desire must be channeled into daily activity that unleashes your imagination. Let every moment speak an idea or opportunity, propelling you toward your Dream.

Most of us view life as a series of mountaintops and valleys. Many relate more to the myth of Sisyphus[52]. Do you remember him?

He's the man who rolls the boulder up the hill, and, just as he's about to crest the hill, his strength gives out and the boulder rolls back down into the valley. He has to start all over again only to have the same thing happen for eternity. But listen: it's a myth. If you have a Dream and desire, you will face hills to climb, and it will be difficult. But **The Shift** can change the story. Here's an example:

For those of us who make **The Shift**, change our minds, Dream and write stories serving us, life is more like this:

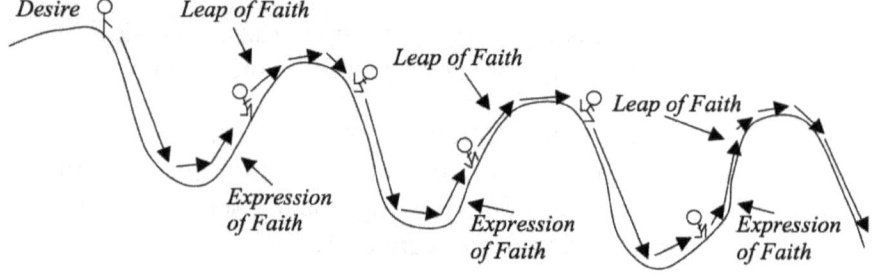

⎯ **Desire, Discipline** and **Determination** over **TIME** create **MOMENTUM** ⎯▶

Do we face hills? Yes, but we know this series of hills is really heading downhill, creating momentum. We gather momentum to finish the race and achieve our Dream. Our momentum carries us up the hills to a point, the point of challenges we've not experienced and must go through. Our Desire, Discipline and Determination help us stretch our faith into uncharted territory, that little bit of the current hill representing Obstacle-Opportunities we have never encountered before. We grow in faith with new knowledge gained, an obstacle overcome, or a skill developed, bringing us closer to our Dream.

Soren Kierkegaard called it *the leap of faith*.[53] We step into the darkness and hope the light rushes in. Even the smallest step can feel like a leap. This leap of faith powered by Desire, Discipline and Determination adds to our momentum. The next time we confront a similar challenge or obstacle, it's easier to overcome, until, after a few similar experiences, what was once a leap of faith is now an expression of faith because we grow comfortable with what was uncomfortable. Whatever obstacles we face, we can confront, go through, grow and overcome because we've done it before. We know we're heading downhill.

Adventurer or Victim?

In Paulo Coehlo's *The Alchemist*[54], the protagonist, Santiago, a young shepherd from Andalusia in Spain, journeys to

Africa to seek his treasure. In Tangier all of Santiago's money is stolen his very first day in Africa. He finds himself penniless, homeless, and hopeless. He begins to feel sorry for himself, and he weeps alone in the town square as the sun sinks in the Western sky. As darkness falls, Santiago fears this strange place.

And then something wonderful happens. Santiago makes The Shift. He changes his mind. He realizes Tangier is not a strange place. It's a *new* place. He realizes he has to choose between thinking of himself as "the poor victim of a thief [or] as an adventurer in quest of his treasure."

As the sun rises on the new day, Santiago declares, "I am an adventurer, looking for treasure." And though he doesn't have a "cent in his pocket. . .he ha[s] faith." He realizes the ups and downs of life are moving him closer to his "treasure," his Dream. He accepts the Obstacle-Opportunities as transformational moments to experience something different, learn, and grow in his Greatness. His leap of faith will become an expression of faith, and momentum will build with each new experience. Even the seemingly negative experiences prepare him for his next adventure on his grand journey and his transformation because of the journey.

What About Us?

Winston Churchill said, "A pessimist sees the difficulty in every opportunity. An optimist sees the opportunity in every difficulty." Be the optimist! How?

Let's say I have an appointment to share a business opportunity I am passionate about. It's part of my Dream. For me, the first appointment is the hardest, because it's uncharted territory and I don't know what to say, or I'm afraid I'll get a no. In my mind I tell myself, "This uncharted territory is the mystery on this grand adventure! I look forward to what it will bring!"

That first appointment will be a great teacher. I will learn a little more of how to say what I need to say. I'll improve my technique, gaining momentum. I'll exchange the story of struggle for a story of adventure filled with triumph and transformation, something like, "I want to add value to others' lives and help them discover for themselves the abundance I'm enjoying in this life. I am compelled to serve!"

I'll learn that someone saying no is not a personal rejection. It is simply the answer of someone who is not interested in or ready for the opportunity I have to offer. It's not their time. And I'll learn that sometimes rejection is protection against those who are not ready for the way I live life so fully! And besides, it's not like I am a young shepherd boy in Tangier, Morocco without a cent in my pocket!

Serendipity? No Accidents? You Decide.

In John Irving's *A Prayer for Owen Meany*[55], Owen tells his friend, John, there are no accidents. Everything happens for a reason. Owen realizes every moment, good or bad, can serve us for this great adventure called life! The Shift enables us to see opportunities when most people see obstacles. When most are shackled and content to see shadows on the wall of the cave, we break loose from our shackles and make a complete one-eighty, seeing the truth behind the shadows and what lies beyond the cave!

Are obstacles, difficulties, and struggles necessary? Well, necessary or not, everyone experiences them, especially those who experience success and significance. Anything worth having, like your Dream, will involve struggles and exchanges of time, money, and hard work. But remember, while Comfort is everyone's friend, Discomfort is the best friend you'll ever have. He'll teach you what you need to hear if you'll listen. He'll give you what you need to grow, and he'll do it again and again because that is how much he wants you to realize your Dream. Remember, When Discomfort shows up, all heaven breaks loose. It just feels like hell for a while.

We must practice seeing all our circumstances in the same light as Santiago, the shepherd boy, and Owen Meany. Whether the glass is half empty or half full, the water is good! So drink it down! Make the most of every moment, and the moment will make the most of you!

An Important Shift: Success and Failure Are Friends

Failure does not exist. However, many people define success and failure as distinctly different from one another, two separate categories that have little to do with each another. We either fail or succeed:

But those who accomplish their Dream understand failure is simply the partner of success. Failure is something we go through to find success:

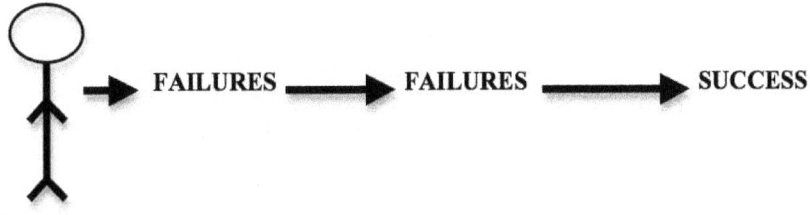

Thomas Edison famously quipped he did not fail ten thousand times to make the filament of the light bulb. He simply found ten thousand ways not to make the light bulb. Edison wrote a story that served the ten thousand events many considered failures. He understood in order to succeed one goes through failure, and learns from the failure so he can succeed.

Remember when you were in elementary school and you learned, "If at first you don't succeed, try try again"? Successful people define failure as something not turning out the way they expected. That's it! No emotional baggage. No depths of despair. It's back to the drawing board with another possible solution to try! It's an adventure! It's growing! It's truly living!

Napoleon Hill writes, "Every failure brings with it the seed of equivalent success."[56] In the midst of a no are all kinds of lessons teaching us about how to get a yes.

As a college basketball player and a high school coach, I always learned more about myself and my team when we lost rather than when we won. In most respects, we learned the irrelevance of the scoreboard. We needed to focus on and practice what to do differently. We just had to get in the game and give it all! As John Maxwell says, "Sometimes you win; sometimes you learn!"

Real Failure

Okay, maybe I fibbed a little earlier. Failure does actually exist. The only way to fail is to not learn from your failures.

Paolo Coehlo writes, "When you repeat a mistake, it's no longer a mistake; it's a decision." Doing the same thing again and again with the same negative results is not only insane, it's true failure. If you want to succeed, try things. When they don't work the way you planned, adjust your plan and try again. Take risks! And keep trying until you succeed. The only way to fail at your Dream is to give up. Never, never, never give up! Keep walking! Crawl if you have to! If you truly want to succeed, double your rate of failure.

When failure overwhelms, attach your significance to the activity and not the outcome. Execute your plan, trying to accomplish the goals you've set. Then, celebrate your activity. Always think "activity not outcome." Know that you will accomplish your goals and Dream as long as you persist, adjusting and executing your plan as you progress. Make no mistake: You are progressing!

Edison and you! It's the same with anyone who experiences defeats and disappointments along the way. Learn, adapt, and adjust to be your very best. Grow at every moment. Grow in your Greatness, until *The Greatness Revolution* grows in you!

What Matters

From this chapter remember:

1. Be intentional about your job; let it inform you on your journey toward your Dream and Greatness. The most successful people can find a connection between what they are doing and how it is transforming them for their Dream.

2. Every hill you face is an opportunity to stretch and grow your faith, building momentum toward your Dream.

3. Failure is the path to success; you **go** through it to **grow** through it. When you fail and learn, you're that much closer to success.

4. As John Maxwell says, "Sometimes you win; sometimes you *learn*."

5. Attach your significance to the activity and not the outcome.

Your Turn

Step One: List five challenges you face in your plan to achieve your Dream. What are five Obstacle-Opportunities holding you back from carrying out your plan or achieving your Dream? These are challenges you may not have known how to overcome.

Step Two: Now, brainstorm! List three possible solutions for each Obstacle-Opportunity. Think outside the box! Nothing is too outlandish. You're just writing down fun, exciting, and adventurous ways to overcome the Obstacle-Opportunities. If you struggle with this, get together with some smart, successful people you admire, and ask them to help you brainstorm some solutions.

Step Three: Implement the solutions in your daily plan toward your Dream. If they work, great! If not, keep Course Correcting your plan by trying another solution.

The Greatest Secret of Great Dreamers

What made Abraham Lincoln, Winston Churchill, Gandhi, Martin Luther King Jr., Mother Theresa, Walt Disney, Thomas Edison, and Steve Jobs outstanding leaders in their fields? There may be many and various character traits they each possessed, but they all possessed the one secret to being a great Dreamer: They never gave up!

Every leader of great influence lived their plan daily to achieve their Dream. No matter the obstacles, they did not give up. Persistence constantly pursued them and was their constant companion. When you look at the Obstacle-Opportunities you face, remember you will become the person you were designed to be if you persist. A person who persists is a leader that inspires because his gyroscope of experience has given him the wisdom to overcome anything time and space throws at him, and in this way, a leader can serve those who follow him.

STOP! DO NOT READ ON UNTIL YOU'VE COMPLETED THE *YOUR TURN* SECTION OF THIS CHAPTER.

10

Spirals: The Listen and Learn Technique

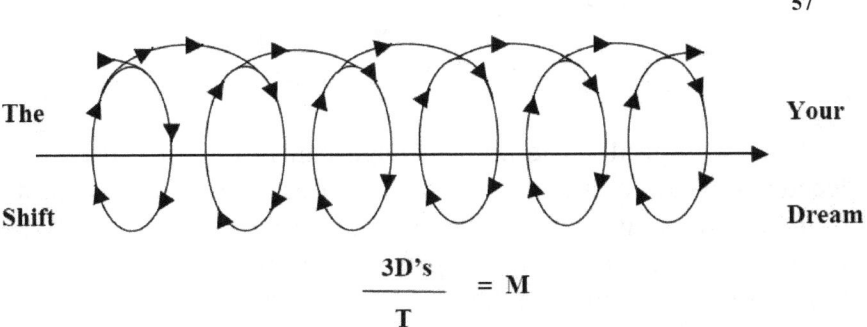

57

$$\frac{3D's}{T} = M$$

It's the circle of life and it moves us all
through despair and hope, through faith and love
till we find our place on the path unwinding.
    - Disney's The Lion King[58]

I love Disney's *The Lion King*, and most of us understand the concept of the circle of life. There's that moment when Mufasa tells Simba we become the grass and the antelope eat the grass, and so we are all part of the circle of life. Most of us are accustomed to a view of life that looks like this:

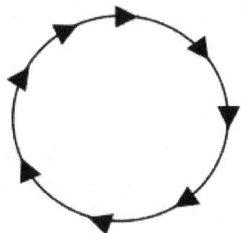

You're born, you pay taxes, and you die! Okay, there may be a little more to life than that! But life is not a circle. In fact, it's *the path unwinding*:

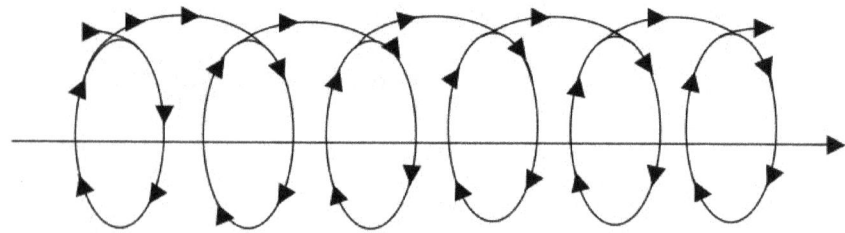

Life is a spiral. The above image can represent a lifetime, a decade, a year, a month, a day, an hour, a minute or even a moment. We may view every day as a circle. Most people view Monday through Friday as pretty much the same day. They believe they are going through the same motions every day. That is their lot in life. It's not a lot, but it's a life, right? Wrong! Here's a quick review from *Chapter Two*:

I recently read about a survey that said about eighty-five percent of Americans don't like their job. Most people spend seventy percent of their existence working a job they are not passionate about. The most often heard refrain at the end of the week around the water cooler is, "TGIF!" Thank God it's Friday! How often do we hear, "TGIM"? Thank God it's Monday! I'm guessing you probably haven't heard that refrain because the truth is most people are going to a job they don't enjoy just because they *have* to pay the bills, right? Wrong! They don't have to pay the bills! They do not *have* to do anything. Whether we recognize it or not, we choose to go to our job. We choose to pay the bills. We choose our life!

What if instead of a job, every day you used your unique combination of strengths, gifts, and talents within and lived each day fully, living and giving who you are to humanity and the world? And what if, by doing so, your job was transformed into your calling?

Soren Kierkegaard said *I must find a truth to live and die for*. We hear a lot about what people are willing to die for: family, friends, country, the list goes on and on. But we don't hear many people talk about *what they are willing to live for*. It seems most of humanity is consumed with death, one brief moment in a lifetime, instead of the myriad of moments of life we have the opportunity to embrace adventurously. And it seems like many people use all those myriad of moments of life to focus on avoiding death.

In fact, many people seem to define life based on longevity, on *quantity* and not *quality*. But is a long life necessarily a fulfilling life? Shouldn't life be defined as more than having a pulse and breathing in and out? Isn't life living your calling every moment of every day? Shouldn't the refrain we hear rolling off our tongues every morning as our feet hit the floor be, "TGIT! Thank God it's today"?

What if we lived every day fulfilling our *Dream*, taking and using every opportunity to live the *Dream* we were made to bring to this world and the people in it? What kind of a transformational life would that be? And what if more people in the world were doing that? What kind of a world would we inhabit? Can you imagine?

Gopher It!

In the classic comedy *Groundhog Day*[59], starring Bill Murray, Phil, a weatherman, goes to Punxsutawney, Pennsylvania to cover Groundhog Day, when the Groundhog, also named Phil, emerges from his den to either see or not see his shadow, thus determining whether winter will last another six weeks or not. Phil, the weatherman, wakes up every morning trapped in February 2nd, Groundhog Day. He actually spends years trapped in the same exact day. Phil, at one point, asks two locals at the bowling alley who are getting drunk, "What would you do if you were stuck in the same day over and over and nothing you did mattered?" One of the drunks responds, "Well, that just about sums it up for me."

Phil lives the same day again and again, at first completely self-absorbed, taking advantage of women, robbing an armored car, and doing whatever he wants. Then, he sets his conquests on Rita, his producer, and spends months in the same day setting up the perfect date to seduce Rita. His attempts end day after day with a slap in the face.

Although he can do whatever he wants with no consequences, Phil finds no fulfillment. Eventually, he sees life as meaningless and tries to commit suicide time and time again, from driving off a cliff to electrocution with a toaster in the bathtub, to stepping in front of a truck to jumping from the top of the three-story hotel. Yet, every day he wakes up on February 2nd in Punxsutawney.

Maybe you've felt like Phil. No, you're not trapped in the same day literally, but they all seem the same. Why is that? Somewhere along the way you may have forgotten who you truly are and what you are meant to bring to your world.

But if you make The Shift and transform your thinking, you begin to see your current circumstances, the positive and negative, as learning experiences. You say, "Today I am living my *Dream*," and you practice *The Listen and Learn Technique*.

A Moment in Time (Event)

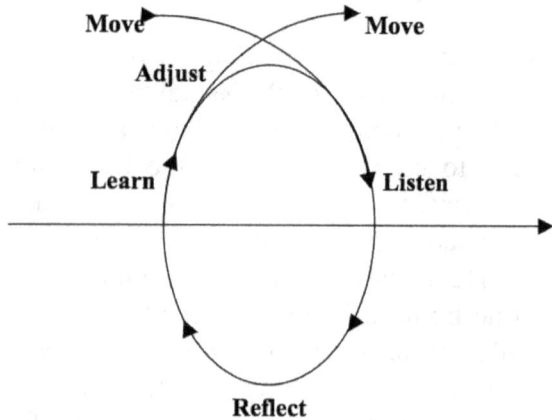

Here I am in a moment, maybe a moment of struggle. Winston Churchill said, "If you're going through hell, keep going!" The bad news is the struggle brings discomfort. The good news is Discomfort is my best friend. He'll tell me what I *need* to hear if I'll listen. As I go through this moment, I do the following:

Listen

Have you ever been in a heated discussion? If you are like me, I often find myself thinking about how I will respond while the other person is still *speaking*. When I do this I *hear* what the person is saying, but I am not *listening*. I am actually thinking more about *how I can win* the argument, sometimes by any means necessary. *I am focused on me*, and the short-sighted two stories most people live by unsuccessfully: *being right* and *looking good*. Ever been there? We know this type of behavior does not bring long-term, lasting success or change.

There's this great ancient saying about people who don't listen:

> *You will be ever hearing but never understanding; you will be ever seeing but never perceiving. For this people's heart has become calloused; they hardly hear with their ears, and they have closed their eyes. Otherwise they might see with their eyes, hear with their ears, understand with their hearts and turn, and I would heal them.*[60]

When we stop listening, our hearts harden, and we stop seeing and understanding others or our circumstances. It's nearly impossible to reconcile with others or change for the better when we stop listening. We can't bring "healing" or a solution.

There's a difference between *hearing* and *listening*. When I *listen*, I *open my mind and my heart*. I am not constructing a response. I focus my attention on the person sharing. I simply wait and receive what he shares, thinking it over, pausing, and reflecting on his words. I approach the person with a *beginner's mind, with no preconceived notions*. When I listen, *I have not already made up my mind* about what I am hearing. If I respond to someone, I wait a few moments between the person finishing his words and my response. This practice lends itself to compassion, *seeing things through another's perspective*.

We can also practice this when it comes to moments in our lives. Sometimes, I am so busy rushing through moments, I fail to learn from them. But if I open my mind and heart, lessons come; the moments teach me. John Maxwell says, "Walk slowly through the crowd." In other words, savor the moment and open your mind and heart. You never know what amazing insight or lesson each moment may teach you.

While it's important to be listening to my own voice, writing stories that serve me and attaching those stories to events, I also listen to other voices with an open mind, even negative voices. I don't have to agree with them, but they may serve me in understanding some aspects of the moment.

For example, if I want to go to college, but a close family member says, "You can't do that! You have no money!" I listen completely and then filter the pertinent information. I will throw out *You can't* but keep *You have no money*. Then, I will think, "I will research people who were in my same position financially and see how they went about being successful." From listening comes a plan to overcome the obstacles I face. Listening can save us from the "school of hard knocks." Listening is invaluable to accomplishing your *Dream*.

Listening entails the following skills:

- Beginner's Mind – approach the moment with an open mind and an open heart, like a child experiencing the moment for the first time, setting aside all preconceived ideas.

- Be in the Moment – be present and think of yourself as a sponge, trying to fully absorb all that the moment has to offer.

- Focus on Understanding – when the moment involves others, as most moments do, focus on seeing the world from their perspective, so that you can learn as much as possible and bring as much as possible to those in the moment.

- Determine the Need in the Moment – identify what you can do to help in the moment with the strengths and skills you possess, and do it.

- Suspend Your Emotions – let go of all emotional baggage from the past, and see the moment for what it is without any emotional coloring. This gives you a fresh perspective.

- Suspend Your Judgment – let go of all preconceived notions about the moment, especially a moment similar to moments you have experienced before. Remember that all moments are unique, even if similar, and lessons from past experiences can prepare you, but be wary of forcing the moment to fit the paradigm, plan, and purpose of previous moments. You can make your judgments during the *adjust* stage of *The Listen and Learn Technique*.

Reflect

When I get up in the morning, as I make my way from the bedroom to the bathroom, I look up and sometimes experience a horror beyond words: my reflection in the mirror! Ever been there? As we look in the mirror at the beginning of our day, we take in all of the minor (or sometimes major) adjustments we must make to our disheveled appearance.

That's exactly what we do when we reflect during a moment. We hit the pause button. We take in all of the moment without filtering the information through our preconceptions. We explore everything in the moment. We look at all the items that are "out of place" or need addressing. Then after letting it all sink in, we begin to determine what ideas will serve us to improve who we are and what ideas we can let go of that don't serve us. We keep what serves us and let go of the rest.

Reflection is a common denominator to the most successful people. Reflection is space where we intentionally stop the busyness that tends to surround, and sometimes, consume us.

Reflection is shutting off the technology, being still, and imagining. Reflection is essential to growth and learning.

Reflecting entails the following skills:

- Sum up the Experience – think through the details of the moment, and identify the trends and major lessons of the moment.

- Ask Questions for Clarity - here are some helpful essential questions:

    - *What am I learning about myself?*

    - *What are my strengths and weaknesses in relation to this person/moment, and how can I play to my strengths and manage my weaknesses?*

    - *What am I learning about my friends, my colleagues, my co-workers, my family, my community, my world?*

    - *How can what I'm learning serve me to accomplish and live my Dream?*

    - *How much and what kind of interaction will I have in future moments with people/moments like these?*

    - *Are people/moments like these a positive or negative influence on me living my Dream?*

    - *How will I adjust how I respond and interact with people/moments like these?*

    - *If I make this adjustment, what consequences may result? If I make a different adjustment, what may happen? (weighing your options)*

    - *What adjustments will I make when I encounter a similar person/moment?*

- *What Course Corrections to my plan and activities will I make to be better prepared for future people/moments like this one?*

By listening and asking the right questions at every moment, I do what most successful people do: *reflect*. Reflection is difficult, *disciplined* work, but it binds my Dream to my action.

Learn

To learn is to *transform, to become more of who you truly are, to grow in your Greatness*. How many of us keep doing the same things again and again, expecting different results? Why? Because we either fail to *listen* and *reflect* or, when we do, we fail to change our actions based on *listening* and *reflecting*. Why? Because what we are currently doing is comfortable and predictable. Because it's easier to do the same thing again and again. Easier and *emptier*.

Learning entails the following practices:

- A Humble Heart – humility is not thinking less of yourself, but thinking of yourself less. Humility is not about seeing yourself as unworthy. It's knowing your strengths and weaknesses and resting in who you are: a person who's open to change and willing to grow in the skills necessary to change, a person who is willing to grow her strengths and manage her weaknesses. A humble heart is malleable and willing to be shaped to change for the better.

- A Decision to Change Your Mind – a commitment to change the way you think based on the lessons learned in each moment.

- A Willingness to Try Something Different – attaching your changed mind to actions, realizing the old adage that *if you always do what you've always done, you're going to always get what you've always got.*

- A Spirit of Adventure – writing a story that sees opportunity in every obstacle and developing an attitude that sees every moment in the best light, moments of mystery and adventure.

Adjust, and Move On

Adjusting entails putting the lessons learned into actions. I change my mind, commit to trying something new, then, *I live it*. I move into the next moment trying something new. As I experience the next moment, I *listen, reflect, learn, adjust* and *move on*. This is the rhythm of truly living.

What About Phil?

In *Groundhog Day*, eventually, Phil, the weatherman, *listens* to Rita, his producer, who tells him, "I don't know, Phil, it's all in how you look at it."

From that moment on, Phil makes The Shift, changing his mind to make the most of every moment, from reading great literature, to learning to play the piano, to saving a boy from falling out of a tree and a man from choking, to fixing an elderly gentleman's back, to changing a flat tire for some elderly women, to providing hospice for a homeless man who dies on the evening of Groundhog Day. He takes every moment and develops personally, serving others in the process. He learns to love himself, and in turn he grows to love others. He appreciates what each moment brings because he understands his calling is caught up in becoming whom he truly is in order to serve others.

Every moment serves us in our transformation to live our Dream. Phil employs the listen and learn technique and begins to live a fulfilling life at every moment. As he acts, he learns, and as he learns, he adjusts, experiencing transformation from the inside out. He serves and loves the people of Punxsutawney and Rita. He *listens* to the moment and asks, "How is this serving me?" He *learns* from each moment and asks, "How can I apply this lesson?" Interestingly, even though Phil faces no consequences because Groundhog Day begins anew every day, Phil moves from *life-is-*

about-me to *life-is-meaningless* to *life-is-about-loving-and-serving-others*. He lives a life of significance, and significance is always part of intentionally living the transformed life of one's Dream. Phil makes The Shift, *listening, reflecting, learning,* and *adjusting*. He escapes the never-ending circle and lives the spiral of life.

What Matters

From this chapter remember:

1. Life is a spiral, not a circle.

2. Every moment is connected to every other moment, and wisdom is found in connecting those moments.

3. Practice *The Listen and Learn Technique*: In every spiral, every moment, listen to, reflect on, and learn from the moment. Then, adjust, better equipped for the next moment.

Your Turn

Step One: List five moments from any time in your life, negative moments that may have been really difficult, where you may have felt emotionally down, challenged or struggling, or positive moments that were fulfilling or rewarding. These moments have stayed with you for better or for worse.

Step Two: **Listen to the Moment** – Take each moment and listen to it. Feel the emotion of the moment (anger, fear, joy, excitement). Then, let it go. Think about what was said or done. What valuable thoughts did you have or what valuable words or actions can you hold on to? What will serve you in the future? Just write those down.

Step Three: **Reflect on the Moment** – Ask essential questions regarding what you have listened to in these moments, questions like the following: *What am I learning about myself from what I did or said? What am I learning about the others involved by what they did or said? What am I learning about humans in general from this moment? What can I take away from this moment that will teach me something about how to pursue my dream more effectively? What can I take away from this moment to help me build a strong moral character within? What will I do differently when a similar moment arises, or how do I keep a similar moment, if negative, from arising? What proactive steps can I take to keep moments like this one from arising (if the moment was negative in my view)? What did I do well in this moment (if the moment was either positive or negative in my view)? What story can I attach to this moment that will serve me?*

Step Four: **Learn from the Moment** – Write down what you have learned from the moment. *Write,* "Realizing that I can only control what I think and do with this moment, I have learned _____(*lesson learned*)____, and I will _____(*action plan*)_____ next time.

Step Five: Repeat Steps 2 through 4 for the five moments you have written down.

Step Six: **Adjust and Move on to the Next Moment** – Apply the lessons learned to the moments ahead and see how these moments turn out differently. Reassess the lessons and adjust them to work even better in your life.

You can begin this practice today and every day. I highly recommend *The Listen and Learn Technique* at the beginning of your day or the end of your day, or both! One of its side effects is peace. When you write down what you've learned that will serve you, along with an action plan, worry dissipates, and, actually, *The*

Listen and Learn Technique is a great practical solution when you find yourself worrying. Give it a try!

STOP! DO NOT READ ON UNTIL YOU'VE COMPLETED THE *YOUR TURN* SECTION OF THIS CHAPTER.

11

Choice

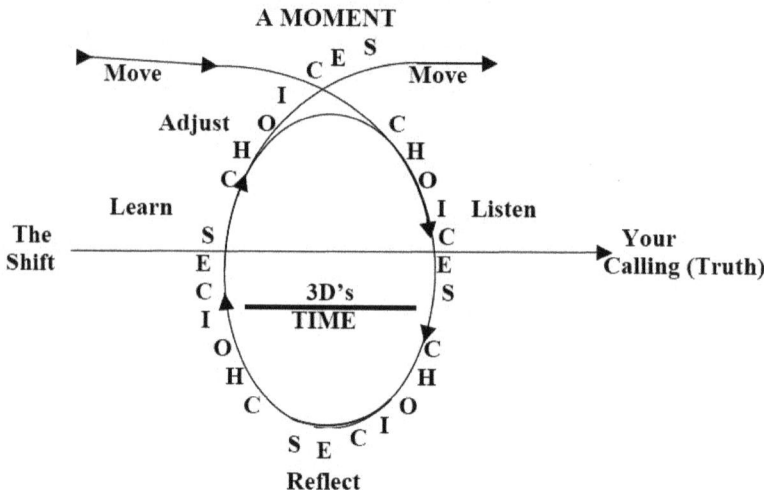

Success and Failure

Two people growing up in poverty and difficult circumstances, one of them overcomes the adversity and becomes wildly successful in life, the other doesn't. We have all heard stories like this. But why do some people overcome all kinds of adversity, while others continue to be victims of their circumstances? The biggest reason is choice. It may be one of the most important ideas to unlocking your Greatness and living your calling, and the good news is you are completely in control of your choices.

While you are completely in control of your choices, you may have little control over many circumstances in your life initially and even throughout your life. However, you do have a choice in the way you respond to those circumstances. Our journey through life is complex, but three main tenets every person embodies in life are subjectivity, individual freedom, and choice.

Subjectivity

You and I are subject to everything. From the moment we are conceived, forces are at work upon us. From our DNA to how Mom or Dad raised us; from where we grew up to our religious beliefs or worldview; from our education to our job opportunities; from our wealth to the weather; from our community's ethics to our own morality. These forces are constantly pressing upon us, from without and within, and they shape us consciously or subconsciously. We are subject to these forces, and we are absolutely free to choose how we respond to these forces.

Life Sentences

Here's a quick grammar lesson. In a sentence, the subject of the sentence acts. The subject is always a noun or a pronoun. You and I are nouns (Okay, literally "you" and "I" are pronouns but you know what I mean.). But there is also another place in a sentence for a noun. It is the object of a sentence. In a sentence, a noun can also be a direct or indirect object. Either way, an object is acted upon. The difference is that *a subject acts* and *an object is acted upon*.

Life is like a series of sentences, and we are the subjects or the objects. When life happens we will either *act* or *be acted upon*. Sometimes we will be acted upon, and then we choose our placement in the next sentence. Will we continue to be acted upon or will we act? Will we choose to be a victor or a victim?

The difference between being the subject or the object is the difference between being either proactive or reactive. Proactive people *act* before a circumstance. They anticipate what is coming, and they plan what they will do. By doing so, they are able to not only anticipate the various outcomes but lead the outcome in the direction they would like to see occur. They are also able to adjust in the midst of circumstances because a plan with a predetermined desired result gives them a goal and set intention to work toward. Reactive people react as a circumstance occurs. They have no idea what is coming, and they choose not to think through ahead of time what they will do. They let circumstances happen to them all of the time, and by the time they respond, the outcome usually is not desirable. Proactive people have vision, and vision is wisdom! Reactive people lack vision and, as a result, wisdom. Proactive people learn from experience. Reactive people just try to survive the experience.

Finding Our Place

Take your place in the sentences of life as the subject and not the object. When the forces of life press upon you, act! Ask, "What will I do?" and do it! Life is not always fair or easy. It does not always turn out the way we'd like. In those moments of struggle remember that success and failure partner with each other, and go through failure to get to success. Those who live their callings recognize they have the power to choose how they see life and what they will do with their life.

Storm Chasers

All of us will face storms in life, some a result of our choices, others a result of forces pressing upon us we have little control over. The one constant in either scenario is what we will do. As we ride out the storm, we can use *The Listen and Learn Technique*: listen, reflect, learn, adjust and move on to the next moment, making choices that will help us overcome the exact same storm, or, at least, prepare us for the next storm.

For the storms we helped create from our choices, leadership expert Tim Redmond says, "Weak people look outward and blame others. Strong people look inward and make adjustments."[62] This applies to all storms, even the ones we didn't play a role in creating. Weak people ask, *What is happening to me? Why is this happening to me?* Strong people ask, *What am I learning? What will I do? How will I adjust?* Strong people confront and go through adversity trying various solutions, and they continue trying until they overcome the challenge. Ralph Waldo Emerson writes, "A hero is no braver than an ordinary man, but he is braver five minutes longer."[63] Practice heroism! Strong people fall down seven times and get up eight.

The Path

In Ray Bradbury's sci-fi short story, *A Sound of Thunder*[64], a man named Eckels goes back in time on a T-Rex hunting expedition. His guide, Travis, tells Eckels to stay on the path the expedition party has laid down. To step off the path and interfere in the slightest way with the environment could change the entire sixty-five million year trajectory of history. Of course, Eckels steps off the path killing a butterfly. Upon his return, the entire world is in ruins under the hand of a tyrant. One person's seemingly insignificant choice has changed the history of the world.

It's Success, Not Succexy

Staying on our personal path matters. It's easy to look at something like a work of fiction on time travel and see that choices matter. It is more difficult to discern what may be more catastrophic or incredibly beneficial: the seemingly mundane or insignificant choices I make at every moment in life. This idea is incredibly profound. In my opinion, the difference between happiness and misery has everything to do with the little, seemingly insignificant choices we make daily.

We Are All Time Travelers

Today is the one dimension in which every one of us is equal. We all have twenty-four hours today. Except Einstein. To him everything was relative. But for the rest of us, we all have three hundred sixty-five days in a year. Those who live their callings, live it every day through daily choices. They realize, living one's Greatness, one's Dream, and one's calling is the difference between seeing life as an event or a process.

Today is not an event. Today is the result of the choices, practices, and disciplines made yesterday. Tomorrow will be the result of those same choices, practices, and disciplines made today. When we see moments in our lives as events, then an event can be inspiring or devastating, motivating or paralyzing. But when we see moments in our lives as parts of a process, then each moment builds on every other moment, creating momentum and powerful results over time.

When crisis, struggle, or obstacles present themselves today, the one who sees today as an event will struggle to get through and make the most of the moment. But the one who develops processes or protocols, like *The Listen and Learn Technique*, on a daily basis will walk steadily with character, integrity, and appropriate actions through adversity when it rears its head because he has been practicing and living character, integrity, and appropriate actions daily for a long time.

Those who look at today as an event believe successful people are just "lucky." People that are "lucky" do not have fewer struggles or obstacles in life. In fact, the more successful they are, typically, the more struggles and obstacles they face. The difference is that so-called "lucky" people are successful because they have a process and protocols in place. They have been practicing *desire, discipline,* and *determination* daily. They examine their mistakes or where they missed the mark and Course Correct, adjust, and move on. They intentionally think positively and practice daily the same activities that develop integrity, character, and positive results despite the obstacles. Their paths point toward their callings, and they stay on the path as best they can, leaning into their strengths and managing their weaknesses.

The power of process is most powerful in the small things. Even the mundane activity that doesn't seem to have any payoff, the extra five phone calls, the extra fifteen minutes a day studying, the extra ten minutes researching, the extra half mile on the morning run, after seven days has turned into thirty-five extra phone calls, an hour and forty-five minutes of extra studying, an hour and ten minutes of more research, an extra three and a half miles of running, which translates into an extra three hundred fifty calories burned. In one year:

- 1,820 extra phone calls

- Ninety-one extra hours studying

- Thirty-six hours researching

- One hundred eighty-two extra miles running

- 18,200 more calories burned

People intentionally living a calling realize that choosing a protocol of a little consistent extra activity compounds over time, creating huge dividends. Those who lock their callings away see today as an event, a circle instead of a spiral. They fail to see the power of today, partnering with time, and the power of staying on the path to Greatness in the seemingly small and mundane moments.

Internal Medicine

Any quick study of former lottery winners shows the tragedy of a life failing to stay on the path of financial discipline. Statistically, within only a few years most lottery winners are either broke, in greater debt than before they won the lottery, or in jail. Why? The way they managed a little was how they managed a lot. The financial disciplines one practices with a million dollars will be the same with ten dollars. How we are in the small moments is how we'll be in the big moments.

This idea is easy to understand but difficult to internalize. We see this so often in education. How students in the classroom behave is how they will behave on the court, on the field, or in any extra-curricular activity. A work ethic does not change depending on the venue. Many students only understand this after they actually experience it. Someone who does not consistently do his homework will not consistently practice his skills for a sport. Someone who takes shortcuts in the classroom will take shortcuts on the field, for which the team pays a price.

In an effort to get into a good college some parents will pressure teachers to give the child a second or third chance after the student has shown he or she is not willing to work, or he or she has missed so much class or coursework his or her grade suffers. In these moments, parents fail to realize bailing their child out of a "C" for a "B" or an "A" simply sets their child up for greater negative consequences later in life.

Sometimes it feels like our entire society is set up on this fallacy: The consequences I experience are not a result of my actions. It's why a country finds itself in trillions of dollars of debt, or a family finds itself in thousands of dollars of credit card debt, or a graduate finds himself with a piece of paper called a degree but cannot read, write, or do arithmetic well. If we do not accept the consequences of our choices, we will never learn to overcome obstacle-opportunities, go through failure, learn from it, and find success.

The student who practices skill development, study habits, time management, and planning in the high school setting, will practice the same habits in college or in his vocation. The student who does not do the little things in high school and does not suffer the relatively minor consequences, such as an "F" in a class, may continue to fail in life when consequences have a greater, negative impact.

The little things matter because they are really big things. Our choices and actions in the small moments prepare us for the big moments. Our good choices and appropriate activities remain consistent; positive consequences grow exponentially as we carry out these good choices.

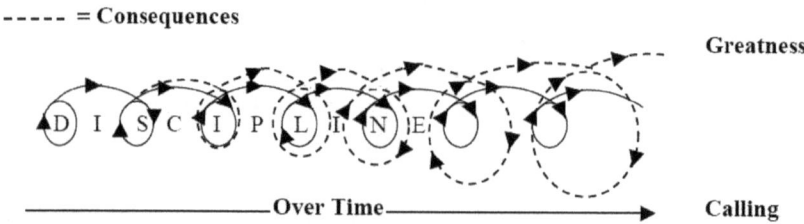

As we follow our plan, practice our daily *disciplines*, and hold to our goals despite great or small obstacle-opportunities, the consequences grow exponentially because each moment in life builds on the next, creating greater results. When we choose the spiral of undisciplined work, we spiral out of control away from our Greatness into a life of mediocrity and victimization. But successful people do daily what unsuccessful people do occasionally.

Change is Inevitable. Growth is Optional.

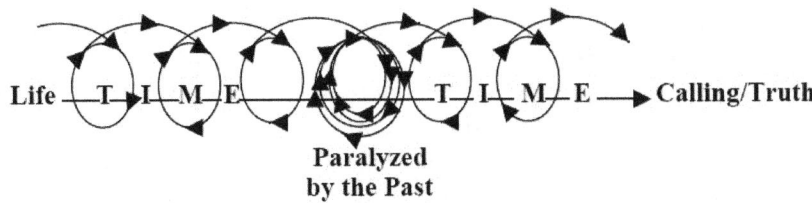

Life ─T─I─M─E ─────── T─I─M─E ──► Calling/Truth

Paralyzed
by the Past

Life is dynamic. As we travel the spirals of life, sometimes we get trapped in the regrets or the guilt of our past, like Phil in *Groundhog Day*. We repeat the same loop in our hearts and minds, but the loops of time move on. We become paralyzed by our past because we don't apply *The Listen and Learn Technique*. We attach stories not serving us to events. When we exchange the stories not serving us for the stories serving us, we mentally and emotionally stop going in circles and travel the spirals of our transformational journey into our Greatness, living our calling.

The Spinning Rainbow Wheel of Death

We're an Apple family. Apple computers use a spinning, rainbow wheel for the cursor when the computer is processing incoming data. Sometimes when we have performed a number of actions very quickly, the computer's rainbow wheel will begin to spin. On some occasions the computer locks up.

In my family we call this *The Spinning Rainbow Wheel of Death* because I'll probably have to force quit or restart the computer and lose the data I was working on. Is it frustrating? Yes, it can be, sometimes a little more frustrating than other times. Is it the end of the world? No. Can I still accomplish my tasks? Yes. It may take a little longer than I thought necessary because of the delay, but I can still reboot, begin the task again, and complete it. All that may have been lost is a little time.

Life is the same. When I become trapped in my past, experiencing emotional overload in an overwhelming and difficult moment for me to process, I experience a real-life *Spinning Rainbow Wheel of Death*.

But guess what? Out of the ashes the Phoenix rises! From a death comes new life! Even in the *Spinning Rainbow Wheel of Death* there is still a rainbow! There is beauty after the storm. During *The Spinning Rainbow Wheel of Death* the only wrong decision is to wallow in the spinning, to live life as a circle, hoping it will change, replaying again and again the keystroke choices that got me here.

Instead I listen and reflect on what I did, learn from my past, reboot, and move on! If I wallow I'll continue to spin my *Rainbow Wheels*. If I practice *The Listen and Learn Technique*, I am free to live again, living my calling and walking in my Greatness. Will I have lost time? Yes, but I'm not going in circles anymore. I'm spiraling on the greatest ride of my life, the ride toward my Dream.

The more conscious I become of the *Spinning Rainbow Wheels of Death* in my life, the sooner I can *listen, reflect, learn, adjust* and *move* beyond simply spinning. A static existence is a shadow on the cave wall. Change is inevitable. Growth is optional. I either spin my wheels, going nowhere, or I spiral, moving into my Greatness and living my calling.

Make the small, unnoticeable, unsexy, seemingly mundane choices moving you towards your calling. Make the appropriate emotional response to the storms of life, writing stories that serve you, then move, and over time watch your Greatness emerge. The Greatness Revolution is a spiral.

What Matters

From this chapter remember:

1. Success is a result of the choices you make.

2. Being proactive instead of reactive generates greater opportunities to be successful in any endeavor.

3. It's the seemingly insignificant choices you make daily that often determine your success. After all, it's called "success" and not "succexy."

4. Putting daily protocols in place, attaching yourself to the activity and not the outcome is essential to realizing your Dream, which manifests over time.

5. See your life as a spiral, getting somewhere, not a circle, a spinning wheel of death, going nowhere.

6. Value the process.

Your Turn

Step One: What habits do you need to fulfill your Dream? What daily practices implemented over time will yield exponential results? List three practices, one in the three areas of skill development, research, and application you can do daily, helping you move toward fulfilling your Dream. For example, if your Dream is to be a graphic designer, you may want to begin by taking a course in graphic design online or at a local community college, or watch Youtube videos on various graphic design programs (Everything is on the internet!) for skill development. You may then decide to spend twenty minutes a day researching various niches in industry where graphic designers are needed and what types of graphic designers are in high demand. For application, you may also begin practicing free graphic design for local firms in need. Since you are just beginning, you have nothing to lose by designing and meeting with a business. They aren't paying you, and they know you are brand new. You may be able to work your way into an internship or even employment where you get to network with other graphic designers or businesses.

Step Two: Take skill development and write a specific attainable daily activity you can implement. For example, "I will take an online course in graphic design and spend 30 minutes a day on the course."

Step Three: Take researching and write a specific attainable daily activity you can implement. For example, "I will spend twenty minutes per day researching various graphic design opportunities online."

Step Four: Take application and write a specific attainable daily activity you can implement. For example, "I will use my graphic design homework for my online class to fulfill the needs of businesses and clients at no charge to establish networks and contacts. I will contact one business or prospective client per week."

Remember: Be certain your action plans are specific, time-based, and easily completed. Better to start with less time than to try to devote too much time and not do the activity consistently.

STOP! DO NOT READ ON UNTIL YOU'VE COMPLETED THE *YOUR TURN* SECTION OF THIS CHAPTER.

12

C.A.R.: The Vehicle to Your Calling

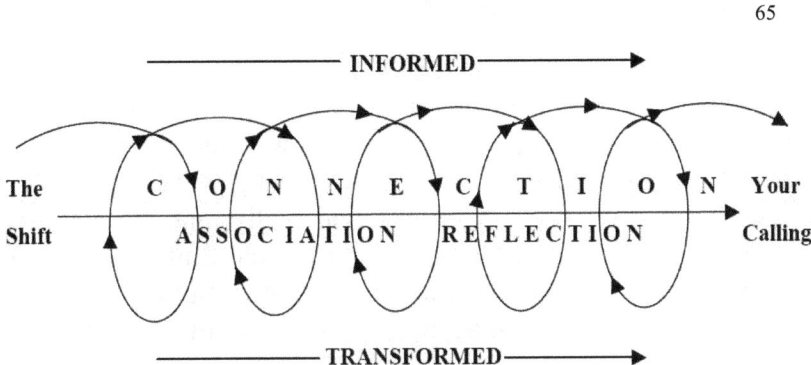

All Terrain Vehicle

If The 3D's of a Dream are the internal combustion engine for your life, then Connection, Association, and Reflection are the external vehicle to get you down the road to your Vocation, Calling, or Dream. While *desire, discipline,* and *determination* foster proper and healthy internal conditions, *Connection, Association,* and *Reflection* foster proper and healthy external conditions, creating a vehicle that can handle any terrain you'll have to cross to intentionally live the transformed life of your Dream. So let's take a look at *C.A.R.*, the vehicle to your *Calling*.

C. Is for Connection

understanding the relationships between moments that bring enlightenment, or insights that inform us (form us within) about our choices and our activity.

Wisdom is vision, and without vision people perish.[66] In Spencer Johnson's wonderful parable, *The Precious Present*[67], a man realizes this truth:

It is good to learn from the past, but it is not good to be in the past. And it is good to plan for my future, but it is not good to be in the future. Because that is how I lose myself. I must live in the present.

Poor Vision Brings Headaches

I called him to the front of the room and handed the student a rubber ball. I was trying to give the class a demonstration of cause and effect. I didn't realize just how effective this lesson would be. The student was a really nice young man. I liked him. However, he was a little high-strung and really enjoyed being the center of attention. In other words, your typical fourteen-year-old. I knew he would enjoy being the demonstrator, but on this day, I think he got a little more than he, or I for that matter, bargained for.

"I want you to throw this ball as hard as you can at the wall," I said.

He broke into a devilish grin, turned to the wall, and threw the ball as hard as he could. Immediately the ball bounced back off the wall, hitting the young man in the forehead right between his eyes. Smack!

There was a silence of disbelief in the classroom, and then the class burst out in laughter. "This poor kiddo," I thought. Rubbing the red welt developing in the middle of his forehead, glaring at me, he whimpered, "Why did you make me do that?"

"I didn't make you do that," I said as compassionately as I could. "You chose to do that. I said, 'I **want** you to throw the ball.' What did you think was going to happen? Haven't you ever played wall ball? Didn't experience tell you if you threw the ball straight at the wall it might bounce back and hit you?" (This just goes to show that experience is not the best teacher. Experience *with reflection* is the best teacher.)

He had no vision; I imagine literally for a few minutes after this incident. He failed to *see*. He didn't learn from his past, plan for his future, and live now. He didn't *have* to throw the ball as hard as he could. He didn't even *have* to throw the ball. He chose, and he chose poorly.

By the way, he was fine, and, I'd like to think, wiser for the wear.

Frames

If wisdom is vision, then vision is making *connections*. Ironically, in a period where technology is supposedly connecting us more and more, we live in a world that teaches us disconnection from an early age. School systems break learning down into subjects such as Math, History, Science, and Literature. We create frames around each subject. There's nothing wrong with this per se. We need frames to focus on the picture before us and to pay attention to the details of the picture of Math, Science, History, or Literature.

In one of my favorite series of paintings, Monet's *Haystacks*[68], we see the hay, the shadows cast by the sun, but interestingly enough in the paintings, guess what's missing? The sun! It's outside the frame. Hopefully, we recognize frames help us focus on specific contexts, but we recognize there's more to the contexts than what's in the frame, and what's beyond the frame matters to the moment in the frame. What's outside the frame and inside the frame are *connected*.

In school, the very best students recognize Math, Science, History, Literature, Art, Music, Physical Fitness, and Language are all *connected* to one another. In business the very best entrepreneurs recognize price, product, demand, culture, inspiration, marketing, human resources, team building, communication, timing and trends, and presentation are all *connected* to one another. In life the person of integrity recognizes who he is at home, at church, in the community, in his business, and alone are all *connected*, all one.

The frames, the courses in school or the areas in business or the circles of people in life, are all illusions, mere shadows on the cave wall. The frame helps one focus on specific contexts, and when context is understood, the frame no longer serves. A different frame is needed.

Frames don't really exist. They are simply tools to help us focus, grow, and understand various parts of the whole. The real learning occurs when the observer *connects* what's inside the frame to what's outside the frame. For example, in the novel *Life of Pi*, by Yann Martel, the symbol π (pi), a transcendent, irrational, infinite equation is an expression of a human being who is transcendent, irrational, and infinite.

We often hear people talk about "thinking outside of the box." The box doesn't exist, we just keep trying to make it real, like shadows on a cave wall. We don't need to think outside the box. We need to think inside *and* outside of the box because everything is *connected*. People who "think outside the box" simply make the connections most don't. A frame is like the box. We must see the little picture (what's in the frame) and the big picture (how what's in the little picture relates to what's beyond the frame).

The Six F's of a Great Life

When we *connect* our past moments to our present and let them help us plan our future, we have vision. We have wisdom. The same is true for the six areas of our lives, what I call the *Six F's of a Great Life*:

- **Faith** – living what we believe in our lives.

- **Foundation** – our core; what we believe; the stories we write and live by.

- **Family** – the way we conduct our relationships with those in our family.

- **Friends** – the way we conduct our relationships with others like friends, co-workers, and acquaintances in our lives.

- **Fitness** – how we care for and treat our bodies through nutrition and exercise which ultimately determines how we think and live.

- **Finance** – how we view and handle money and what kind of meaning we attach to it in our lives.

Realizing these six areas are frames to help us focus on living a healthy, whole life, we actually experience freedom. Frames don't restrict us. They serve us, just as rules or plans bring freedom as long as we remember the bigger picture. When we practice focused activity in the *Six F's of a Great Life*, we don't just *survive*. We *thrive*!

Wisdom comes when we remove the frames around the *Six F's*, seeing the interconnection of all life. Our practices in Fitness impact our practices in Finance. Our Foundation determines our Family and Friends relationships. They are all one. Those who see the connections between seemingly disparate experiences have vision and thrive, walking in Greatness.

Oftentimes, we forget connection and focus on the frame. Students do this in school when they focus more on a grade for a course and less on learning and growing. In business, people do this when they fill their calendar with ineffective activity. Parents do this when they fill their kids' time with activities but lose sight of the family relationships in the process. In community or church organizations people do this when they focus on accomplishing a service project and less on the people they serve. The *what* (the grade, schedule, activities, or project) displaces the *why* at the center of *Greatness* (see *Chapter 3: The Why is Your Calling*).

Soren Kierkegaard writes, "If a person does not become what he understands, then he does not understand it either."[69] Knowing is not the same as being. And being is not the same as doing. We're not human knowings or human doings. We're human beings! When what you know, do, and feel are one, you are connecting **why** you do **what** you do with **who** you truly are, and though challenges arise as you do this, mentally, emotionally, and physically the will to live that way is effortless. Connection keeps us from throwing a ball as hard as we can at a wall, ending up with a terrible headache.

Connection helps us identify desire, discipline, and determination:

- **Desire** – Does my desire (what's written within my heart) line up with what I'm doing? Am I being *who* I am in *what* I am currently doing? Do I possess integrity?

- **Discipline** - Are my daily actions (my protocols and processes) based on the lessons learned from my past, and are they propelling me toward my calling?

- **Determination** – Am I persisting on my unique path, or am I on an ineffective path, a path that is not me?

A. Is for Association

When the young man in the class threw the ball and suffered the consequences of a ball to the head, he had to make a decision: *What will I make of this moment? Will I blame Mr. Thomas for the event because he told me he wanted me to throw the ball? Will I make excuses out of embarrassment in front of the class? Or will I learn a lesson about my choices and the consequences of those choices?* He was going to write a story about the event, but the story he would write was entirely in his own hands.

Associate the events in your life to the story that serves you. We can't control all the events in our lives. The events we cause from poor vision, like a ball to the head, we can take responsibility, ask for forgiveness, forgive ourselves and learn. However, we do write every story, and if a story isn't serving us, we must change the story! We can *associate* the appropriate story that serves us to the event.

As mentioned previously, Carl Jung writes, "Until you make the unconscious conscious it will rule your life, and you will call it fate." One of the greatest dangers we face regarding our perception of who we are (positive or negative), what the world is (friend or foe), and how we live our lives (faith or fate), rests in not allowing our minds to run on its default setting because the mind on its default setting will always go negative and protective.

The proactive person not only has a plan, establishes goals, and practices positive affirmations, she also consciously writes stories that serve her around every event in her life. She intentionally associates a story that moves her closer to her Dream, and consequently her Greatness.

Proper Emotional Responses

Associate the proper emotional response to an event. Have you made a mistake or failed? If so, how did you feel when you did this? Here's the big question: How long ago did this happen? If not recently, are you still filled with guilt? Do you still feel bad? Do you find yourself feeling regretful? Are you trapped in your past? If the answer to any of these is yes, then examine the story you've attached.

You may need to change the story. If you have done everything you can to correct your mistake, then you most definitely must let go of your guilt and inappropriate feelings because they do not serve you. Forgive yourself. As long as you hold onto these feelings, you are paralyzed by your past. You cannot live right now.

While real, emotions can either line up with what is true, or they can be completely false. Your emotions are not bad things, though many of us will do just about anything to avoid dealing with them. You must accept how you feel, but you don't stay there. Say, *I am angry* or *I am hurt* or *I am sad*, and admit you are human. Emotions are actually blessings because they alert you that it is time to grow by remembering what you know to be true. And that's a great thing!

When intense emotion comes on us, many times physical activity helps resolve that intensity. Go for a walk, hike, run or bike ride. All the chemicals released when emotions overwhelm us will dissipate sooner through physical activity, and we can let go of the raw emotion much more easily. As we exercise, we'll find that the heart will begin to clear and our minds will begin to reflect on the event, seeing how the event that brought so much emotion will serve us in the future in similar moments.

Create processes and protocols in your life. Staying with a process or protocol when difficulties arise and negative emotions come, will help you release those negative emotions because daily processes are not sentimental. They are simply activities with an intentional vision and a plan. For example, when someone offends you, if you have a process in place like *The Listen and Learn Technique,* you can move systematically through the five-step process to grow your understanding of who you are and what you are learning. Remember, protocols and processes protect you and others from the Accuser's lies (See *Chapter 3: The Shift*).

Here's what we can hold on to from emotional responses to our failures or offenses: the lessons we have learned. With what we've learned we can adjust our activity when a similar moment arises. If we have wronged someone, we apologize. If it happened a long time ago and it is not possible to apologize, we say to ourselves, "I am sorry." Then, let it go. We *listen, reflect, learn, apologize, and move on* better prepared for the next moment.

Remember in *The Lion King*, Simba tells Rafiki his past regrets, believing he is responsible for his father's (Mufasa) death; Simba has attached a story to Mufasa's death based on his emotional response rather than the truth that Scar, Simba's uncle, was sinister and cunning. Rafiki smacks Simba on the head with his staff. Just like the student and the rubber ball, rubbing his head, Simba yells at Rafiki:

> Simba: What did you do that for?
> Rafiki: It doesn't matter. It's in the past.
> Simba: Ya, but it still hurts.
> Rafiki: Oh, yes, the past can hurt, but the way I see it, you can either run from it or learn from it.[70]

Simba learns from it. He exchanges his story for a story that serves him, returns to Pride Rock to face his uncle, Scar, and overcomes his *obstacle-opportunities*, becoming king.

When we make a mistake, it's appropriate to feel disappointment and regret for a time. However, at some point we have to let go of the feeling, hold on to the lesson, and move on with adjusted behaviors. Successful people do not take failure personally, internalizing it. They say, "Well, I missed that one," or "I made a mistake." Those with a calling *associate* events with the proper emotional response. They don't blow their mistakes out of proportion. They realize the past is over and unchangeable, but today can be different.

Excellence

Many people tend to equate perfection with excellence. Perfection is defined as "freedom from fault or defect; flawlessness." Excellence is defined as "a virtue, transcendence, or eminence."

Perfection is so much easier to understand, mostly because all of us know we don't possess it. When it comes to imperfection, we're all in the same boat. But what, exactly, is excellence?

Excellence finds its roots in *virtue* (another word for truth), in *transcendence* (meaning to go beyond, to exceed, to surpass), and *eminence* (meaning high repute). Excellence relates to a person's moral compass, not whether he or she lives perfectly. Excellence is about being whole.

The Ancient Greek View of Humanity[71]

The ancient Greeks believed humanity consisted of three components. The first part was *cerebral man*. This was the mind of man, the logical, thinking element of humanity. The second was *visceral man*. This was the gut of man, the animal nature of humanity, or instincts. By *cerebral man*, humanity is spirit. By *visceral man*, humanity is animal. But the third element of man, according to the Greeks, made humanity unique. This third element was the place of grace (or love); it was the compromising element between humanity's logical and animal nature. It was the place where emotions rested, emotions taking the middle ground between a purely logical and a purely animal existence. This was *the heart* of man.

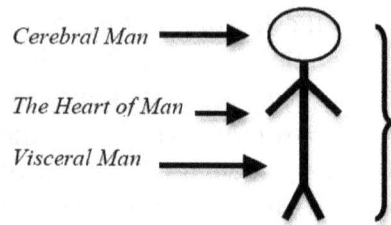

By *cerebral man*, Humanity is *spirit*.
By *visceral man*, Humanity is *animal*.
By its *heart*, Humanity is *human*.
The balance of *cerebral* and *visceral* man in the *heart* makes humanity *whole*.

This triune view of humanity tied into the ancient Greek's idea of "arête," meaning virtue or excellence, the highest state someone could reach. When one practiced moral virtue, fulfilling his purpose or calling, living up to his full potential, he was said to possess "arête." What he thought, what he felt, and what he did were one. His head, heart, and gut danced together as one, inseparable from one another. A person like this was not perfect, but he was whole, possessing integrity. "Arête" can only be accomplished when we listen to our hearts (our emotions), letting it mediate between our head (intellect) and our gut (animal nature).

What the Dante!

Dante Alighieri's *Inferno*[72] establishes a view of hell we might find odd today. Dante based his entire work in large measure on Aristotle, the Greek philosopher. The Greek view of humanity figures prominently in Dante's taxonomy of hell.

We might assume murderers would inhabit the deepest part of hell, but Dante places murderers somewhere in the center of hell. He places those who succumbed to sins of passion, like adultery or gluttony, in the upper levels of hell. Why? Because these were sins of passion, of *visceral man*, of the gut, of humanity's *animal nature*. Dante places the sins of malice and fraud in the very lowest levels of hell. Why? Because these were sins of cold, calculated, premeditated thought, of *cerebral man*, of the mind of humanity.

In Dante's view, those in hell were out of balance. They weren't whole. They failed to listen to their heads and their guts, and find a compromise in their hearts. It's easy to see why Dante would place a glutton or adulterer in hell. We get the idea of letting your selfish proclivities overtake you, ending up in ruin, but we may not understand in our modern era the dangers of listening solely to intellect, for intellect alone fails to take into account the deepest of values: love, compassion, and mercy.

Instead, what we find in our world today are what C.S. Lewis called *men without chests*.[73] According to the ancients, the two greatest teachers are pain and love, and often those two great teachers accompany each other. And where do these two great teachers reside? In *the heart*.

We all probably know someone who has escaped from pain through such things as alcohol, drugs, sex, and entertainment, things of *visceral* man. We understand that idea. But perhaps an even more insidious way to avoid the pain of the *heart* is the escape of *cerebral* man, the intellect, which detaches any emotion to whatever causes our pain. This occurs far more often than we may be aware. Why? Because intellectualizing a problem allows us to believe this illusion: We have conquered the problem causing us pain. We are in *control* of the pain and the problem.

We build a fortress around our hearts, using *escape* and *control*. We *escape* to our gut, using alcohol, drugs, sex, or entertainment (the list goes on and on), or we avoid our emotions by running to our heads, trying to *control* the pain of our *hearts*. Either way, when we face obstacles, struggles, or painful moments, many of us either run to the gut or the head to escape the heart, winding up imbalanced, unhealthy, and un-whole. We are literally broken in pieces. Not being whole is our form of *personal disconnection*.

Like the caterpillar we must struggle to become great. We must embrace our struggles and pain. We must go through, feel, and learn from them. If we don't, we end up paralyzed by them, stuck in a moment we cannot escape. Any struggle we face where we do not listen to our hearts will continue to haunt us. All the alcohol in the world will not drown the issue. All the intellectual analysis in the world will not *control* the issue.

Only through *listening* to and *embracing* the heart, experiencing the mental anguish, crying the physical tears, receiving the lesson of the moment, and going through the struggle will we emerge transformed and whole. We must go through it to grow through it. We come to a full understanding that *escape* and *control* bring paralysis, and what we resist will persist.

When the Greeks said follow your heart, they did not mean, do whatever you feel like! I'm ok. You're ok. The Greeks meant find a compromise between your head and your gut. Don't let one rule the other. Let them dance with one another to the music of the heart. Only in this way can you be one, a whole person, a person of excellence.

Ice Cream

It had been a particularly hard year of teaching. On my way home from school I was feeling sorry for myself. I decided to stop off at the local supermarket and pick up a gallon of ice cream, not the cheap, generic knock off stuff. No! The expensive, soft and smooth, absolute-perfection ice cream: Chocolate Chunk Chip Cookie Dough Ice Cream! Oh yah! A little touch of heaven!

I purchased the ice cream, arrived home, put the ice cream in the freezer and greeted my wife and kids. Later that evening after dinner together, I was ready to drown my sorry teaching life in absolute delight. I headed for the fridge, opened up the freezer, and proceeded to dole out a huge, I mean *huge*, bowl of Chocolate Chunk Chip Cookie Dough Ice Cream.

I looked at my wife across the counter who was staring with wonder at the bowl I had just overfilled and asked, "Would you like some?" She said, "No thank you." I put the ice cream away and walked to the couch to sit down and flip on the TV, remote at the ready and ice cream in hand. It was going to be a grand *escape* from the struggle, pain, and obstacles of, well, the school year!

I ate that ice cream with absolute delight. By the time I had finished the bowl, I was alone on the couch. My wife and kids had gone upstairs. I looked at the bowl, the empty bowl. The bowl begging me to lick it clean. I heard *visceral man* say, *You know you want more. Go on . . . go get another bowl. You **deserve** it. It's been a rough year. You **know** you want it.* Then I heard cerebral man: *Don't do it. You've already had too much. If you eat more **you will regret it tomorrow**, if you know what I mean! It's not going to feel good tomorrow.*

I slowly got up, crept over to the kitchen, opened the freezer door and doled out another giant bowl of Chocolate Chunk Chip Cookie Dough Ice Cream. I sat back down, ignoring *cerebral man's* advice, holding hands with *visceral man* while I downed a second bowl of deliciousness.

And once again, the voices were back. More? *Visceral man: Go ahead! Why not! Cerebral man: "You seriously must stop! You will be a disaster tomorrow!* What to do?

I scraped out the last of the ice cream from the container from the fridge into my bowl, threw the ice cream container away, and sat back down on the couch. One gallon gone!

Then, the real fear began. I heard footsteps on the stairs.

I knew it was my wife coming back downstairs. I stared at the television screen, remote in hand, pretending to be watching, but all the time praying, *Please, please, please don't go to the freezer!*

I heard her footsteps on the hardwood floors of our house that led to the kitchen. I heard her footfalls stop. There was a pause and I prayed, *Please don't open the freezer door!*

I heard the freezer door open. There was another pause and I prayed, *Please don't look for the ice cream.*

From behind me I heard, "Hey, Honey, where's that ice cream?" Sheepishly and as matter-of-factly as I could I said, "Oh . . . umm . . . I thought you said you didn't want any."

I had been caught! I had *listened to my gut,* and I had been caught! *Cerebral man* said logically *you should not eat all that ice cream because it is not good for you and you will regret it when all that lactose and chemicals get into you,* but *visceral man* won out, and I lived to regret that decision the next day, if you know what I mean!

I had not listened to my heart. I did not compromise. I was out of balance. I was not a *whole person* in that moment because I ignored *cerebral man* and failed to listen to *my heart.*

When mind (cerebral), body (visceral), and heart (soul) all work together to find what will serve all of me best, then I experience *wholeness.* Then, I practice *excellence.* I may not be flawless. I may not be perfect. *But if I unite my head and my gut in the heart I practice excellence.*

Celebrating Excellence

When we do listen to our *head*, our *gut*, and finally find a compromise in our *heart* we must celebrate those moments. When we experience a moment of excellence, we must celebrate our success with an appropriate emotional response. Celebrate when you accomplish something in your *Greatness*, and let go of negative emotions attached to failures.

Successful people define failure as an outcome that differs from what they thought would happen. Through processes and protocols, Thomas Edison discovered ten thousand ways to *not* make a light bulb, but those ten thousand ways taught Edison how to make the ten thousandth and first way matter. I am certain Edison celebrated the ten thousandth and first way. And he got there by letting go of the negative emotions of the previous ten-thousand ways!

Neuroscience tells us memory is six parts emotion and one part information. This explains why childhood memories filled with sensations and feelings remain vivid and reading a dry, laborious textbook doesn't stay with us. We all must feel the pain and cry our tears. We can't ignore our emotions and hope to get beyond them. If we hang on to the negative emotions of events and downplay the positive emotions of successful events, *association* will not serve us. We must let go of the negative emotions, remember the lesson, and celebrate excellence, moving toward our *callings*.

Associating with Excellent People

You are the combined average of the five people you associate with most – including the way you walk, talk, act, think and dress. Your income, your accomplishments, even your values and philosophy will reflect them.[74]
-Jeff Olson, *The Slight Edge*

Ever been crab fishing? Anyone who has will tell you if you only have one crab in the bucket, you need a lid. If you have two or more, you can leave the lid off. Why? Because if there is only one crab it will climb out of the bucket, but once you have several crabs in the bucket, they will continually pull each other down, and, as a result, by the end of the day, you are ready for a crab feast!

It's the same way with people. We may find ourselves around crabby people who have given up on their Dreams and will do all they can to drag others down, keeping others from achieving their Dreams as well. But in the end, those crabs are going to be building someone else's feast instead of rising above the bucket of life and fulfilling their own. You don't have to be a crab. You don't have to enter the bucket. How?

Your *why*. What do you want? Whatever it is you want, find people who have achieved what you want and form relationships with them. The more time we spend with people, the more we tend to look and behave like them. Associate with positive, responsible, reflective, empowered and empowering people with vision. Dissociate from negative, irresponsible, blaming, entitled and enabling people without vision. This may be the most difficult and painful part of walking in our Greatness, especially if we love these "crabby" people.

Henry Ford said, "My best friend is the one who brings out the best in me." The more time we spend associating with negative people, the more likely we will write stories that do not serve us. At first, it may not be evident, but over time those negative stories will manifest, growing more toxic in our lives. What we focus on will grow.

There is a difference between a negative friend and a challenging friend. Friends who challenge us to grow by speaking the sometimes-painful truth or asking the tough questions are challenging relationships. Friends who simply look to drag you down, leaving you feeling empty and defeated are negative relationships. True friends rejoice with your change and growth!

Remember, "as iron sharpens iron, so a friend sharpens a friend."[75] The more time we spend with positive people, the sharper we become, writing stories that serve us. At first, it may not be evident, but over time those positive stories will manifest and bring positive results from the positive, proactive practices in our lives, moving us toward our Dreams, growing our Greatness, creating *The Greatness Revolution*.

Dissociating While Practicing Compassion

Dissociating with negative people does not mean ignoring, withholding or being cruel. We can still give negative people time, but perhaps instead of an hour, we give ten minutes. Often, we can sense when our encounters with these people begin to head down a road of negativity. When that moment arises, we bring our time to a close and move on. We still practice compassion.

Adversity is not a reason to dissociate with others. Sometimes, friends or family experience a difficult season in life. Many responsible, positive, reflective, and empowered people struggle, and they want to grow in their Greatness.

However, others, no matter how blessed, see a half-empty glass, what's wrong with every situation, and do not want to get better. They have resigned themselves to a life of *quiet desperation*. They choose to wallow in the *The Spinning Rainbow*

Wheel of Death (without the rainbow, of course). Even the Great Physician asked the paralyzed man by the pool, "Do you **want** to get well?" Unless we answer, "Yes!" to that question, there's not much anyone can do. As Henry Ford once said, "Whether you think you can or you think you can't, you're right!"

With people who wallow in what's wrong, unfair, and impossible, sometimes we have to compassionately let them go the way they choose. No person has the power to heal another person all on his own, period. A Buddhist proverb reads, "When the student is ready, the teacher will appear." A person must **want** to be healed, must want to get better, and must want to be transformed in his Greatness.

R. Is for Reflection

Reflection in western society is scarce, but successful people use reflection to connect desire, determination, and discipline to their Dreams. Just as we look in the mirror and prepare for our day, those who reflect assess what actions and practices they need to implement. Reflection is pausing, listening, learning, and adjusting. When we reflect we ask:
- How did my day go?
- What did I do today that went well?
- What did I do today that didn't go well?
- What served me today for my calling?
- What adjustments can I make to practice the disciplines that will move me toward my calling?
- What struggles did I have and was I determined enough?
- What might I adjust when I face the same struggle tomorrow?
- Did I listen to my head, gut, and find a compromise in my heart?
- What will I keep doing?
- What will I stop doing?
- What will I add to my activity?
- Am I still walking in my Greatness and on the path to my calling?

Daily assessment is vital to making connections. Reflection helps us associate the proper emotional responses to events occurring in our lives. Reflection empowers us to live each moment to its fullest, to appreciate what each time and place has to offer, to be grateful for the adventure of living our calling daily, and to enjoy the journey.

Driving the C.A.R.

Connection, Association, and Reflection, if we don't practice these consciously, we will practice them unconsciously. And until you make the unconscious conscious it will rule your life, and you will call it fate.[76] The question is, will I take control of the C.A.R. and drive it in the direction I desire, toward my calling, or will I remain a passenger, letting my subconscious determine the road I travel? If you don't know your direction, any road will take you there.[77] And any vehicle will serve!

Those who walk in their Greatness and live their calling daily take the wheel and drive the C.A.R. They connect every moment. They associate the proper emotional response to events along the highway. They associate with like-minded, positive, proactive drivers headed in the same direction. They reflect on what they have learned and how they will adjust. Then, they move on down the road, applying the lessons to the next mile, enjoying the journey as they grow nearer their destination: Greatness.

What Matters:

From this chapter remember:

1. Intentional connection, association, and reflection are three indispensible practices you must implement to live the transformed life of your Dream.

2. Connecting lessons from previous experiences and applying them in the current similar moments, as well as to your plans, will move you toward your Greatness and Dream.

3. This type of connection is wisdom. Wisdom is vision.

4. Frames help you focus on one goal or purpose, but the frame is an illusion, and you must connect the goal or purpose in the frame to your larger calling or Dream beyond the frame. It helps you remember why you are doing what you're doing.

5. Associating past lessons learned to your current vision, plan, and actions help you progress more efficiently and effectively.

6. Associating the appropriate emotional response to an experience, eventually letting go of the intense emotion and remembering the lesson, serves you.

7. We're not human knowings or human doings. We're human beings.

8. Practicing excellence using your head, your body, and your heart is essential. It's not about perfection. It's about being whole, having integrity, every part of you moving in the direction of your transformation and Dream.

9. Associate with excellent people, and see your transformation rise before your eyes.

10. Reflection, like practicing *The Listen and Learn Technique*, on a daily basis makes desire, discipline, determination, and Course Correction easier and more effective.

Your Turn

Step One: **Vision:** Write a brief personal Vision Statement for your life. What is the ideal result of your life, the state you would like to attain from pursuing your Greatness and your Dream? Who are you? What do you value? What do you see? What is the most important thing you are doing in the Vision? In what do you excel in the Vision? What makes you unique in the Vision? How does the Vision bless others? Your Vision must inspire you every time you read it, say it, and see it. Your Vision must excite you. Your Vision must give you a sense of purpose for the actions you take to attain it. Your Vision is what you turn to in the midst of Obstacle-Opportunities and seasons of struggle. Write the Vision in the present tense: "I am. . ."

Examples:

- I am a financially sound international, inspirational and motivational speaker and author, empowering thousands of people to live their unique gifts and dreams for the world.

- I am a progressive, motivational, and dynamic teacher who upholds the highest standards for my students and uses the best practices of education.

- I am a compassionate, energetic, and positive team leader with my own successful business, casting a strong vision of what is possible for my team members and what is possible for their lives.

- I am a sober, happy, and healthy recovering substance abuser who inspires, encourages, counsels and empowers other recovering addicts to live sober, happy, healthy lives full of love, joy, and peace.

- I am a consistent, hard-working, happy and high-performing student who creates continuous, multiple opportunities for myself from which to choose from, so I can pursue my dream to be a wealthy, healthy, and happy contributing member of my community.

Step Two: **Connection:** We will be going in-depth with the *Six F's of a Great Life* in chapter sixteen. For now, brainstorm briefly how you can practice your

Vision statement in each of the *Six F's*: Faith, Foundation, Family, Friends, Finances, and Fitness. In chapter sixteen we will flesh these out more, but for now, think about how you will live your Vision in each of these areas. Write a sentence or two for each area.

Step Three: **Association:** On a piece of paper, create two columns. Title the first column "People Who Will Bring Out the Best in Me." Title the second column "People Who Suck the Breath Out of Me."

In the first column, write down people you know and would like to know better who have the traits, the lifestyle, the knowledge, or the success you would like to possess, people who inspire you. These people bring life to all they do, and they bring life to others. They also have accomplished some or all of what you want to accomplish.

In the second column, write down people you currently associate with who are negative, people who leave you feeling low after you leave their presence, people who seem to suck the life out of you, who seem to make your Dream and your Vision impossible. These are "glass is half-empty" people.

Step Four: Take a look at your lists. Write an action plan. What will you do to create opportunities to be in relationship with those in the first column?

Examples:

Perhaps one of the persons you wrote down on your list goes to your church. One action plan might be to approach this person at church and begin a weekly relationship by greeting this person and having a casual conversation with this person. This will lead to an opportunity to develop a deeper relationship.

Perhaps you have a teacher or a boss at work that possesses traits you want to emulate. During passing period or on breaks, you might enter into conversation with questions that play into that person's expertise or interests. You may offer to bring back some lunch for that person and eat with the person once a week or once a month.

Now, take a look at the second column. Write a strategy of how you will spend less time associating with these persons on the list.
Example:
Perhaps one strategy you employ is as simple as limiting the amount of time you are on the phone with this person, or limiting the length of your personal conversations with this person. Simply write, "I will limit my face time with this person to seven minutes."

Perhaps you plan to shut down the conversation as soon as it goes south into negativity. Simply write, "When I sense things going negative, I will say, you know, I have some other errands to run. I have to get going. It's great to see you. Have a great rest of your day."

Step Five: **Reflection.** Be intentional about reflecting. Create a plan to spend time reflecting. Have the plan consist of the following:

1. **When** – when will you spend time reflecting (morning, evening)?
2. **How Long** – how much time will you spend time reflecting (ten, fifteen, thirty minutes)?
3. **What Key Questions** – what key questions will you ask and answer during your

reflection time (see potential sample questions in the chapter)?

4. **How often** – how often will you reflect (daily, weekly, bi-weekly)?

Implement your plan and be consistent. Use a journal to record your thoughts and plans that come out of this reflection. You will grow exponentially in achieving what you want.

STOP! DO NOT READ ON UNTIL YOU'VE COMPLETED THE *YOUR TURN* SECTION OF THIS CHAPTER.

13

Time Flow

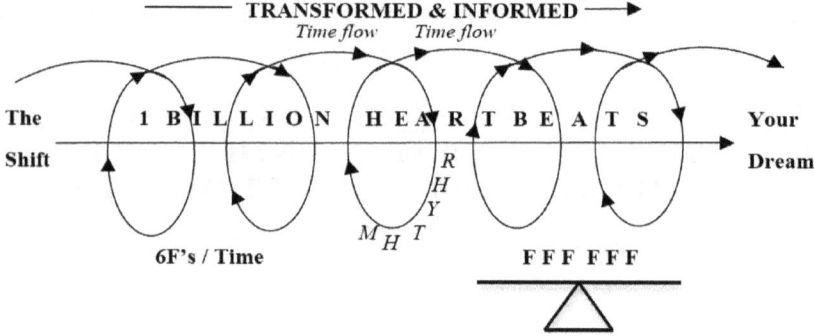

One Billion Heartbeats

One billion heartbeats. This is a lifetime. Not just for humans. The life span of humans, amphibians, birds, fish, mammals, and reptiles, when counted in heartbeats is one billion *on average*. Humans live sixty-five years on average, hamsters three years, and Arctic whales one hundred fifty years. The hamster can have a heart rate of up to four hundred fifty beats per minute, the whale as little as ten beats per minute, thus explaining the difference in the number of years they live, but the number of heartbeats in a lifetime on average is about one billion.

When we exercise, our heart rate increases so we "use up" more heartbeats, thus shortening our life span. However, when we exercise regularly over time, our resting heart rate slows, and we "save up" heartbeats. Each year exercising three to four times per week costs us one entire week of heartbeats, but our improved fitness adds about thirteen weeks to our life expectancy. That means we gain a year (fifty-two weeks) of life about every four years of consistent exercise three to four times per week. We see desire, determination, and discipline over time (exercise three to four times per week) leads to The Greatness Revolution in Fitness.

The Swiss-born Max Kleiber, a professor and researcher at U.C. Davis, developed these ideas from his research. He called it the *Kleiber Ratio* (of course!). *The Kleiber Ratio* is based on the metabolic rates of various animals. A hamster's metabolism is much faster than an Arctic whales, but on average the number of heartbeats over a lifetime remains the same: one billion.

Some scientists speculate that different sentient life forms experience time differently because of this phenomenon. A fly, which only lives from twenty-four hours to a few days, seems to move rapidly when we brush it away. To us the fly's movement seems rapid because our metabolic rate and our heart rate is slower than the fly's. But to the fly does the hand coming at it seem to be moving much more slowly because the fly has such a high metabolic rate? If Kleiber is correct, then time flows differently for each life even though on average all life forms live the same amount based on heartbeats: one billion on average. Perhaps each life has a unique rhythm, and each must live that rhythm.

Time Flow

Now, I don't want to go all Harry Chapin on you and talk about *Cat's in the Cradle.* . .but I am going to. Chapin sings *As I hung up the phone it occurred to me, my boy was just like me.* In Chapin's classic song a father realizes that his habit of being too busy with the cares of the world keeps him away from an intimate relationship with his own son. He realizes this towards the end of his life when his son tells his father over the phone that he is too busy to give his father any time because of all the cares of the world in the son's life. With the last, slowing notes of the song we understand what really matters.

It is so easy to say, "Relationships are the most important things in life." It's easy to say, "You can't take it with you!" But if you're like me, it's often tough to be fully present and to give time to family and friends because of all the other concerns of life on one's plate. How I see my life and the time I have every day determines whether I am spending my life truly living and loving, fostering what really matters to me, or whether I am spending my life dealing with all kinds of stuff that feels shallow and unfulfilling. And this begins with my view of time.

Time flow differs from time management just as being productive differs from being busy. Doing things won't create success; doing the right things strategically, efficiently and with proper timing creates success. Having a full calendar does not guarantee success. Having a calendar with rhythm brings success. Thinking time flow versus time management requires The Shift.

In the *Tao Te Ching*, Lao Tzu writes, "The highest good is like water. Water gives life to the ten thousand things and yet does not compete with them. It flows in places that the mass of people detest and therefore is it close to the Way."[79] Elsewhere Lao Tzu writes, "Be still like a mountain and flow like a river."

The Masking Tape and Rhythm

One day in class, I was directing an activity with my students. I can't remember the topic. I was holding a roll of masking tape in my hand, and I was sitting on a student desk in the front row of the class facing the students. The roll of masking tape accidently slipped out of my hand, fell to the floor, and rolled all the way down the aisle to the back of the room near my teaching desk. I watched it slowly roll to the back and finally fall over, twirling faster and faster until it lay flat on the ground.

At that moment the *Tao* principle, "Be still like a mountain and flow like a river" came to my mind. I decided to practice the principle. As students continued to work, I fixed my eyes and mind on the roll of masking tape. Sitting in the front of the room on the desk, I began to meditate on a phrase: "Return to me." I did not know how the tape would return to me. I only knew I was going to be still like a mountain and let my mind flow like a river. I saw the masking tape in my hand. I meditated upon this a little less than a minute or so as students were working individually at their desks.

Suddenly, a student in one of the desks near me, stood up, walked to the back of the room, picked up the masking tape, walked with it to the front of the room and handed me the tape. I had not moved. I had not asked the student or any student to do anything. I simply meditated on the tape, thinking, "Return to me," and I saw it I my hand.

If I had gone and picked up the tape on my own, I would have accomplished the task more quickly, but I would have exerted more effort. Instead, I simply fixed my mind on the objective and let it come to me.

I know it is a silly illustration, but it raises the idea that everything has its timing, its rhythm, including us with our one billion heartbeats on this earth.

Plant, Cultivate, Harvest

What we do, what we don't do, when we do, when we don't do, how we do, how we don't do, why we do, why we don't do, what we think, what we don't think, how we see, how we fail to see, our daily rhythms transform us over time, in our minds, actions, and hearts.

Our daily rhythm determines who we are and who we are becoming. Despite technological advances in a rapidly changing world, the human rhythm remains the same, deeply embedded in our existence for thousands of years: plant, cultivate, harvest. Many people in our instant-gratification-culture want to skip to the harvest, but planting and cultivating prepare one for the harvest. "The harvest is plentiful, but the workers are few."[80] It's the work that makes the harvest plentiful. It's the rhythm of life that creates the symphony.

- Plant: The Shift and a vibrant Vision of my Calling.

- Cultivate: A plan designed with daily desire, determination, and discipline, acting daily on that plan.

- Harvest: The manifestation of my Greatness and my Calling in my life and transforming or blessing the lives of others.

Here's the thing, if I want to grow weeds in my garden, I don't have to do anything, right? They're going to come up regardless. But if I want to grow flowers and plants, those tomatoes for my salsa this summer, I am going to have to do some things! I am going to have to plant the plants, water them, pull the weeds, protect the plants from pests and certain types of weather and let time do its work. Over time, with some tending to the garden, tomatoes will grow, and I will reap some killer salsa! Our minds, heck, our lives are gardens! If we don't tend to them intentionally, time marches forward and we get weeds. We must tend our minds, hearts, and bodies and, in turn, our lives!

When we make The Shift and express our Calling, we plant a new perspective in our minds, just as the gardener plants the seed in fertile soil. The gardener waters the ground, ensures the sprout gets sunlight, spreads fertilizer, and pulls weeds threatening to destroy the sprout. Likewise, we practice activities based on The Shift, helping our Dream take root and blossom, and we weed out any ideas, practices, people, and stories not serving The Shift and our Dream.

Over time the plant the gardener has nurtured produces fruit, and he harvests, tasting the fruit of his labor. The gardener shares the abundance of his harvest with others. Likewise, over time our Dream comes to fruition, and we taste our success. Our Dream serves others, and they are blessed by our labor. Like the gardener, when it comes to our Dream, we plant, cultivate, and harvest.

Time-Lapse Photography

And this leads me to time-lapse photography (OK, I know it's a stretch, but go with me.). It is really cool to watch time-lapse photography. Maybe you have seen some with, say, a flower, the seasons, or the transformation of a caterpillar to butterfly. Whatever you have seen, here's the thing about it that I find so fascinating. You see an entire cycle of growth with a flower or you see the entire change of seasons in just a few short seconds or minutes.

But here's the kicker: If you were an observant person (who never slept of course!), you could see the same exact thing without a camera or fast-motion. What happens in time-lapse photography is happening in real-time first! It's just that the change is so seemingly subtle, we never really notice. We take the transformation of the seasons for granted. We don't see the clouds change throughout the day. We don't see the flower grow and blossom throughout the week. All of a sudden, or so it seems, one day it's cold and snowing! We didn't notice the chill in the air of the morning the past two months. We didn't think about how the daylight hours were diminishing. Nope. Just *boom!* It's winter!

Now, like me, you might be saying, "I don't have time to sit around and look at trees change in the season! Who does?" Well, a time-lapse photographer does evidently! But the way time works in the world and my view of how time works is very different it seems. Let's just be honest, it seems like nature is so slow! And isn't that the rub? We take for granted the constant, powerful changes in the world because it seems to be moving so slowly.

But here's the thing. Time-lapse photography always shows me just how incredibly active creation is. I think what I really need to do is view my daily life through the eyes of a time-lapse photographer. The seemingly insignificant things I do every day add up over time, until huge changes have taken place in my life? I realize the rhythm of my life and the rhythm of the world, while seeming very different, are actually one, so I continue to live my rhythm with patient, time-lapse eyes, pointed toward the prize, my Greatness and my Dream. I plant, cultivate, and wait for harvest.

What Matters

From this chapter remember:

1. Time flow differs from time management.

2. Plant. Cultivate. Harvest. When you skip either of the first two, the results are meager and short-lived.

3. Patience must overrule instant-gratification.

4. Your head, heart, and body are your garden. **Tend your garden.**

Your Turn

The Monthly Time Flow and Non-negotiables

How do we practice Time Flow in our lives? We start with the *Six F's of a Great Life*: Faith, Family, Friends, Foundation, Fitness, and Finances. In *Chapter 16* we will spend time on each of the *Six F's*. For now, just being aware of them is enough for this *Your Turn* action step. As we walk through the *Monthly Time Flow and Non-Negotiables* keep the *Six F's* in mind. Here are the steps:

Step One: Get a monthly desk calendar, a monthly calendar, or a calendar app (I use Google Calendar) of some sort. You will be making a Time Flow Chart for the next month.

Step Two: Get some multi-colored markers or crayons unless you are using an app.

Step Three: Lay out the next month of the calendar unless you are using the app on your phone or laptop.

Step Four: Determine the Non-negotiables of your life. For example, my Non-negotiables are the following:

- Sunday morning worship, as I am a worship leader on a regular basis at my church. (*Faith, Foundation*)

- Self improvement time Monday through Friday from 5:30am to 6:30am. This is when I read, listen to talks by one of my

- mentors, write, reflect, meditate or pray. (*Foundation, Faith*)

- Teach High School from 7am to 3pm.

- Client Meetings Tuesday and Thursday from 3pm to 4:30pm. (*Finance, Foundation, Friends*)

- Exercise Monday, Wednesday and Friday from 3:15pm to 5pm and Saturday mornings from 7am to 10am, depending on the activity. (*Fitness*)

- Work on writing and research from 5:30am to 6:30am and/or 5pm to 6pm, splitting time with Self Improvement time. (Finance, Foundation, Faith, Friends)

- Family Dinner 5:30pm Monday through Friday. (*Family*)

Notice each of my Non-negotiables is tied to at least one of the *Six F's of a Great Life*. Practice something daily in the Six F's. Have a Non-negotiable in every area. This keeps each of us mindful of rhythm in our lives.

I'd also like to suggest when it comes to Family, you write in all the known dates in the next six months related to family functions, things like birthdays, band concerts, theatrical performances, plays, sports game schedules, graduations, one-on-one times with your kids and spouse, vacations, weekend family getaways, regular date-nights with your spouse, anniversaries, etc.

Besides Faith, Family is the most important of the Six F's because success and significance in life flow out of relationships, particularly the foundational relationships of your spouse and children. Make sure you schedule them by putting them on your calendar. Why? Because if you don't schedule it and plan for it, you will inevitably schedule something else that conflicts, and this will bring internal conflict for you. Being intentional and proactive rather than reactive allows for rhythm and flow in life.

Step Five: Choose a color to represent each Non-negotiable. Fill in the days and time of your Non-negotiable on the calendar for the month.

Step Six: When done, you should see a colorful array of parts of the days in which you perform on a regular basis the various Non-negotiables of your life. You will also see the white spaces in your month. These are the areas you can dedicate to other activities that will empower you to live your Dream every day and discover your Greatness. Seeing the colored-in areas and the white spaces helps us create a vision of how our days will flow. We notice some days have more white spaces than others, and we may cluster certain activities in a white space on a specific day of the week.

Step Seven: Commit to your Non-negotiables. They are **NOT** negotiable. Exceptions may arise, and you may have to adjust occasionally. This is normal. Just make sure you are not adjusting all the time. When you do adjust all the time, you've made the Non-negotiable a negotiable. When this occurs, re-assess your Non-negotiables and the *Monthly Calendar* and adjust your times.

Step Eight: Stay with your *Monthly Calendar* for six months. It takes six months to see any results from any activity change. Most people give up on change after a few weeks, thinking the change isn't working. Be patient. If you don't see the results you expected after six months, then adjust your calendar and try something else. When you practice time flow versus simply filling your calendar with appointments you will begin to feel the rhythm of your life. Your mind will be more at peace, and one activity will flow into another because you grow accustomed to what activities to expect on certain days at certain times.

An Example of Non-Negotiating

Sometimes when we adopt a time flow calendar, we find the times and days we have designated on any given week do not seem to accommodate all the activities we confront. How do we handle keeping our Non-negotiables during those times? Here is an example from my own personal experience:

A potential client wants to meet with me. My time to meet with potential clients is Tuesday and Thursday from 3pm to 4:30pm. The client is not available, but he tells me he is available on Monday at 3pm. My Exercise Non-negotiable occurs during this time. I tell him I am not available on Monday, so I book a meeting with him the following week on Thursday at 3:30pm.

Limiting Access

If I had booked the client for Monday, I would then have to switch gears in my mind. Switching gears constantly will make me less focused and productive, leaving me feeling unorganized, a bit frantic, and conflicted. By booking the client the following week I maintain a better time flow, and I am more focused, productive and peaceful. Being unavailable is not necessarily a bad thing. Sometimes limiting access can be good. Limiting access will do several things for us:

1. Give us more freedom.

2. Keep our mind flowing, not disjointed or jumbled, by reducing interruptions and abrupt transitions.

3. Signal to others we are disciplined, serious, and focused.

4. It may make others value us more.

5. It conveys we value others more because we want to give them all of our attention and not just fit them in.

You may be thinking, "One change isn't a big deal," but imagine three or four changes to a Non-negotiable. Once we start down that path, over time we only have negotiables. Putting a process in place when it comes to time will create greater productivity and will consistently, over time, move you closer to the life you desire. Going with the flow does not mean have no plan. A plan brings rhythm and freedom.

Making an Exception to a Non-negotiable

Sometimes we must make exceptions. Here is an example from my own personal experience:

I must meet with a client this week because of completion dates that cannot be moved or adjusted. However, my calendar is already full Tuesday and Thursday from 3pm to 4:30pm. I decide to practice what is called "chunking" or "clustering." I arrange to meet with my client at 4:30pm on Thursday during the week, the time just after my regular calendar time for meetings with clients. By "clustering" the meeting before or after my other client meetings I maintain my flow, increasing productivity and peace of mind. I maintain my rhythm. The transitions of my day remain clear and planned, so I can flow from one area of my life to another.

Our *Monthly Calendar* is set up with flow in mind. When we approach our time with flow in mind, we see how much time we really have and how much time we have not been using productively. As we "let go and let flow," we experience peace because we maintain priorities in the *Six F's* of our lives. Everything falls into place. Exceptions arise, and we adjust our plan on occasion. However, having a monthly vision and a plan brings freedom because *wisdom is vision*.

Making Room for Something New

What do we do when we decide to take on something new and the activity that goes along with it? We can do anything we want, but we can't do everything we want. If we add something new, we will have to exchange it for something else. We will have a price to pay. That's just how life works. We will have to give something less time or no time. However, we will not exchange our Non-negotiables, though we can modify or adjust our timing and placement of them.

Instead of thinking of time management and filling up our calendar, think time flow. Think rhythm. Think plan. Think freedom. Think tend the garden. Think one billion heartbeats. Think Greatness. The Greatness Revolution!

What Matters

From this section remember:

1. Create non-negotiables

2. Limit access.

3. Make an exception to a non-negotiable when no other alternative exists.

4. When you add something new to your calendar (and subsequently your life) on a regular basis, you are going to have to exchange something for it. Make sure it isn't something essential and non-negotiable, like family time.

STOP! DO NOT READ ON UNTIL YOU'VE COMPLETED THE *YOUR TURN* SECTION OF THIS CHAPTER.

14

The Three "R's" of Self-Destruction

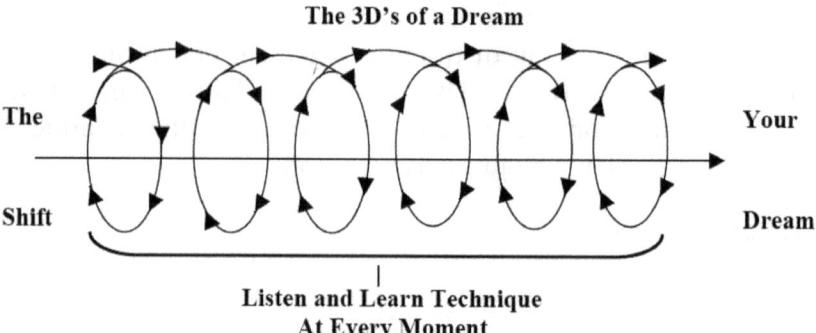

> *I saw the tears of the oppressed— and they have no comforter; power was on the side of their oppressors— and they have no comforter. And I declared that the dead, who had already died, are happier than the living, who are still alive.*[82]
>
> *-Qoheleth*

Qoheleth describes human history. Throughout human history the oppressed have no comforter because, well, they are oppressed. But Qoheleth writes that the oppressors have no comforter either. Really? You'd think those in power would be comforted because they hold sway over their subjects. And aren't we all guilty of this assumption? *If I were the boss, I'd definitely be happier, do things the right way, and have it so much easier! If I were the president, I'd certainly be better off, and so would the country! If I was a billionaire and owned those corporations, man, that'd be awesome!* Ever thought these kinds of things? I have, and when I do, I always think of Julius Caesar of course! OK, stay with me for a minute here.

Julius Caesar was *the* most powerful Roman ruler, and he was the person to whom all the other Caesars compared themselves. This even extended into the 19th century with the Russian *Csars* and German *Kaisers*, both variations of the name Caesar. But here's the deal: Julius Caesar worked politically to consolidate his power and ended up ruling the Roman Empire and dampening the power of the Senate of Rome. While married to Calpurnia, he had an affair with Cleopatra who gave birth to Caesar's son (at least that's what Cleopatra said) so that Caesar could consolidate his power over the entire Roman world. Caesar, who conquered the "Barbarians" of Gaul and seized control of Egypt was the very definition of an oppressor. But his oppression brought him no comfort at all. He had to continually watch his back, staying one step ahead of his political enemies. This doesn't sound to me like a life of ease, comfort, and peace. Caesar constantly ran the risk of someone stabbing him in the back, until it actually happened.

We can understand how the oppressed have no comfort, but even the oppressor, like Caesar, has no comfort. Caesar simply exemplifies what we see repeated throughout human history, whether we speak of a Napoleon, a Hitler, or a Stalin. This is life viewed as a *circle* instead of a *spiral*:

- The oppressor oppresses the oppressed.
- The oppressed rise up to become the oppressor.
- The *circle* begins again.

Societies rise and fall, but no *transformation* occurs. Yes, it's perplexing and depressing. How do you go from a *never-ending circle* to a *transformative spiral*?

First, you've got to recognize the problem. We humans keep doing the same thing again and again. And when we do, according to Qoheleth, we start to believe we'd be better off dead. Because the living in this cycle of violence and destruction are the miserable walking dead! Zombies!

Second, you've got to believe there is a better way, and you have to live a different way than the way of the circle. We humans have to choose *faith* over *fate*, *transformation* over *repetition*, and *service* over *self*. In Shakespeare's *Romeo and Juliet*, Friar Laurence says, "Two such opposed kings encamp them still / In man as well as herbs - / grace and rude will. / And where the worser is predominant, / Full soon the canker death eats up that plant." The battleground every one of us faces is in the small clearing of our heart, and two armies are gathered under the colors of two kings: King Grace (or love) versus King Rude Will (or selfishness). If you are really paying attention to *Romeo and Juliet*, you'll see that practically everyone, except perhaps Benvolio (whose name means "good will"), is consumed with his or her self-interest, even Romeo and Juliet, and that leads to death. Shakespeare's biggest message in the so-called greatest "love story" ever written is that there is so little actual love in the story at all. Some argue Shakespeare actually wrote this story to show what love is *not*! Everyone is living in a circle of self-interest over the spiral of serving others with grace and love, and their circular, petty, self-interest ends in the utter destruction of two families and a community. We have to choose the *spiral* over the *circle*.

Third, you've got to recognize that larger changes and exponential growth begins with small changes and incremental growth. We humans have to choose to change ourselves individually if we hope to see the entire world change. If it's to be, it's up to me, right? Be the change we want to see in the world, right? Love others as you love yourself, right? We must each make The Shift within our minds and, subsequently, our hearts and choose to put in place *desire, discipline,* and *determination* in the small things of our life. Then, and only then, will our incremental change influence change in others and, eventually, over time, exponential growth in the world. How do you change the world? One person at a time, and it starts with you.

Finally, one of the greatest illusions in our world is that we are not connected. As long as we can deny this truth, we can justify just about anything we do or say. But when you realize that everything you do and say has consequences for good or harm to you and others, then the responsibility of The Greatness Revolution rests inside your mind and heart, and is either realized or thwarted by your actions. Qoheleth writes:

> *There was a man all alone; he had neither son nor brother. There was no end to his toil, yet his eyes were not content with his wealth.*

Isolation and separation bring, at best, discontentment, and, at worst, destruction. To be alone brings endless and meaningless work because if what you do isn't your calling and doesn't serve others, then it's an empty motion. Conversely, "wealth," whether physical, emotional, or spiritual is only fulfilling when it effectively connects others physically, emotionally, or spiritually. Qoheleth continues:

> *Two are better than one. . .If either of them falls down, one can help the other up. But pity anyone who falls and has no one to help them up. Also, if two lie down together, they will keep warm. But how can one keep warm alone? Though one may be overpowered, two can defend themselves. A cord of three strands is not quickly broken.*[83]

Two can defend themselves. Why? Because they've got each others' back, something I am pretty sure Caesar would have liked, oh, I don't know, maybe on March 15, 44 B.C.E.[84]

When you connect with another person, something powerful occurs. It's that third cord that cannot be broken. A spiritual bond, an invisible cord, wraps around the two creating greater physical, emotional, and spiritual strength. The sum is greater than its parts. This is where The Greatness Revolution begins, with each individual connecting to another, loving others one person at a time forever.

So, life is a spiral and not a circle. Throughout the ages there have been a few who understood this. They saw the connection between each unique moment in their lives, the connection between themselves and others, and the power of the *spiral* of life.

While many of the moments throughout a day may *seem* to be the same as the day before, each moment in life actually is unique and has something to teach us if we are willing to learn. We make The Shift, transform our minds, and see our lives transformed by *listening, reflecting, learning, adjusting* and *moving* into the next moment (See *The Listen and Learn Technique* in Chapter 9). This *discipline,* coupled with *desire* and *determination over time* creates exponential growth mentally and spiritually, and manifests in our material lives as well.

However, the enemies of this type of transformative life are *The Three R's of Self-Destruction: resentment, resistance,* and *revenge,* and we must proactively overcome them by being conscious of their existence and their plan to thwart our Greatness!

Resentment

any negative emotional reaction oftentimes to what we think was said or done.

Resentment toward another person is like drinking a poison and expecting that person to die. Have you ever been there? Perhaps someone has hurt your feelings or offended you. Whenever this happens, our pain can lead us to think extremely irrational thoughts. When we find ourselves carrying around resentment towards someone, a good practice is to say to ourselves, *"Most people are people of good will,"* which is absolutely true. While they do exist, very few people are people of ill will.

Often, people say and do inconsiderate things, and we hold on to the offense. Ironically, they may not even be aware of what they've done. But even if they were intentional, we still must tell ourselves, *"I must not let the voices outside override the voice inside. The only person I can control is myself, and I know how hard that can be! And I know that someone's hurtful comment or action toward me ninety-nine percent of the time has little or nothing to do with me and much more to do with his or her current circumstances. I will seek to understand rather than be understood. I will try to see through the eyes of the person who has hurt me."*

Sometimes we overestimate another person's interest in us. There's that old saying by Winston Churchill I previously mentioned: "In my twenties I cared what everyone thought about me. In my forties I didn't care what anyone thought about me.

And in my sixties I realized that no one was ever thinking about me." I am convinced that all behavior is explained, and in almost all circumstances, most people's rudeness or offense has nothing to do with me and everything to do with them.

Resentment will never serve me. It simply infects me, and, as I waste away, the one I resent remains untouched. When I resent, *I give away my power.* I no longer own my life. Instead, I place my life in the hands of a person I cannot change nor control, the one who has offended me. And that is futile. And by the way, it's the same when we resent institutions, political, religious, or educational. In those moments we must shake off resentment and be the change we want to see in the world.

Resentment has little to do with what actually occurred. Oftentimes, when I resent someone, my perception of what occurred stems from *my limited knowledge* about all the factors around the moment. Quite often my interpretation of what happened *rests solely on my experience,* so I have to be careful about *rushing to judgment.*

"But, Brad, what if my perception is accurate and the person really did say or do something hurtful or inappropriate?" Great question!

In the classic film *To Kill A Mockingbird,*[85] Atticus Finch tells Scout and Jem, his children, "You never really understand a person until you consider things from his point of view – until you climb into his skin and walk around in it."

This practice is the beginning of dispelling resentment. If I understand someone's point of view, it becomes much easier to overlook the offense. Understanding is like reflection in *The Listen and Learn Technique,* where you open your mind and heart to see and hear from another person's perspective. To clarify, *understanding* and *agreeing* with a person's point of view are not the same, but *understanding* is a huge step in overcoming resentment.

"A truly compassionate attitude toward others

does not change even if they act negatively."[86]
-The Dalai Lama

Practicing compassion is another step to dispel resentment. However, when it comes to resentment in any circumstance, there is only one practice to eradicate it, and we'll get to that in the next chapter.

Resistance

the act of opposing or withstanding

Resistance may serve us in some instances. Resisting unhealthy choices and immoral practices serves us, but in many cases, resistance is futile! Most forms of resistance lead to negative escalations in relationships because the motives of the resistance are flawed. You push, so I push back, and soon we are exhausted from resisting.

Gandhi said, "An eye for an eye only ends up making the whole world blind."[87] He was talking about the ancient law employed in much of the world. The idea behind "eye for eye, tooth for tooth" was to do away with the third R of self-destruction, revenge. If you take an eye, justice demands I can take your eye. The problem is most people don't want to just take one eye in return. *They want to pluck out both eyes!* Soon everyone involved is eyeless, toothless, limbless, or worse, dead! When we employ resistance, someone loses.

Saint Peter writes, "If it is at all possible, as far as it depends on you, live at peace with everyone."[88] If it is at all possible to find a beneficial resolution to any circumstance without using resistance, by all means, practice that solution. Our resistance uncovers our lack of compassion, the inability to see through another's eyes, to try and understand another's point of view. Compassion and cooperation are keys to win-win solutions.

Why do we resist? In the West perhaps we can chalk it up to "rugged individualism." Perhaps it is pride, or a competitive nature. Most reasons relate to the two big stories: the need to be right rather than be successful and the need to look good.

Most people would rather look good than look inward. Weak people look outward and blame others, putting control into others' hands, but strong people look inward and make adjustments. What you resist will persist! What you focus on grows!

We may resist because it gives us the illusion of control. When we resist, we often tell ourselves we are in control or in power. Ironically, when we resist, we actually relinquish control or power because those we resist determine our behavior. Resisting does not give us control. It controls us! In reality we only control ourselves. As long as we resist, we will find ourselves in lose-lose situations. We must make The Shift, change our minds, and transform our thinking.

Who We Aren't Instead of Who We Are

Another reason we resist may be because it is so much easier for us to define who we aren't. Most people can tell you what they don't believe, what they are against, or what they don't want to do, but ask them who they are, what they're for, or what they want to do, and many have no response. That's why it is so easy for us to criticize others without looking at our own behavior.

Protesting against an unjust law or a verdict in a trial is far easier than living daily the answer to injustice. Protesting against injustice is healthy if it is coupled with proactively living the solutions. The challenge is that it's easy to just be against something. It's far more difficult to live **for** something bigger than yourself. But who you are and what you do speaks much more loudly than your words. Treat others the way you want to be treated.[89]

Gandhi abhorred the violent mistreatment of the Indian people, but he knew resisting with violence simply created a monster to defeat a monster. Resistance often turns us into what we resist and is based solely on *being right* and *looking good*. Resistance of this kind has little to do with justice or morality and everything to do with revenge and immorality. When we resist in this way, we are thinking only about ourselves, looking for an excuse to put ourselves first, and this self-centered thinking tends to be the major reason we resist.

Gandhi's *Satyagraha* was about serving all of India, encouraging the British Empire to see his and others' humanity, not by animalistic violence, but through non-violent protest or by breaking unjust laws that brought attention to oppression and the dehumanization of the people of India. This resistance defined who Gandhi was and whom the Indian people were, not what they weren't. Henry David Thoreau's writings on the man of conscience, even if a majority of one, is the beginning of the change we'd like to see in the world. You must be someone whose resistance is not really resistance but a proactive way of living the life of the person of conscience.

Lao Tzu writes, "The highest good is like water. Water gives life to the ten thousand things, and yet does not compete with them. It flows in places that the mass of people detest, and therefore is it close to the Way."[90] A drop of water remains water and combined with many drops of water overcomes all obstacles to reach its goal. It doesn't resist. It flows. Like water, our individual integrity combined with others' integrity helps us find a common path to living our Greatness and having a community of Greatness!

Tearing Down the Walls

The real problem in a relationship is when the arguing stops.[91]
                                                                -Bono

One of the major forms of resistance is putting up a wall or cutting off communication. As long as people are talking there's a chance of reconciliation. The word *hate* has been grossly misunderstood. Rather than an emotion like anger or fear, the essence of the word *hate* is *separation and isolation from someone or some thing*. If I hate broccoli, I don't want it near my plate. *Hate* is a form of resistance. A marriage where spouses stop communicating may be more *hateful* than a marriage where spouses are discussing passionately values dear to them. When silence turns to distance, and wounds become walls, destruction comes calling.

Most problems in life emerge from poor communication: ruined friendships, broken marriages, parent-child conflict, faltering businesses, even warring countries. So resistance in the form of deliberate wall-building or cutting off communication is bound to create self-destruction eventually. Focus on the obstacle, and it will grow. Focus on the solution, and *it* will grow. Avoid the obstacle, and it will grow. Embrace the Obstacle-Opportunity, and *you* will grow. *Be like water.* Move toward your goal. Embrace the obstacles along the way. Keep the conversation going. Leave them better than when you found them. Bring them life, and life will transform all involved.

Revenge

an opportunity to retaliate or gain satisfaction, especially in a resentful or vindictive spirit

Gandhi's statement about an eye for an eye leaving the whole world blind shows that revenge is more than an attempt to get even. In our world revenge is dolled up as "justice," but revenge has little to do with justice and much to do with the need to be right. The need to be right creates lose-lose situations and compromises one's ability to find peace, happiness, and joy. Being right and simply being are two very different ways of life.

Gandhi masterfully found and practiced win-win solutions. Sometimes these solutions caused him great suffering and struggles, but he knew the momentary suffering[92] would eventually bring about win-win solutions for the people of India and the British. When the British left India, they left as friends because of Gandhi's desire, discipline, and determination to bless and be blessed.

When we practice the *Three R's of Self Destruction* all suffer.

High Beams

I remember driving many times at night down two-lane highways, and meeting drivers who would not dim their lights when I met them. It was very annoying, and I grew angry. I fumed inside with *resentment*, and I wanted to keep my lights on high beam (*resistance* and *revenge*). I will confess that on occasion I left my high beams on, and only looking back on it did I realize I was not only jeopardizing the lives of those in the oncoming car, but I was jeopardizing my own life by deliberately trying to blind someone who was coming straight toward me with only a small yellow line separating us. I know, crazy!

I couldn't be bothered by *why* someone might leave their high-beams on, whether from being discourteous, having poor eyesight, or distracted by children perhaps in the car. How absolutely ridiculous is that! You'd think I would have the sense to minimize the danger and to do my very best to produce a win-win solution by doing what made sense: dimming my headlights.

How many of the lessons in the spirals of our life have been wasted because we are blinded by high-beams coming at us, driven by *resistance, resentment, and revenge?* How many opportunities have we squandered to produce win-win solutions because we did not take the time to try to understand others and do what we knew would be best for everyone involved in the moment? How often have we forgotten our integrity, to treat others the way we want to be treated because of *The Three R's of Self-Destruction*?

Instead, let's make The Shift and change our stories. Let's decide to be our true selves and to walk in our Greatness by renouncing the *Three R's* from our lives? Let's replace resistance with *relationship,* resentment with *optimism,* and revenge with *compassion*!

Distraction

Distraction is a form of *resentment, resistance,* and *revenge*. Life, inherently, contains hurdles. As we run the race of life, we must not get distracted by the critics in the stands. To stop and argue with those telling you that you're running too slowly with the wrong form and the wrong way keeps you from winning the race. The critics aren't even running! When you stop to explain yourself or argue your case, you become one of them, standing on the sideline, letting life pass you by.

As Teddy Roosevelt so aptly stated, getting even with the critics by explaining who you are, all the while taking time away from your Dream and calling, defeats your purpose. People on the sideline may think they know better than you, but if they aren't in the race, they don't. Be careful about accepting criticism from them. Run, walk, crawl if you have to, but don't stop to listen to those who have no idea of and no desire to run the race you are running. Just be the runner you are, and stay focused on the course before you, not distracted by the voices in the stands. Listen to fellow runners and those who have run the race before you.

The One R of Self-Preservation

"R-E-S-P-E-C-T, find out what it means to me!" sings Aretha Franklin. There's a lot of talk about respect in our world.

In one of the classes I taught, part of the curriculum units centered on respect. One of the main questions the curriculum asked was "How does one get respect?" It's an absurd question.

"I only respect those who respect me. If they don't respect me, I don't respect them," answered one student in my class.

"It's a trick question," I told the class. "You can't *get* respect. *You can only give respect.*"

"Are you serious?" responded that same student. "If someone is disrespectful, I'm not going to give them my respect."

He didn't realize he was keeping his lights on high beam.

"What does someone else being disrespectful have to do with you?" I asked. "Whether someone shows you respect or disrespect has nothing to do with you, whom you choose to be, and what you choose to do."

Giving respect to someone, whether he or she deserves it or not, is a statement about you. When you base giving respect on the behavior of another person, you place your power into their hands. Don't give away your power! Showing respect for others, whether they deserve it or not, is a statement about who *you* are.

Respect is a key to overcoming *resentment, resistance, and revenge.* Respect yourself enough to show respect to others regardless of their behavior. You may not respect what they do or say, but if you show disrespect for them, you essentially have become the monster in order to defeat the monster.

Mandela

After experiencing many years of great adversity, after "knitting his cocoon" and "struggling to emerge" from it, Nelson Mandela created a *win-win* culture in South Africa, exchanging the cycle of oppression (a *circle*) with a united society working together to create a community of infinite possibilities (a *spiral*). He called upon what was best in humanity to overcome the ugly scar of Apartheid. Mandela shared his thoughts on the day of his release after twenty-seven years of prison: "As I walked out the door toward the gate that would lead to my freedom, I knew if I didn't leave my bitterness and hatred behind, I'd still be in prison."

Nelson Mandela made The Shift. He began with himself and influenced a group of transforming, like-minded individuals banding together. As American cultural anthropologist Margaret Meade writes, "Never doubt that a small group of thoughtful, committed people can change the world; indeed it's the only thing that ever has."

The cause of all war, civil unrest, and the cycle of oppression reside in *The Three R's of Self-Destruction*: *resentment, resistance* and *revenge.* Only The Shift, changing our minds, seeing life as a *spiral* and not a *circle,* will create win-win solutions.

One thing remains to be said. Neither Nelson Mandela, Gandhi, nor Henry David Thoreau were perfect people. There are many people who changed the world for the better through the way they lived, and with the exception of one man, none of them were perfect. They said and did things that were wrong and that they regretted. They made mistakes. But isn't that the point? First, they practiced excellence, not perfection because perfection is impossible but excellence is absolutely necessary. Secondly, I am not perfect, and you are not perfect. However, excellence is available to both you and me today! Since no one's perfect, we don't have to be the judge and jury of anyone except ourselves. This liberates us to look at the log in our own eye and not worry about the speck of sawdust in others' eyes.[93] We focus on progression in our own transformation, not perfection. Essentially, this is humility, an essential component to ending the Three R's of Self-Destruction and practicing the One R of Self-Preservation.

An Answer?

How do we rid ourselves of the two self-destructive stories: *being right* and *looking good*? How do we stop *resenting, resisting* and seeking *revenge*? We make The Shift. We begin trying to see from others' perspectives, practicing compassion, filled with respect. But in order to do that we move to the ultimate and only way to eradicate the *Three R's of Self-Destruction*, and that is what the next chapter is all about.

What Matters

From this chapter remember:

1. Life is a spiral. Each moment, whether a year, a day, an hour, or minute, is unique and offers you an opportunity to grow, learn, and bless others. All moments are connected to one another, just as you are connected to all others, whether they recognize it or not.

2. What you do impacts not only yourself but others for harm or for good. Your choices have consequences.

3. To live the transformed life of your Dream you must avoid the *Three R's of Self-Destruction*: resentment, resistance, and revenge.

4. When you practice one or more of the Three R's, you give away your power over yourself and your choices.

5. Resentment is like drinking a poison and expecting the other person to die.

6. Resistance with revenge in mind is about being right and looking good rather than being successful.

7. Most people find their identity in who they aren't; the exceptional find their identity in who they are.

8. Practice reconciliation with others.

9. When silence turns to distance, and wounds become walls, destruction comes calling.

10. Look for win-win solutions.

Your Turn

Step One: Make a list of those people you resent and what they have done that causes you to resent them. You will use this list at the close of the next chapter.

Step Two: Make a list of people or things you have resisted. After making that list, create at least two potential alternative ways to approach these people or things allowing you to overcome what you have resisted and also bring life to those people or the things you have resisted. Think win-win situations.

Step Three: Employ your possible solutions to what you have resisted. Make a plan. Adjust your plan as you go to find win-win solutions and outcomes.

Step Four: Make a list of those people with whom you have tried to get revenge or those people from whom you want to get revenge. These are people if something bad happened to them, you would have that awkward and uncomfortable but smug and secretly pleased feeling they got their comeuppance. This list may be identical to the list in Step One. Keep this list for the next chapter activity.

STOP! DO NOT READ ON UNTIL YOU'VE COMPLETED THE *YOUR TURN* SECTION OF THIS CHAPTER.

15

Forgiveness

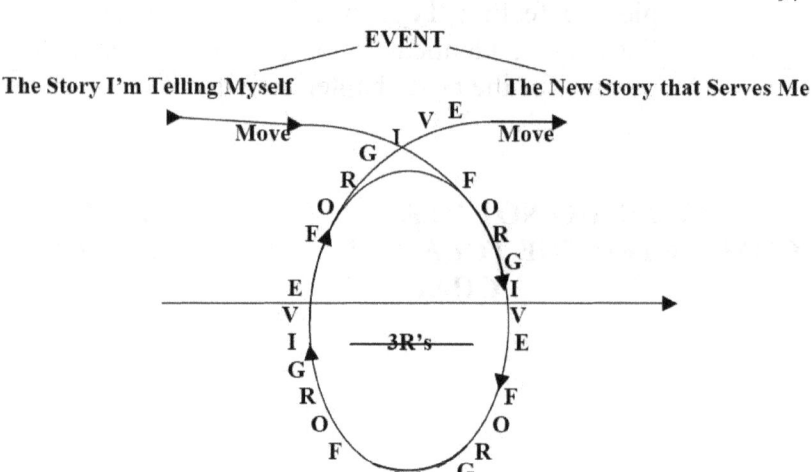

Seventy-Seven Times

Once there was a man who fervently desired integrity, living a life of freedom and love in relationship with the people in his community. He met a teacher and became his student.

One particular day, after several encounters with people who were inconsiderate, self-absorbed, and cruel, he grew frustrated. He *resented* these people. He *resisted* them, secretly wishing they "would get what was coming to them." Frustrated, he approached his teacher. Knowing the teacher was a great man, full of compassion, he wanted to know how compassionate he must be in relationship to these people.

"Teacher," he asked, "how many times do I have to forgive my brother or sister who wrongs me? Seven times?" for he considered forgiving seven times was an outlandishly generous act very few, if any, could practice.

"Not seven times but seventy-seven times," the Teacher replied. The student stood open-mouthed, staring wide-eyed at his teacher. After letting the answer sink in, the teacher continued:

There was a man who owed several million dollars to a wealthy and powerful businessman. He could not pay his debt. He went before the businessman and begged, "I cannot pay my debt right now. Be patient with me, and I will pay it back." The powerful businessman had compassion for the man and said, "I forgive your debt. You don't owe anything. Go and live free, giving to others what I have given you." The man was overwhelmed with his good fortune, and he went out from the businessman's office jubilantly.

Later in the day that same man came upon someone who owed him one hundred dollars. He grabbed the man in debt by the collar, screaming, "Give me my money! Now!" When news of this got back to the businessman, he filed suit against the man and in court he testified, saying to the man, "You cruel and wicked man! You should have forgiven that man his one hundred dollar debt! Now, before this court, you will have to pay back the millions I had forgiven you."[95]

The teacher turned to his student and said, "We all have wronged others at some point in our lives. We're all indebted to others in some way. We must always remember, 'There, but for the grace of God, go I.'

"Hardness brings hardness, and softness brings softness. Inside each of us rests all the secrets of our heart that if the rest of the world knew, it would be horrified. And so, we always see the seven offenses of our brothers and sisters through the lens of the seventy-seven horrors within us.

"We can never change another's heart. But our hearts of compassion are bridges some will cross, and as they rest in our hearts of compassion and forgiveness, they too, like us, will become one of The Seventy-Seven Warriors of Love."

Before you take out your notebook and get ready to mark off forgiving someone seventy-seven times before you either give them your two-cents worth or cut them loose from your life (yes, I have thought about this at times too when it comes to some people in my life), realize that the teacher called on his student to continually forgive.

Forgiveness is the only way to truly live your calling and walk in your Greatness. All other ways are ultimately dead ends, specifically, your death, either mentally, spiritually, or even physically.

It's a tall order, isn't it? How do I forgive *even them*? Yes, that's right, picture *them* in your mind right now (you know who I'm talking about – there's always at least one person in our lives we find it very difficult to forgive). So, let's figure this out.

Forgive

> ***to grant pardon for an offense or debt; to cease to blame or hold resentment against someone or something; to free or pardon someone from penalty***

When you get what you deserve, that's justice. When you get what you don't deserve (the good stuff!), that's forgiveness.

To forgive actually means *to give before*; to give yourself to another as *before they wronged you*, to treat them as if nothing has changed in your relationship.

Why don't we want to forgive? Because many of us would rather be right than be successful. Filled with resentment, we would rather drink the poison than find the cure.

Monsters of Depravity

British playwright and novelist Somerset Maughm writes, "If I wrote down every thought I have ever thought and every deed I have ever done, men would call me a monster of depravity."[96] Ouch!

We know the horrors of what we have thought and done, and we think it impossible to be free of those monstrous deeds. And sometimes something weird happens when we hold on to our wrongs. We begin to view others as cynically as we view ourselves. We assume the worst about others because we know what we ourselves have done. As American author Anais Nin writes, "We don't see things as they are. We see them as we are."[97] This illness (and, rest assured, it is an illness[98] according to Dostoyevsky) leads us to view others cynically, or it paralyzes us from walking in our Greatness, absorbed in a negative view of others, the world, or ourselves.

The Beautiful Mess of Excellence

Perfection is impossible, but *excellence is attainable*. The Greeks called it arête, meaning "excellence of any kind," but particularly moral excellence and the striving of fulfilling one's purpose. You can see this has little to do with perfection. It's about process as we have been talking about throughout this book. In other words cerebral man, visceral man and the heart of man work as one. We all make mistakes, but we also do beautiful things. I like to think of us as a beautiful mess! If you are to live your calling and walk in your Greatness, you must:

1. Admit your wrong-doings.

2. Let go of your guilt by apologizing to yourself, others, and God.

3. Let go of mistakes daily. Lift them up and let them go.

4. Learn from your mistakes. Don't repeat them.

5. Change your behavior.

6. Celebrate the beautiful and positive things you are doing daily.

7. Embrace the beautiful mess you are!

Shift your mind right now! Write down these steps and practice them daily. In twenty-eight days you will be amazed how much happier, healthier, and free you are.

Where Does Forgiveness Begin?

Forgiveness begins with love, and the first person you must love is yourself if you ever want to forgive others. Change the stories not serving you, keeping you from loving yourself. We've all heard, "Love others the way you love yourself."[99] We call it *The Golden Rule* when actually it's not a rule at all. It's a reality. We cannot love others unless we love ourselves also, and we will only love others as much as we love ourselves. If I view others cynically, it's likely I am just as cynical about myself and my behavior.

Ironically, the only way we will love ourselves appropriately is to forgive ourselves, to accept grace regarding our own imperfections and wrongdoings. Most often my harshest critic is myself. When harshness takes root, I hold others to an impossible standard because I hold myself to an impossible standard. Hardness brings hardness, and it leads to one's own self-destruction and the destruction of others.

Forgiveness and Consequences Are Not the Same Thing

Accepting or giving forgiveness is not the same thing as ignoring the consequences of wrong-doing or offense. While I must forgive myself and in turn others in order to live a healthy life, sometimes negative consequences linger for a short or long time depending on the offense. I cannot excuse myself from the consequences of my wrong-doings, just as I cannot excuse or get rid of the consequences of others' wrong-doings. Consequences, both positive and negative, result from the choices and actions I and others make. I do not have control over the consequences of my actions or the actions of others, but I do have control over my choice to forgive the negative choices and behaviors of my self or others. But even in the midst of forgiveness, negative consequences will necessarily play out in a cause-and-effect world.

Remember in 2007 the massacre of Amish school children? A gunman shot ten children, and five were killed. The gunman then took his own life. The parents of those school children forgave the man. The consequences of this horrible crime were devastated families whose lives would never be the same because their children were gone. But the parents forgave the gunman, and showed that forgiveness by donating money to the gunman's widow and three children, as well as attending the gunman's funeral and consoling his widow. While the consequences of loss from the horrible crime will forever be with the families of those children and community, the families and community were set free from a spiritual and emotional prison because the parents of those children chose to forgive.

Make The Shift, change your mind, and believe you are lovely. You are worthy of love and belonging. Forgive yourself so you can love others as you love yourself.

Truth

Here's the truth: It is impossible to love another person if you don't love yourself.

Someone once said to me, "That's not true. I can serve others. I can love others no matter how I feel about myself." Yes, you can do the right and loving act, and it is good to do the right act in relationship with others, but the action alone is not love. Doing the right act without love in your heart is an empty motion.[100] Many people don't love themselves, but do "loving" acts for others. Why? It's who they really are trying to get out, trying to live, even when they are burdened with *resentment*, *resistance*, or *revenge*, three indicators of someone who does not love himself or herself. However, in most cases, many seek their identity in what **they** think others think about them or how **they** think others see them, trapped in the "looking good" story, which eventually leads to self-destruction.

I am not advocating that you stop performing loving acts to others if you don't really feel love. That just adds fuel to the fire of un-loveliness. By all means, continue to act in love, and you will see your emotions change when you see the gratitude of those you are serving. Our feelings often follow our actions. Sometimes what I know to be right and how I feel don't line up, but often when I do what I know to be right, noble, true, and loving, my feelings come along and I am overwhelmed with love. So keep practicing love.

The Growth-Gap

I had coffee with a friend of mine who had recently been through a divorce. He was confronting Obstacle-Opportunities regarding a new relationship. He said to me, "Brad, I am bad: I am a bad father. I am a bad friend. I am a bad. . ." After he listed off several of these, I stopped him. I said, "I want you to think about the language you use in regards to yourself. If a friend spoke to you the way you speak to yourself, would he still be your friend?"

James Allen writes, "A man is literally what he thinks. . .the complete sum of all his thoughts." When we shame ourselves for our mistakes, we think we are worthless or unlovable, but when we see our shortcomings, learn from them, and change our approaches, we build our self-esteem in the midst of obstacles, struggles, and difficulties.

Instead of basing our self-esteem on our *performance* or one event, we build our self-worth and identity through *process*, the continual process of getting better in our relationships, leadership, and life. We take responsibility for our mistakes, but we don't let them define us. There's a huge gap between, "I am a failure," and "I made a mistake." It is the *growth-gap*. The first statement is final, paralyzing, and destructive. The second statement is *process-oriented*, empowering, and constructive, literally helping us build ourselves up into the people we want to be and are meant to be.

You are your best friend. When you use negative self-talk you sabotage your success. When you focus on what's wrong, you focus on who you aren't instead of who you are. As author and speaker Marcus Buckingham says, "When we focus on what's bad and try to reverse that, we get *not bad*."[101] We don't get excellence. We are not our very best!

Game-Changer

It was a tight basketball game. Grant was fouled and had a chance to seal the win by making two free throws. The opposing team called time-out to "ice" him, and several of the players on the opposing team started talking to him about "choking" as he walked to our bench for the time-out.

Any coach knows to never say, "Don't miss these free throws!" because the only thing the player hears is "miss these free throws," and the only picture planted in his mind are free throws bouncing off the rim. Instead, I said, "After Grant makes these free throws we will drop back to half court in man to man defense." What did he see? Excellence! He saw himself making the free throws to win the game. And he did!

Grant was a good free-throw shooter. He had practiced a lot, making hundreds of free-throws. He also missed many, but he let go of his mistakes, tried to emulate his successes at the line, and saw the good in himself. He had even pretended in practice to be at the end of a game with two free-throws to win it. So, when he stepped to the line during the game, his mind, body, and heart were one in the moment.

This is exactly what we must do at critical moments in our lives when we are called to forgive or love ourselves or others. Forgiveness takes practice. It is in the process of practice that we conquer in crisis.

The Voice Inside, Not The Voices Outside

I told my recently divorced friend struggling in his new relationship, "There's something I've seen in you for a long time. You care more about what **you think people think of you** than you do about what **you think of you**. Don't let the voices outside override the voice inside."

I told my friend, "Shame is part of life, and all of us experience shame. It actually helps us stay connected to others when experienced appropriately. But when shame drives us to guilt, and we stay in that place, we sabotage our growth, our relationships, and ultimately our lives. You are guilt-driven. Conviction is healthy, but guilt is destructive. People of conviction act from the inside out. Guilt-driven people struggle with forgiving themselves first and then others because they operate from the outside in. Grace-driven people operate from the inside out."

- Guilt-driven people see **duty,** but Grace-driven people see **beauty**.

- Guilt-driven people think **the moment is taking something away from me**, but Grace-driven people think **the moment is making something great of me.**

I told my friend, "Listen to what you are saying: I am a *bad* father. I am a *bad* friend. I know you. I see you with your daughter, and that's just not true. You've got to make The Shift, change your mind, and change your stories because your guilt is not serving you."

Guilt Versus Conviction

There's a difference between *guilt* and *conviction*. When we do something wrong and recognize it, we feel guilty about our actions. That is appropriate. The problem arises when we hold on to guilt and stay wrapped up in it. We end up trapped in our past, unable to live now where we are. Guilt is accompanied by shame. Most human beings feel shame, and that is good because shame is what keeps us connected to each other.

The only people unable to feel shame are sociopaths. They're unable to feel any connection to others, and connection is a fundamental need of all human beings to live a fulfilled life. Guilt is simply a stage in the learning process. Guilt and shame should lead us to conviction, a conviction to change our thoughts and behavior. Conviction should lead us to action, action that does something differently to make the wrong right in the future.

Tunnel Vision vs. Humility

Your life is epic.

Homer's *The Odyssey* tells the ten-year journey of a man trying to find his way home to his kingdom, his wife, and his son. Like all epic tales, upon the journey Odysseus confronts many "monsters of depravity." Every monster represents a trait within Odysseus he must confront and overcome, traits like pride, greed, and lust.

On one occasion Odysseus confronts the Cyclops, Polyphemus. The monstrously large Polyphemus doesn't respect the gods. In other words, he has no humility, and he has no concern for things of the heart or spirit. He represents the animal nature of humanity. He cannibalizes several of Odysseus' men to placate his unchecked appetites. The Cyclops' every action is concerned with only one person: himself. He has one eye, meaning he has no depth perception (He is shallow!). He focuses solely on the surface of things: filling his belly, getting what he wants, drinking to the point of drunkenness. He is full of pride.

Polyphemus suffers literally and metaphorically from myopia, *a medical condition resulting especially in defective vision of **distant objects**,* or *a lack of **foresight**, a **narrow view** of something*. He has no vision for distance, for the future. And wisdom is vision! He does not see the negative consequences of his self-centered actions. He does not learn from his past and plan for his future. In short, he is a creature of habits. . .bad habits, poor protocols and processes. He practices instant-gratification, and ends up suffering humiliation at the hands of the seemingly insignificant Odysseus.

Odysseus and his men escape when they use a sharpened pole to stab the Cyclops in the eye after the "monster of depravity" falls asleep, drunk from wine Odysseus serves him. Polyphemus' spiritual and intellectual blindness, from undisciplined habits and unrestrained instant-gratification, leads to his physical blindness at the hands of Odysseus.

In the narrative Polyphemus mirrors Odysseus, who himself suffers from myopia. As he and his men escape on their ships, Odysseus taunts the Cyclops after having blinded him, and in the taunting nearly causes the death of himself and his crew as Polyphemus hurls a mountaintop in the direction of the ships. Like the Cyclops, Odysseus also believes he does not need the gods, and he can do everything on his own. He is blind to "the seventy-seven horrors" within. He is filled with pride, lacking any humility whatsoever.

The encounter with the Cyclops is Odysseus' personal encounter with his myopic view, his inability to see the consequences of his arrogance and self-centeredness. It takes him several more episodes to find humility. From this episode we learn the importance of healthy protocols, humility, and the grave consequences of the poor choices we make every moment that over time lead to our demise.

The Three Most Important People in Your Life

Think of the three most important people in your life. Write them down right here, right now. If you have several siblings or kids, sorry, you will have to choose. Do this before reading the next paragraph. Go!

_____

_____

_____

Now, are you on that list? If not, add your name. You must be on that list! *Just make sure you're not the only one on that list!*

Forgive yourself. Love yourself. Once you forgive and love yourself, only then can you love and forgive others.

Forgiveness is the antidote for *resentment, resistance* and *revenge*. Forgiveness brings protection. Mercy is new every morning![102] When forgiveness goes before me in all my actions and relationships, I am protected from my self-destruction. I can truly live, which is to say, I can truly love . . . myself and others.

Are you guilt-driven or grace-driven? It's time to make The Shift. Live a grace-full life. Open your eyes, live your calling, and walk in your Greatness. Begin the revolution within . . . The Greatness Revolution!

Grace, The Greatest Way

> *You see, at the center of all religions is the idea of Karma. You know, what you put out comes back to you: an eye for an eye, a tooth for a tooth, or in physics; in physical laws every action is met by an equal or an opposite one. It's clear to me that Karma is at the very heart of the universe. I'm absolutely sure of it. And yet, along comes this idea called Grace to upend all that "as you reap, so you will sow" stuff. Grace defies reason and logic. Love interrupts, if you like, the consequences of your actions, which in my case is very good news indeed, because I've done a lot of stupid stuff. But I'd be in big trouble if Karma was going to finally be my judge. I'd be in deep s#!%. It doesn't excuse my mistakes, but I'm holding out for Grace. I'm holding out that Jesus took my sins onto the Cross, because I know who I am, and I hope I don't have to depend on my own religiosity.*
>
> —Bono, U2

Forgiveness is absolutely essential to rescue yourself from the poison of what others say and do to you. But if you ever hope to walk in your Greatness and influence your world for the better, you'll have to take another step. And it is a giant leap into freedom and fulfillment. At the beginning of this chapter I mentioned that forgiveness means to "give as if before" someone wronged you, to see them in the same way as before they wronged you. And this is where forgiveness falls short.

Forgiveness looks backwards into the past. Yes, it keeps us from a present and future scarred by the wrongdoing of others, but it does not assure us that we ever forget the wrongdoing that was done. So, forgiveness is good.

Mercy is when you forego justice. You have the power to punish someone for wrongdoing, but you choose not to punish him and instead hold him as one who never did wrong. In a very real sense, the wrongdoer gets what he doesn't deserve. Forgiveness is good. Mercy is even better. But the best is revolutionary. The best is Grace.

For the Greeks, grace was about form, physical appearance or elegant or refined movement. Think of the sculptures of Greek athletes with a literally perfectly sculpted body. But Grace took on greater significance with the teachings of Jesus of Nazareth. It was a revolutionary idea that has set billions of people free.

Grace looks forward. It sees someone in his truly transformed state, even while that person may be imperfect, still making mistakes. One who sees through the lens of Grace sees who the person will be, but right now, at this moment. If you are a parent, haven't you ever caught glimpses of your children, seeing what they will be like when they are grown? Or if you are married, don't you remember glimpsing what your fiance would be as a spouse or parent? Don't you remember thinking, "I want this man to be the father of my children," or, "This woman is going to be an amazing mother to my children"? Those were glimpses of Grace.

When you are filled with Grace, you actually see that people's potential has already come to pass. You don't see who they are now. You see who they are becoming, their true character. It is a miraculous gift given to those who receive that Grace from their Maker. Karma is natural. Grace is supernatural but accessible to every person walking the earth. You simply have to receive Grace within you, first, in order to practice it in your life.

There's this story in the New Testament when Jesus is walking through town with some of his disciples. They see a man blind from birth. The disciples ask Jesus, "Why was this man born blind? Was it because of his sin or because of his parent's sin?" They believed in a Karma theology. In their view, the man's blindness was punishment because of either his or his parent's wrongdoing. But Jesus shows the Truth.

Jesus tells the disciples, "It's not because of his sin or his parents sin. It's so that the power of God can be seen in him."[103] And Jesus walks over to the man, and heals the man, revealing the deepest intention of God, of Jesus, and, consequently, of you and me: the Grace to encounter any adversity and turn it into something beautiful through Grace, to make beauty from ashes.[104] Even though we may not understand why adversity occurs, Grace gives us the strength and power to see and trust that something beautiful will come from it. For the healed blind man, his faith was rescued and renewed. For the disciples, their minds were changed not about the way of the world but about the way they were to live in the world, under the influence of Grace.

Forgiveness is good. Mercy is better. Grace is best. All three have a part to play in allowing us to live fulfilled in our Greatness. But Grace differs from the other two in one essential way. Grace comes only from God. As Bono says, the way of the universe may be Karma, but Grace is an idea beyond nature, beyond the universe and comes into nature by a supernatural presence. Jesus called it the Holy Spirit, which dwells in the heart of every person who receives God's Grace through Jesus' physical life, death, and resurrection. Karma demands death from wrongdoing. Jesus did no wrong as a human being. Therefore, he takes on death, the result of all wrongdoing, and conquers it by dying because justice demands Jesus live forever because he was perfect, morally, physically, emotionally, and spiritually, the perfection that is unattainable for us as mentioned earlier in this chapter. Because Jesus was a human, we have the opportunity as his brother or sister, fellow humans, to reap the reward of his sinless life. In the name of justice, a reality of the Creator's creation, if one human is redeemed from death, then all can be redeemed from death.

Do you remember the Greek View of Humanity? If you were paying attention, you will see that the doctrine of the Trinity is not a doctrine at all. It is a way of life. The Father, the Son, and the Holy Spirit. Father: Cerebral Man; Son: Visceral Man; Holy Spirit: Heart of Man. The Old Testament tells us that we were created in the image of God. It is a triune image. And whatever you believe about how man became broken, this triune image is imprinted on each of us. But only with a fourth element can we receive and practice Grace. It is the actual Spirit of God dwelling in us. I believe it is already there, waiting for each of us to let down the walls we've built in our hearts because of all the lies the Accuser has been telling us. Remember the Advocate in chapter three? That is the Holy Spirit. By making The Shift, changing our minds, deciding to accept Grace, accept the Spirit, to be seen as we truly are, already transformed, we can live the transformed life of our Dream.

There are these ancient verses that most Christ followers believe are about Jesus Christ. And while I believe that as well, these verses, I believe, were meant to apply to anyone who receives the gift of Grace through surrendering to it in Christ. Imagine and put your name in the blanks of these verses, and catch a glimpse of what a life of Grace and Greatness looks like:

> *The Spirit of the Sovereign Lord is on _____, because the Lord has anointed _____ to proclaim good news to the poor. He has sent _____ to bind up the brokenhearted, to proclaim freedom for the captives and release from darkness for the prisoners, to proclaim the year of the Lord's favor and the day of vengeance of our God, to comfort all who mourn, and provide for those who grieve. . .to bestow on them a crown of beauty instead of ashes, the oil of joy instead of*

mourning, and a garment of praise instead of a spirit of despair.[105]

What Matters

From this chapter remember:

1. Forgiveness is as much for you (probably more for you) as for the one you are forgiving.

2. Forgiveness is good. Mercy is better. Grace is best.

3. Grace is supernatural, superseding the natural Karma.

4. Forgiveness looks backwards. Grace looks forward into the future, allowing you to see someone's potential fully realized now in this moment. It is a gift of God.

5. The gift of Grace is available to anyone who chooses to accept it.

Your Turn

Step One: From the previous chapter's **Your Turn** section, take a look at the list of names you wrote down, people on whom you want revenge and people you resent.

Step Two: Write out the following statement, filling in the name of each of the people on your list: *I forgive _____ for _____, and I let go of any and all ill-will I may have held on to regarding him/her. From this day forward I hope he/she will find joy and peace in his/her life, even as I find joy and peace as I pursue my dream to*

_____

_____.

Step Three: Repeat this statement daily until the feelings of resentment or the need for revenge have dissipated within you, and you no longer find it necessary to speak forgiveness over the person and the situation. Sometimes this takes a few days, and sometimes it takes months or even years depending on the situation, but a day will come when you will know that you no longer need to do this.

Step Four: Do you want to live a life filled with Grace? If so, read on. If not, go on to the next chapter.

Aren't sure where to start? I would invite you to repent. That word simply means to change your mind about the way you see life. Make The Shift. Instead of viewing living your life as your ability to achieve everything perfectly under your own power alone, change your view, seeing that with God's gift of Grace in your heart, head, and body, anything is possible, and you can live a life of freedom and fulfillment, doing more than you could possibly even imagine. This is all possible through the God-man, Jesus Christ. God entered into the universe he created that fell because of man's choice to no longer walk with God as one in the garden (see Genesis 1). So God became a human being, Jesus Christ. He was sinless and showed us all that it was possible to live a whole life, head, heart, and body all dancing together as one with the Spirit of God filling us. Jesus said he only did what His Father told him to do. In other words, as a human being, he walked with God like Adam in the Garden before the fall. Jesus showed us that through Grace we could live the transformed life of our Dream, the Dream He placed in us, unique to each person. This was made possible by Jesus, the sinless human being who was one with God, dying on the cross, taking on the sin of all of us as well as the broken natural world we live in. But God raised him to a new life because it is not just for one who is sinless to die. In doing this, God adopted us into his family, like a Father, seeing us as brother or sister to

Jesus. So God has promised to give each of us the same Holy Spirit to live in us that raised Jesus from the dead to become the first of a brand new type of being. Our life on earth from the time of our acceptance of this gift of Grace is forever. Heaven is now. When this happens, we see through the lens of Grace, the very same eyes of God because of His gift given to us. That gift is Jesus Christ's life, death, and resurrection and God's Grace, His Holy Spirit, living in us. This is not religion. This is an intimate relationship with God, and like all relationships, you have to start somewhere, letting it blossom over time.

If you want to live this life, simply tell God, "I want your grace in my heart. I am tearing down my walls and surrendering to your gift of Grace. Forgive my sins, and fill me with your Spirit through the life, death, and resurrection of Jesus Christ."

If you have said the above with all your heart, welcome to the Kingdom! There is much more to this. I need to hear from you. You can email me at discoveringyourgreatness@gmail.com, and I will tell you your next steps on this amazing journey.

Note: Living a life of Grace will take time and practice. I struggle to be Grace-full at all times in my life. Just like anything, you will struggle and fail, but by employing the practices in this book, you will find yourself practicing Grace more and more as you walk your transformational journey toward the life of your Dream.

STOP! DO NOT READ ON UNTIL YOU'VE COMPLETED THE *YOUR TURN* SECTION OF THIS CHAPTER.

16

The Six F's of a Great Life

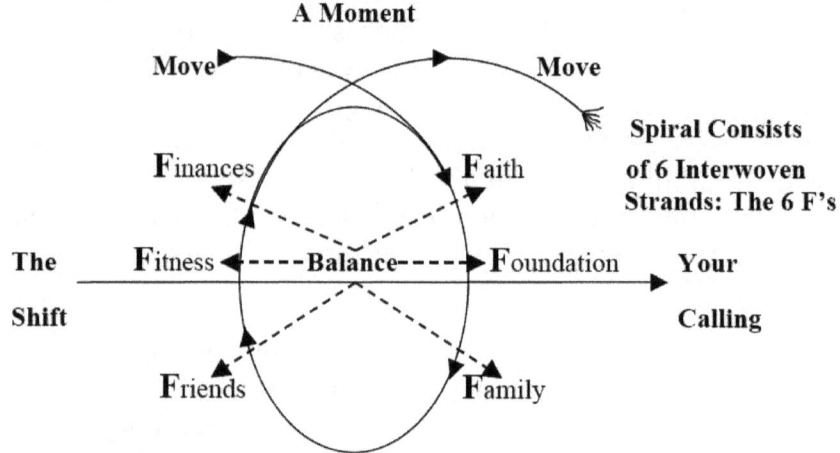

Walking in Your Greatness in Every Moment

To accomplish your Dream, your calling, you must make The Shift, live your calling daily, attaching *desire, determination,* and *discipline* to your calling by practicing *connection, association,* and *reflection*. When the *Three D's* and *C.A.R.* pervade every area of your life, even though you have to Course Correct because you get off track, because you are whole, practicing excellence, not perfection, you find rhythm in life. You recognize that how you are in one area of your life is how you will be in other areas of your life. When you implement planned, disciplined practices over time in all areas of your life, you experience the fruits of your labor, and, what was once foreign to your being becomes natural, first in your actions, then your thoughts, and then your heart. You're being transformed. In your life you begin to see traits like:

- integrity
- a smart and strong work ethic
- compassion
- sound and sober judgment
- peace

- prosperity
- patience
- kindness
- goodness
- gentleness
- self-control
- faithfulness
- joy
- forgiveness
- contentment
- humility
- quiet strength
- abundance
- a heart of service

These traits come from balance in the *Six F's* of your life: Faith, Foundation, Family, Friends, Fitness, and Finances.

The First F: Faith

Because of its importance to a life of Greatness, I have dedicated an entire chapter to *Faith* (chapter twenty-one). For now, here is a brief explanation.

In *A Prayer for Owen Meany* John Irving writes, "Belief poses so many unanswerable questions."[107] In *Life of Pi*, Yann Martel writes, "Love is hard to believe. Ask any lover. Life is hard to believe. Ask any scientist. God is hard to believe. Ask any believer."[108] In *Hebrews* faith is "confidence in what we hope for and assurance about what we do not see."[109] Faith is the practicing of one's beliefs despite the uncertainty. Faith answers many questions while bringing up more "unanswerable" questions. This is one of the great adventures in life. Faith transforms us and transmutes our callings.

We all put our Faith in something. We'll explore this more fully in chapter twenty. Meanwhile, think on this: Faith *connects* our Why, How, and What (from chapters four, six, and eight). *How* we live our lives shows *what* we believe. *Why* we are here at this time in this place shows in *how* we interact and *what* we do in relationship to people and circumstances confronting us daily. Faith is a way of life.

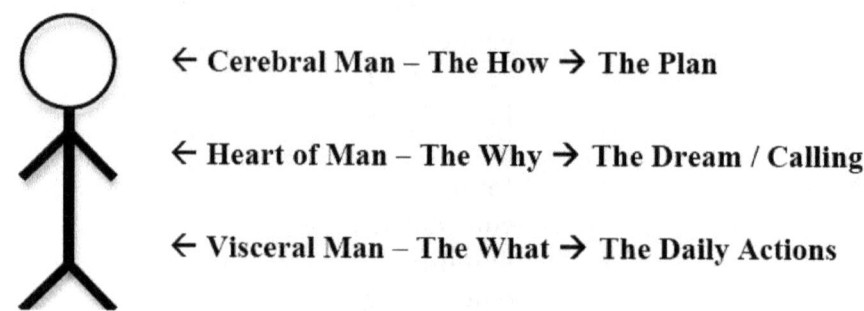

You may have already figured this out, but in the taxonomy of *The Greek View of Humanity* from chapter twelve the **how**, the plan, is cerebral man. The **what**, the daily action, is visceral man. The **why**, the dream or calling, is the heart of man. When **what** I do and **how** I do it line up with my **why**, I have Faith. When my mind, body, and heart are one, I practice Faith. I am not perfect, but I am whole. When my how, what, and why don't line up, I may believe in something in my head, but I don't have Faith because Faith has to be lived, and if I am not living it, my heart is not in it.

Whatever my Faith, whatever I choose to believe about myself, my world, and my calling, I develop daily activities to grow it. If I am intentional and consistent in my daily actions, my Faith grows. With an open mind, I practice *The Listen and Learn Technique* in my daily actions, Course Correcting my trajectory toward my Dream or Calling. My open mind leads to open doors of opportunity. If the room behind the door serves me, great! If not, I can move on after exploring the room, but to close the door before exploring may keep me from discovering an aspect of my Greatness.

In life, *everything is permissible, but not everything is beneficial.*[110] When I remain open, I freely experience the permissible to learn the beneficial. And this is where forgiveness (as we discussed in chapter fifteen) plays a major role. Just because I *can* do something, doesn't mean I *should*, especially if it damages others or detours me from my Dream, my calling, and my Greatness.

Sometimes what I do is detrimental or hurts me or others. It's not beneficial. In those cases I will learn from my mistakes. I will forgive myself of my failures and mistakes. If necessary, I will apologize to anyone my actions may have hurt and try to make it right by changing my behavior, realizing I can't go back, only forward. I will fail forward. I will close the door on that plan of action and try something else.

If I make a mistake or fail, I learn from it because I recognize that *there's no such thing as failure as long as I am learning*, that *I must go through failure to get to success*, and that *I can't take failure or a mistake personally*. Failure is simply *something not working out the way I thought it would.* It's back to the drawing board.

My Faith propels me into my Greatness, and my Greatness propels me on to my calling, and my calling is always caught up in adding value, serving, and being beneficial to others in some way.

The Second F: Foundation

Our Foundation is our heart, our moral compass regardless of the circumstances of our lives. The core values we hold in our hearts determines *how* we live our lives and *what* we do. I will not let just anyone or anything inform (literally form within) my heart or my core values. I will limit access to my Foundation because it determines the way I live. I trust my heart to my God, my spouse and children, to my inner circle of friends, or trusted advisors, mentors, or life coach.

My Greatness is built on a solid Foundation. Faith plays an integral role in my Foundation. What I *think* and what I *do* find common ground in my *heart*. I build a strong Foundation by filling my mind with stories that serve me. I choose to remain open to all that life brings. I *listen, reflect, learn*, then *write a story that serves*.

My solid Foundation is built with daily *disciplines,* using one or a combination of something like the following:

- Spending at least fifteen minutes per day in personal development.

- Reading ten pages per day of an inspirational or self-improvement book.

- Watching an online video or reading a blog by someone I have on my *People that Bring Out the Best in Me* list.

- Keeping a journal.

- Spending time meditating, praying, envisioning.

- Seeking counsel from a mentor.

- Spending time in a Mastermind Group, a group of like-minded people who are positive, empowered and empowering, and have similar ambitions.

- Creating positive affirmations and saying them daily.

- Employing the *Listen and Learn Technique* for personal growth and development.

- Filling my heart with stories that serve me.

Those who practice these types of daily *disciplines* are like the wise man with vision, building his house upon rock. Those who don't are like the foolish man without vision, building his house on shifting sand. When the storms come, the wise man's house stands, but the foolish man's house falls.[111] Daily *disciplines* are the bedrock of a strong Foundation. Inconsistency chips away at daily *disciplines* until all that's left is sand. Build a strong Foundation, leading to a sturdy house able to stand in any kind of weather.

Vulnerability

"The single-most neglected and necessary component to living your calling and discovering your Greatness is making your heart vulnerable."[112] The difference between people who feel loved and have a sense of belonging versus those who don't, all comes down to vulnerability.

While I don't recommend letting just anyone into your heart, I do recommend that if you want to live a fulfilling life, you must risk being hurt, disappointed, sad, or rejected. The original definition of the word courage is *to tell the story of who you are with your whole heart*. Be courageous. By now you might realize that when Faith, which is just another word for risk or trust, and Foundation, your heart, intersect one another, the result is you living an authentic life, being who you truly are.

One morning at the gym I took a spin class. As we got to the most challenging part of the one-hour class, the instructor yelled, "Get out of your head and get into your heart." I immediately had a flashback when I was a child watching Saturday morning cartoons (Do you remember when cartoons were only available on Saturday morning? Me neither! That'd make me way too old.).

Anyway, I remember, when Pepe LePew, the skunk, would fall in love with that poor female cat. Do you remember how when he looked at her, red hearts would appear all around him and his heart would stick out of his chest, beating? After the instructor yelled, "Get into your heart" during spin class, I saw myself riding up a mountain on a bike, my heart stretching the skin of my chest, sticking out of my chest in front of the handlebars. My heart pulled me up the mountain. Then, in a very cartoonish fashion, I imagined that someone could come along with a big pair of scissors and just clip off my heart. . .*snip-snip*! I know, weird! And a little gross! But I think it's a perfect picture of vulnerability, of leading with the heart. To live your Greatness, you'll have to lead with your heart, and that takes risk.

It will take your mind and body to live your calling, *but without your heart, you can never be whole.* When you think about living your calling, do you see a person, walking chest out, leading the mind and body? Inevitably, when we lead with our heart, taking risks, being vulnerable, we will sustain several wounds, but we know this vulnerability is necessary to living our Greatness.

A whole person is willing to be who she is, not what she thinks others think she is. A whole person loves her unique self as part of the body of humanity, so that she can love others. A whole person believes she is worthy of love and belonging because of who she is, and she sees others as worthy of love and belonging. A whole person is authentic and transparent about her triumphs and failures, her beauty and flaws. She sees herself and others as what I call "a beautiful mess." A whole person experiences negative emotions like sadness, heartache, and longing. She knows that to avoid them means she will not experience the positive emotions of joy, excitement, and fulfillment. A whole person leads with the heart.

The Third F: Family

You can pick your friends, but you can't pick your family. Depending on the family you grew up in you might be thinking, "What is he talking about?" when it comes to family, or you might be thinking, "I know *exactly* what he's talking about" when it comes to family. How do we live The Greatness Revolution when it comes to family? How do we become a great father, mother, brother, sister, son, daughter or spouse?

Partner or Spouse

Surveys of couples whose marriages ended in divorce and couples who stayed happily married found both groups of couples fought the same amount. *How* they argued and the techniques they used differed. Here are some practices for success:

- **Express your love for each other.** Before you begin working through difficult issues, conversations, or disagreements, tell each other, "I love you, and I want to work through this because you are the most important person in my life." This can disarm anger, cut to the hurt of the situation, and foster compassion between both you and your partner.

- **Don't try to be right. Try to be successful.** Don't get caught up in wanting your spouse to see things exactly the same way you do. Honestly, that gets pretty boring. Appreciate each others' views. Appreciate differences. They are just differences, not necessarily deficits. Find a solution through compromise.

- **Agree to disagree.** When you don't see eye to eye, that's ok. Remain open. Who knows? Maybe your perspective will change. If the disagreements center on questions of morality (your Foundation), you may want to seek counseling because being on the same page in values bodes well for raising children and having a successful relationship.

- **Don't go hysterical.** Yelling and screaming at someone you love never produces permanent desired results. They may stop their behavior for a time because of fear, but hysterical behavior does not make lasting change. It is simply a bandage on a wound that needs to be cleaned out and disinfected. A polite, calm, and honest tone of voice lends your perspective credibility and influences your spouse or partner to listen to your heartfelt concerns. You have two ears and one mouth, so listen twice as much as you speak.

- **Don't go historical.** Bringing up behaviors from several years ago, even if they fit the same pattern, is a sure-fire way to sabotage the present discussion on the problem facing you currently. Solve the problem at hand, and find a different time to address past events. If an unhealthy pattern of behavior exists, counseling may be a good course of action, but "historical" items usually need a mediator. And by the way, that mediator should not be your kids, friends, or relatives. That's called triangulation and breeds an unhealthy household. Get an impartial, trained counselor or unbiased, trusted friend for mediation.

- **Play the Two-Minute Game.** When a conflict arises, use a protocol where each person gets two minutes to speak and the other person must listen with no interruptions. Between rounds wait at least ten seconds before the next person begins to speak. This ensures two things: one person cannot monopolize the conversation, and the ten second delay helps each person to listen more attentively because he or she is not thinking of how to respond while the other person is speaking. This makes the conversation more centered on being successful and less on winning or being right. If either you or your partner is reluctant to try this, that may be a sign of insecurity and a desire to want to control the situation or the other person. Get help!

- **Use "I" statements.** When working through difficulties avoid "you" statements. For example, "You don't care what I say." Instead, "I feel like you don't listen to what I say." We cannot control anyone but ourselves, and that is why "I" statements serve us so well. We can say how the other person's behavior affects us, and it shows our spouse his or her behavior has impacted us negatively without an accusatory or judgmental tone

- **Use What-I-hear-you-saying statements.** For example, "What I hear you saying is that when I do that, you feel I am not listening. Is that accurate?" This keeps us from putting words in someone's mouth, and it also keeps us honest by seeing if we are coloring the other person's words with our own prejudices and emotions.

- **Avoid vulgarities.** Conversation peppered with name-calling or four-lettered expletives will not serve the relationship ever! If you have children, this models an unhealthy relationship they may adopt from your example.

- **Forgive.** Extend forgiveness to one another, realizing most people are people of good will. Your spouse or partner loves you, but for whatever reason (probably rooted in hurt), he or she has said or done some misguided things. Giving him or her the benefit of the doubt allows you to approach your conflict with the attitude of wanting to be successful in your relationship.

- **Respect your partner.** Just like the importance of respect in chapter fourteen, *The Three R's of Self-Destruction*, remember behaving appropriately in moments of conflict has nothing to do with the other person. Your spouse's or partner's rudeness doesn't excuse your rudeness. Showing respect to your spouse or partner is more of a statement about you. If your respect for someone else is based on his or her behavior, that's not love. That's self-justification, and you are more concerned with *looking good* and/or *being right* than being a successful person of good moral character.

- **Create boundaries with extended family.** Sometimes in a new marriage, couples fail to create healthy boundaries for their extended family and friends. Your parents may not see eye to eye with you or your spouse regarding various issues such as how to raise children, the expectations of a spouse's role in a marriage, the role of faith, and especially the role of Grandma and Grandpa with your children. Your immediate family, your spouse and children, are your priority. Your extended family, though important, is not on the same level as your spouse and children when it comes to each others' needs, familial roles and duties, and how the family will live. While a conversation about boundaries is difficult when the parents of the new couple go beyond proper boundaries, it is necessary for a husband to support his wife and vice versa, setting healthy boundaries through a conversation with one's parents or in-laws about what the newly formed family considers appropriate behavior from extended family and friends.

The Exception

When physical or emotional abuse is involved in a marriage relationship, immediately remove yourself from the relationship. By staying in a physically or emotionally abusive relationship, you do not love nor have the best interest of your spouse or partner in mind. The loving thing to do is to remove yourself from that relationship immediately so your spouse or partner sees what he or she is doing: destroying his or her life. This is the only course of action in these circumstances that may bring transformation, health, and reconciliation.

Love

Love is a choice. When I chose to marry my wife, Margaret, I chose to surrender my heart to her. I basically took my heart and handed it to her. What she did with my heart was up to her. She could throw it on the ground and trample it. She could stick it on a shelf and forget about it. Or she could nurture it and reciprocate my love. I had no control over what she chose to do. I chose to give my heart freely and give my life to help Margaret live her calling. I've not always been perfect in this regard, which Margaret would openly tell you is the case, but she knows my intention. She's given me the benefit of the doubt. She's extended forgiveness and grace.

Love is not a mutual arrangement to give love if you get it. That's a contract. Love is not a business arrangement. Love is not possession. Possession is just another word for control. Love has nothing to do with possessing another person. That's slavery. Love has nothing to do with controlling another person. That's oppression.

Love centers on freedom. We've all heard, "If you love someone, set them free." Love is letting your partner or spouse be who he or she is intended to be. I love Margaret not *in spite* of who she is but *because* of who she is. No, she's not perfect. Neither am I. I want her to become fully who she is on this epic journey of life. The more she becomes who she is, the more I can become who I am, and the more united, whole and complete our hearts and minds become. Love is hard work, and it must be practiced with daily *discipline*. Love walks through pain and pleasure, comfort and discomfort, ease and hardship, life and death, sickness and health dedicated to the one you love. Love is a choice.

Daily Family Practices

What can we practice daily to help us live *The Greatness Revolution* with our family?

- **Evening Dinner.** This has been a main component for our family. During this time we reconnect and have conversations with each other and our children about the day and what we're all doing. This sends several messages to our children: We love them. They are important enough to demand special time every day. They can count on a strong, consistent Foundation. Dinner is a deliberate choice to meet and connect with each other, and although we laugh and goof around at times during dinner, we also have discussions about serious issues and what we believe. We grow together on our journeys through life, and we look forward to being together.

- **Schedule Family First.** Before marking your calendar with work related duties and appointments, first mark your calendar with all family events: birthdays, anniversary, ball games, theater, dance, and band performances, special ceremonies, date nights, dinners, etc. If you don't plan ahead, you will lag behind in your family relationships. What is the point of being successful in your business or dreams if you falter in the most important relationships in your life, your family. If family comes first, and your family relationships prosper, all other areas of life will fall in place eventually. If the family falters, other areas will too.

- **"I Love You" Daily.** Another simple practice is telling every person in your family daily, "I love you." Hugs and kisses daily are good too, even when your teenage children seem annoyed. I guarantee they appreciate those hugs and kisses because it lets them know they matter. Those are seals of approval. You are saying, "I am yours. I am on your side. I am here for you. I am proud of you. I am your advocate. I will never leave or forsake you. You belong and you are loved." And feel free to say these things to your kids as well.

- **One-on-One Time.** On a weekly basis try to schedule one-on-one time with every person in your family, spouse or partner and your children. This is a time to just hang out, go get a meal, a drink, something where you can visit. This is a time to ask your children about what's going on this week, how school is going, activities or sports, or relationships in their life. It's also a time to volunteer with them what is going on in your life. Sometimes children will not ask about your life because, well, they're kids. But it is healthy to let them into your world beyond the family a little bit. When you share triumphs and failures and how you handled those things, it informs your kids about how they can possibly handle their own triumphs (with humility and grace) and failures (with humility and grace).

  With your spouse or partner, this is a time to share what's going on at work or other community activities, how your heart is doing, how you and your spouse or partner are doing. It's a time to assess your relationship, your life together, if you are on the same page in your trajectory for your family. It's also a time to goof around, play, and have fun together.

- **Make it Right Before the Sun Goes Down**. No matter what conflicts you have with family members in the day, before the sun goes down, everyone needs to hear those three most important words: "I love you." Parents, tell your kiddos every day, "I'm proud of you." Before the sun goes down apologize and ask for forgiveness if you need to, or forgive fully if you need to. It is never too late to start again with a clean slate.

- **The Excellence Emphasis.** You might ask, "What if I'm not proud of my child or spouse?" You might consider what I call *The Excellence Emphasis.* If you begin telling your child, or anyone for that matter, "I am proud of you, and I appreciate you," something often happens over time. The person begins to respond with excellence.

    Telling someone you are proud of him or her doesn't mean you don't spend time working through struggles or difficulties he or she may have. It sends the message that no matter the circumstances you will stand beside him or her. When your spouse, partner, or children know this, they will be more inclined to approach you about life challenges, particularly children in those teenage years when so much adversity with self-image and social acceptance occurs.

    Practice excellence in your own life, engaging cerebral man, visceral man, and your heart to be a whole person, and look for moments of excellence in others to praise. Over time you'll be amazed at the transformative power of practicing *The Excellence Emphasis.*

- **Compliment.** Look for others' beauty and compliment them. Catch people doing the beautiful thing and play it up! Celebrate them. Watch how their behavior changes. It is amazing how we repeat what others notice. So notice excellence and celebrate it!

- **Mind How You Treat Your Partner.** Make no mistake, your children listen to what you say about yourself and your partner or spouse, not just your words but how you "speak" with the way you live the *Six F's of a Great Life.* You teach in every moment. How you honor your spouse or partner will influence how your children honor their spouses or partners. No, you cannot be perfect, but you can be a *whole person*. When you make a mistake, humbly admit it. Ask for forgiveness. This allows your children to see how to handle their own mistakes. Extending forgiveness allows your children to see how to deal with the relationships they have in their lives.

The Fourth F: Friends

You can pick your friends.

Association is a key component of building healthy, positive friends. Our behaviors, values, and worldviews mirror our five closest relationships. Who we associate with matters in regards to our *Why, How,* and *What*:

- What is my *Why*? Who do I know with a similar *Why*? *How* will I accomplish my *Why*?

- Who do I know with a similar *How*?

- What is my *What*? Who do I know with a similar *What*?

These people are your tribe! Find these people and develop friendships.

How do I find these people? By moving in circles of influence where your *Why, How,* and *What* are prevalent. If your desire is to be a writer, join writers groups in your community, or attend writing workshops with the intention of fostering relationships or to form a writer's group. If you want to build an entrepreneurial business, attend a BNI Group, Rotary Club, Kiwanas, and similar community groups with the intention of connecting with like-minded people. If you want to be a motivational speaker, attend a Toastmasters group locally or training events and seminars with the intention of building relationships with others who have a similar vision as you. Whatever your desire, develop relationships with like-minded people. Create what Napoleon Hill calls a "Master Mind Group," a group of like-minded people with similar *desires*, pointed in a similar direction, who bounce ideas off of each other and share daily, *disciplined* practices with each other, empowering each other to persist with *determination* to accomplish their callings.

Do your current relationships serve you, and are you serving them? If the answer to either of those questions is no, you may need to *listen, reflect, learn,* and *adjust* your current activities and focus. Sometimes that may mean limiting access to a relationship or adjusting the relationship to better serve one another. Some friends have access into our *House* (our *lives*) but not our *Foundation* (our *hearts*). A few friends have access into our *hearts*. You can pick your friends.

The Fifth F: Fitness

Your body is a temple. It is where you dwell. It only takes a bad cold to remind us how integral our bodies are to our thoughts and emotions. How we honor our body speaks to our integrity. Health and wellness are major components of our quality of life. Upon its release, the documentary *Forks over Knives*[113] shared some alarming statistics about the U.S.:

- Heart disease and stroke claim the lives of 460,000 women per year.

- There are 215,000 cases of prostate cancer per year.

- A half million Americans have open-heart surgery every year.

- Type two diabetes in children is at an unprecedented level.

- Forty percent of Americans are obese.

- Fifty percent of Americans are taking prescription drugs.

- Lipitor (a cholesterol fighter) is the most prescribed drug in the world.

- One in five U.S. four-year-olds are considered obese.

- The U.S. pays more in health care per person than in any other industrialized country in the world.
- Americans spend about $120 billion per year on diabetes, heart disease, and high blood pressure.

- Every minute a person is killed by heart disease in the U.S.

- One in three Americans will have diabetes in their lifetime.

Fitness isn't simply about weight or dieting. Fitness (or lack thereof) is a way of life. How we treat our bodies speaks to how we will treat other areas of our lives. My fitness journey is one of the pivotal journeys in my life, and it has shaped the way I view the other *Six F's of a Great Life*. The keys to Fitness call for The Shift, and here are some:

- Exchange the stories not serving you about your health for stories that will serve you.

- Implement a healthy approach to what you eat to live the best life possible.

- Exercise consistently over the course of your lifetime.

- Do daily what will serve your body to be healthy, and realize, over time, healthy practices will bring a better quality of life today and down the road while unhealthy practices will bring a poorer quality of life today and down the road.

Most health and wellness experts agree, when it comes to fitness and quality of life, genetics, exercise, and nutrition are three essential components. However, a major misconception pervading the Western world is that genetics play the major role in health and wellness. Most people fail to realize when it comes to fitness and wellness, study after study shows genetics have about a ten percent impact, exercise has about a ten percent impact, and *nutrition accounts for a whopping eighty percent impact*. This means we have a lot of control because *what we eat determines our health and wellness*. We choose our health and wellness or lack thereof. So what are some simple steps one can take to live a balanced life in the area of Fitness? Here are some healthy habits to get you started:

Eat whole foods instead of processed foods. While forty percent of Americans are obese, many are malnourished because processed foods remove much of the nutrients that build a good healthy body. While whole foods may be more expensive than processed foods, *we choose to pay for our wellness or subsidize our illness.* A cheeseburger is not going to kill you. But a cheeseburger every day for thirty years will.

In a society where medical costs are rising astronomically, the greatest health insurance plan is proper nutrition. The cost of health care later in life because of poor nutrition far exceeds the few extra cents spent on a whole foods nutrition plan. While the life spans of most Westerners has lengthened, the quality of the latter thirty years of life rest on the nutritional exercise habits in the first fifty years of life, but, even with that said, no matter your age, it is never too late to change your quality of life with proper nutrition.

Exercise regularly. Some studies show just twenty minutes of exercise four days a week can dramatically improve life span and quality of life in later years. In his *RSA Animate*, Mike Evans asserts just one-half hour of exercise daily can create improved results in Dementia and Alzheimer's, Diabetes, Anxiety, Depression, fatigue, high blood pressure and heart health.[114]

Keep it simple when you start exercising, but *do exercise.* Walking is a great way to begin your exercise regimen. Exercise as a family by going on a family walk, and visit about everyone's day. If thirty minutes seems like too much, begin with ten minutes, but start with something you can be consistent doing.

Start somewhere and build. If cutting all processed food out of your diet seems like too much, start with one food. It is about progression and not perfection. As you begin to feel better from eating nutritional foods and exercising regularly, you will find yourself gravitating toward the fruit and vegetable aisles at the grocery store and looking forward to time at the gym or on the run at the local park.

Put a process in place. Remove the emotional turmoil that so many of us attach to food and exercise by methodically practicing daily disciplines. Remove from your pantry unhealthy foods. Just don't buy them. Do something consistently over time, and you will begin to see results as your momentum builds.

It Is Never Too Late

The human body is amazing! In *Forks Over Knives*, several of the people studied actually reversed their heart damage simply by switching to a whole foods diet combined with some exercise. These were people who had been written off by traditional medicine and were expected to die in months. Thousands of years ago Hippocrates, the physician, said, "Let food be thy medicine and medicine be thy food."

So, if you're thinking, "Well, I'm too old to change. It won't make a difference," you need to know two things: I thought that too, and then I started researching and found that was not a true story. Secondly, that story was not only false, it's not serving you! So, make The Shift! Change your mind! Change the story! Start today! It is never too late!

The Sixth F: Finances

"It's not how much money you make. It's how much money you keep." This is one of the first of several key insights in Robert Kiyosaki's book *Rich Dad Poor Dad*.[115] And Kiyosaki should know. He went from living in his car to living the life of his dreams. How we view and use money is central to having a healthy and productive lifestyle.

Liabilities and Assets

Kiyosaki writes, "While many people work for money, those who are successful make money work for them."[116] Anything that takes money away from us permanently is a *liability*, while anything bringing money to us consistently is an *asset*. Money can empower us to serve others more effectively. How we manage a little money is how we will manage a lot of money.

When we stop working for money and start making money work for us in order to accomplish our callings, then we are free. We cannot serve money and find balance in our lives. Money is a tool that serves us.

Residual Income

Putting in place a plan where we buy *assets* (residual income producing items) and not *liabilities* (expense producing items) will lead to a life of abundance. Residual income is income you receive time and time again but only do the work for that income once. A simple example is purchasing a rental property. You buy the property, but the rent you receive from the property covers the mortgage, all the expenses for the property, plus some profit every month. Every month you are *making money work for you* because, eventually, you will own the rental property.

Those who *make money work for them* know a car is a *liability*.

Those who *work for money* think a nice car is an *asset*.

Those who *make money work for them* know buying retail is a *liability*, and instead buy wholesale.

Those who *work for money* think buying retail is the only way.

Those who *make money work for them* remain unconcerned with the two stories: *looking good* and *being right*.

Those who *work for money* think about *looking good* and *being right*.

Those who *make money work for them* know buying a home through traditional ways is a *liability*.

Those who *work for money* think buying a home through traditional ways is an *asset*.

Those who *make money work for them* live off their *assets* and pocket their paychecks.

Those who *work for money* live off their paycheck and have empty pockets.

Debt Free

The average credit card debt for adults in the United States is about $15,000. Credit cards can charge up to 22% or more per month of interest on debt. That's $3,300 on $15,000. *If you have credit card debt, get rid of it as soon as possible.* If you cannot pay off your credit card every month, *get rid of it*. If you pay off your credit card every month, you will not be charged interest. A credit card can be great for convenience on vacations or earning things like plane tickets, but *if you do not have the discipline to pay the credit card off consistently every single month, don't have a credit card.*

If you have credit card debt and are being charged a high interest rate on your credit card, *call the credit card company and request that they lower your interest rate.* Many companies will do that just because you called and asked. Sometimes, *if you tell a credit card company you are thinking of transferring your debt to another credit card company, they will be willing to lower your interest rate.* You can even ask them to cut your debt, *to actually lower the amount of money you owe.* All this will cost you is a little time to hear a *no*, but it is worth a shot. If the company does lower your interest rate, *realize you did not just save money. You still have debt and are paying money to have that debt.* Pay off your credit card and cut it up. Close your account. Once more, *if you cannot pay off your credit card every month on time, do not use a credit card.*

A debit card is a good alternative to a credit card because it is based on the amount of money you have in your bank account, so it is difficult to go into debt. Credit cards are great if you pay them off monthly. Otherwise, they are a *liability*.

Budget

Live below your means. Most people live above their means and turn to credit cards to cover their debts. Instead, live on

70% of your income. Rent an apartment or buy a house you can afford on 70% of your income. Pretend that 70% of your income is 100% of your income, and put the other income away in a savings account or even better an investment for retirement, like a Tax Deferred Annuity. As your income increases, your cash flow will increase, and you can adjust your living standard when you can pay cash for that car you've had your eye on for a while.

When you create a budget, create categories like the following: Savings: 10%, Mortgage/Rent: 30%, Taxes: 30%, Living Expenses: 30%. If you are not saving at least 10% re-think your budget. Ideally, at a minimum, you want to have three months salary in your savings in case of a lay-off or a medical emergency. A full year's salary is better. These suggestions are basic and common sense. Remember, make money work for you not the other way around, and strive for residual income along with assets and not liabilities.

With the advent of on-line business models, such as social-marketing companies, residual income (doing the work once and continuing to generate income) is a brilliant way to create a stable and growing income.

The Key

So what is a key in Finance? We create a plan allowing us to save money and purchase assets (residual income producing items), or we live slightly below our means. We fix our monthly spending for our family even as our pay increases. We take the difference and save in order to purchase assets. Over time we will cover monthly expenses with income from our assets, and any extra asset cash flow or paycheck from our employer we will invest in more assets. We will eventually be able to decide whether or not we want to work toward our calling in our current employment circumstance or go live our calling in a different capacity.

I Don't Need A Lot of Money

I have some friends who sometimes say with disdain, "I don't need a lot of money," priding themselves that money is not a factor to their decisions. I agree. I don't need a lot of money either. Sometimes my friends make remarks leading me to believe they think money is evil. I understand this. I used to believe this way, as well. But. . . .

Money is not evil. The *love* of money is evil. When it solely becomes about the money, you may have a problem. Some seem to believe a life of poverty is an inherently better or nobler life, that being poor makes you a nobler or more holy person, and being wealthy makes you an inherently evil person. However, having or not having money has nothing to do with good or evil and everything to do with The Shift.

Abundance is a state of mind, and scarcity is a state of mind. I have known people with a lot of money who were afraid of losing it, filled with anxiety and unhappiness. I have known people with very little money who were afraid of losing what "little" money they had, filled with anxiety and unhappiness. I have known people with a lot of money who looked for ways to give away what they had because they knew there would always be more. I have known people with very little money who looked for ways to give away what they had because they knew there would always be more. Abundance and scarcity are states of mind.

If you had more money working for you, think of all the good you could do with it. Think about the opportunities you could give to those who might never have opportunities otherwise. There's a saying: "Some people are praying for your extra!"

An abundance thinker always looks for opportunities to give and receive so he can give even more. Jim Rohn said, "Asking is the beginning of receiving." If you want to receive, you have to ask, but the receiving is not just for you. When you don't ask, you are not just denying yourself the opportunity to receive. You also deny those you could bless because you do not ask.

If you don't ever ask, the answer is always, "No." You've got to ask for opportunities to manifest. Knock and the door will be opened,[117] but you must choose to knock! Once the door opens, then you must decide whether or not to walk through the doorway of opportunity with action, by stepping through the doorway. I always advise those who are good at making money work for them to make as much as they can, so they can do more good in the world and give away more of it, serving others with their means.

Showing disdain for money and holding your self "above" it seems shortsighted. Ironically, someone who does this has given his power away to money. It obviously holds sway over his life. I suspect these people work for money instead of making money work for them. When I work for money, I have given away my power. Money controls me. When money works for me, I retain my power and channel it in ways to serve others by living my calling.

It's not about the money. It is more blessed to give than to receive. . .and to him who has been given much, much is expected.[118] Live a life of abundance, and see ways to give what you have received. Knock and the door will be opened. Then, walk through the door. Ask, and you will receive, and then give! Repeat this process as often as possible.

The Common Denominator of the Six F's

The *Six F's* common denominator is consistent, patient, appropriate activity over time. Implement at least one non-negotiable activity in each of the Six F's, and, over time, you will see your Faith grow, your Foundation strengthened, your Family and Friend relationships blossom, your Fitness and quality of life improve, and your Finances bring freedom all so you can not only live a healthy and whole life, but the transformed life of your Dream.

What Matters

From this chapter remember:

1. Live the Six F's of a Great Life.

2. Faith involves your head, heart, and body, moving as one, living a whole life.

3. Foundation is your heart: what you believe, your passion, and the very core of your existence.

4. Vulnerability is central to leading with your heart. Courage is to tell the story of who you are with all your heart. Risk is a part of a fulfilling life.

5. Family relationships, your spouse and children, are the most important relationships in your life. Practice positive protocols. Those listed in this chapter are a good place to start.

6. Love is a choice, not simple sentimentality. It involves desire, discipline, and determination and a never-wavering commitment.

7. Friends who sharpen you, make you better, and vice versa are necessary to live the transformed life. Surround yourself with friends who share a similar *Why*, *How*, and *What*.

8. Fitness is eighty percent nutrition, ten percent exercise, and ten percent genetics. Eat to give your body proper nutrition, and weight and health will take care of themselves. (This does not mean stop going to the doctor if you have a condition.)

9. It's never too late to get fit.

10. Exercising moderately four times a week for twenty minutes each time is enough with proper nutrition.

11. Finances are not about how much money you make but about how much money you save.

12. Don't work for money. Make money work for you.

13. Create a residual income stream.

14. Get out of debt and stay there. You will experience freedom.

15. Live below your means. Save, and invest.

16. Some people are praying for your extra. The more money you have, the more you can help people who need it and don't have the means.

Your Turn

Step One: **Faith.** Create a Statement of Faith. What do you believe and how will you live your belief in your everyday life?

Examples:

- I believe in Love as the defining principle of my life, and I will practice compassion, kindness, and service to those I encounter on a daily basis in my life by listening to others.

- I believe in the power and strength of my family and our relationships, and I will practice fidelity, love, excellent communication, and service to my family. In everything I do I will bring honor to my family, to myself, and to others.

- I believe in God, and I will practice love, joy, peace, patience, kindness, goodness, gentleness, faithfulness, and self-control in my daily life relationships. I will bring honor to God, myself, my family, and others.

- I believe in the inter-connectedness of all things, and I will practice unity with my mind, body, and soul, unity with others in this world, unity with all sentient and plant life by respecting all of nature and loving and serving humanity and all creatures great and small.

- I believe in individual freedom, and I will practice respect for every individual's freedom by listening and learning from others, giving others the same rights and privileges I desire in my life, showing gratitude for my and others' ability to choose the way to live.

- I believe in humanity's unlimited potential progress, and I will practice imagination, innovation, and positivity in my relationships and with myself, continually seeking my Dream and encouraging others to live their Dreams. I will seek out and develop Master Mind groups pushing me and others into greater potential and accomplishment.

Step Two: **Foundation.** Create a list of core values. Then create a short list of trustworthy and wise people whose words and counsel you value and will allow into your Foundation.

Examples of Core Values:

- Grace, Mercy, Love
- Forgiveness
- Kindness
- Strong Work Ethic
- Integrity
- Service to Others
- Freedom

Examples of Foundation Counselors:

- Spouse or Significant Other

- Parents
- Close Friend
- Priest or Pastor
- Mentor
- Sibling
- Counselor / Psychologist / Psychiatrist / Therapist
- Fellow Entrepreneur or Business Associate

Step Three: **Family and Friends.** List three practices you will implement to foster healthier family relationships, and list three practices you will implement to foster healthy friendships.

Examples to Foster Healthy Family Relationships:

- Nightly Dinner
- Weekly Family Activity (Games, Movie Night, Hiking, Biking)
- Tell Every Person in My Family, "I Love You" on a Daily Basis

Examples to Foster Healthy Friendships:

- Daily/Weekly Correspondence (Email, Text, Telephone, Coffee Shop Talk)
- Monthly Dinner or Get-Together
- Imagination or Vision Breakfast/Luncheon/Dinner (Master-Mind Group Session)

Step Four: **Fitness.** List three practices you will implement over the next several weeks to have better health and wellness. Make sure these practices are simple and attainable.

Examples:

- Walk four times a week in the park for thirty minutes.
- Get eight hours of sleep per day by going to bed earlier.
- Limit myself to one cup of coffee per day.
- Pack a lunch for work with whole foods, such as fruits, and vegetables.
- Drink eight cups of water per day.
- Use a vegan protein shake with banana and strawberries as a meal replacement (breakfast).
- Count my caloric intake daily and modify what I eat to match anywhere from 1500 to 2200 calories per day (depending on my gender and size).
- Replace processed foods with whole food choices (i.e. brown rice instead of white rice).

Step Five: **Finances.** List three simple practices you will implement to improve your financial situation.

Examples:

- Save an additional $50 per month by creating a budget below my means.

- Automatically deposit $50 per paycheck into an interest bearing savings account.

- Purchase all items with cash (no debt).

- Pay off credit cards monthly so as not to accrue interest.

- Save monthly for a down payment on a rental property. Once saved, purchase the first rental with cash down and rent charged to cover all mortgage payments and expenses plus generate a monthly positive cash flow.

STOP! DO NOT READ ON UNTIL YOU'VE COMPLETED THE *YOUR TURN* SECTION OF THIS CHAPTER.

17

Mentors

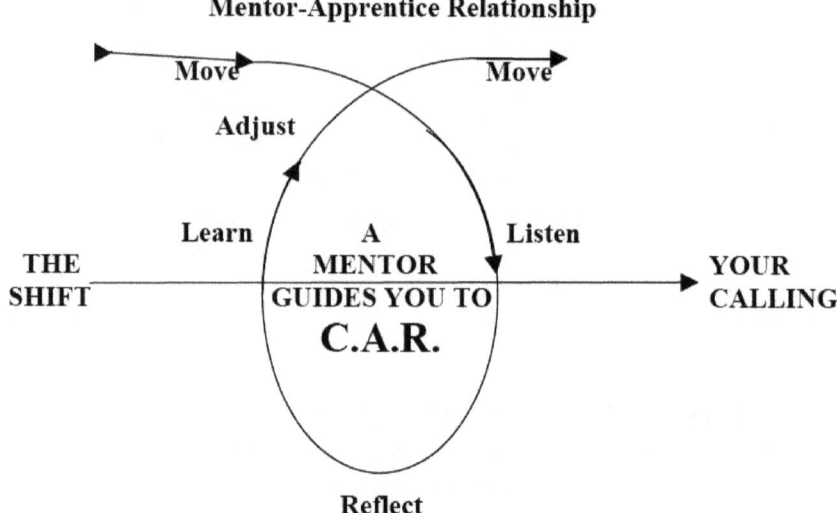

We live in an era of lost art. Up until the Renaissance the word used for business was "art." Most persons a few hundred years ago were tradesmen, like bakers, blacksmiths, and tailors, artists actually. Each of these tradesmen spent anywhere from three to seven years, maybe even longer, as an apprentice. Apprentices still exist today in many trades, though they are less common.

A mentor was an experienced, trusted expert and advisor. If you were a good apprentice, when you were released, you began your own artist studio, or your own business.

Inherent in the Mentor-Apprentice relationship was *desire, discipline,* and *determination.* An apprentice wanted deeply to be a Master Tradesman, like his mentor, to be the best baker, tailor, or blacksmith he could. The work involved long hours, little pay, and struggle. Much of an apprentice's initial training was seemingly mundane, like cleaning up the kitchen, the shop, or the stable. It wasn't sexy. If you were working in the blacksmith shop, it might be years before you even began working with metal. You probably shoveled a lot of manure and fed the livestock, so *determination* was crucial to enduring the mundane and the difficult, seeing no measurable results in your skill development. This long period of mundane and menial tasks instilled *discipline* in the apprentice. He learned continual, consistent activity over time, so when the time came to fire the bellows and work with the metal, he understood the *little things* he had been doing for years had to be in place so the *more important tasks* could be accomplished. He understood everything mattered. They were all one thing.

Throughout the seven years of training by the mentor, the apprentice learned built-in controls, eventually empowering the apprentice to practice his trade as well as, if not better than, his mentor. The apprentice imitated the mentor's behavior until it became his own, until eventually the difference between the mentor's and apprentice's work was indistinguishable.

At first the apprentice's imitation of his mentor felt awkward to the apprentice because he was practicing skills he did not know, but eventually a time came when the apprentice could not remember if what he was doing in his art came from his mentor's teachings or if what he was doing originated in his own head and heart. The apprentice imitated his mentor's practices so many times they became second nature and appeared to be natural in the eyes of customers. At that point the apprentice was ready to move beyond the skills, imitation, and practices of his mentor. He was now ready to bring his own personality and creativity to his craftsmanship. The Master Tradesman released his apprentice who would become a Master as well.

Built-in Controls

Confucius said, "Knowledge without practice is useless. Practice without knowledge is dangerous."[120] Just ask a professional glassblower. It takes years of training. The word *fiasco* actually comes from the Italian root word for flask or bottle because glassblowers who were inexperienced created many misshaped bottles.

A karate master does not go home and kill his wife when he gets angry. He's learned from his mentor that his hands are lethal weapons and should only be used to neutralize and redirect oncoming attacks. Over the years of training he has developed built-in controls, *discipline*, and morality.[121]

A mentor can lead his apprentice down the path that points toward the apprentice's calling, a path of *desire, discipline*, and *determination*, empowering the apprentice to grow in his Greatness. This is the power of mentorship. Even with apprenticeship, things can end up a fiasco, but without apprenticeship *they stay that way!*

An educated man is one who achieves what he wants without infringing on the rights of others. Mentor-apprentice relationships empower this lifestyle.

Unless, of course, you're a dark, Sith Lord. Then, your loud-machine-like-breathing, helmet-wearing, black garbed apprentice gallivants about the galaxy wreaking havoc, which is *not* a healthy Master-apprentice relationship. I don't recommend this, though watching it on film is fun!

Finding a Mentor

How do you find a mentor? Do some research. Identify people who are living a calling similar to yours. Find a person or a community of people who have already mastered what it is you want, and model what you do after them. Write down heroes who have achieved some aspect of your calling, then emulate their behavior.

It is possible to have a mentor who has accomplished a goal or aspect of your calling and not your calling. It's also possible to have a mentor in one of the *Six F's of a Great Life* but not another. You may have multiple mentors for various areas of your life. Identify someone who has the same kind of life you *desire* and figure out how to build a relationship so you can learn. Don't leave this to chance. Intentionally seek people who have the skills, knowledge, and the way of living you want.

I heard a story about young woman who wanted to be financially wealthy. She had very little and lived in a lower income neighborhood. She deliberately chose to drive an extra twenty minutes to a wealthy neighborhood to do her grocery shopping, banking, coffee shop visiting, and more with the intention of being surrounded and mentored by those who were living the life she wanted. Over time she established friendships and apprenticeships with people in the wealthier neighborhood. And guess what? She became a wealthy and successful businesswoman.

What does this story teach us? Be intentional. Do the little extra things others won't, like performing your daily life errands in a wealthy neighborhood in order to become wealthy and live what you want.

Remember, association is a powerful force. You tend to become like those with whom you spend your time. If you want to advance or improve in some area of your life, or if you want to advance on the path to your calling, then surround yourself with and emulate those who are closer than you are to achieving similar goals. Create opportunities for relationships with those who raise your level of awareness and performance.

How do you create a relationship with someone who has succeeded in a similar way you want to succeed? Add value to their lives. What skill can you give? Find what you can do for that person. Offer to work for them. Mow their lawn and wash their cars every week. Word-process documents for them free of charge. Offer to make phone calls for them for which they don't have time. Your service will gain you access.

Come right out and tell them you want them to be your mentor. You can tell your mentor you admire them for who they are and what they do, and once you begin to serve, maintain your level of service, becoming a reliable and trustworthy person in the eyes of your mentor. Always remember *give and it will be given to you*.

Oh yah, one last thing. If your mentor wears a creepy black hood and gown and tells you to use the force and strike down your loud-machine-like-breathing father, don't do it! Get a different mentor.

Practicing The Greatness Revolution to Find a Mentor

The young man had heard of an inventor who was re-imagining the world. So, he decided, "I will become that man's partner. I will do whatever it takes to work for him, and I will stop at nothing until I am his partner." He packed up where he was, and because he could not afford a passenger train ticket, he hopped on a freight train and moved to the city where this man's laboratories were located. He knocked on the man's front door and said, "Sir, I admire your work, and I am here to become your partner. I will do anything to get on board. You don't even have to pay me."

The man at the door was unimpressed, but, not being one to ever turn down potential breakthroughs in even the most unlikely places, he consented to give the young man a position with little pay in one of his offices. The young man's eyes had a look this mentor could not ignore.

Over the next several months, whenever a project no one else wanted came up, this young, ambitious apprentice ran with it and always accomplished more than anyone expected. One such moment came when the inventor who owned the laboratory created a device used in offices that recorded someone's voice and could be played back. The inventor was very excited about this "dictating machine," but none of his employees saw any potential for it. That is, all but one. The young apprentice jumped at this opportunity, and he began to produce major income, earning millions of dollars for the company by marketing the "dictating machine" all over the country.

The inventor took notice, and soon the young man was outperforming and out-imagining those who had been with the company much longer in higher-paying positions. The young man's performance was so outstanding, the inventor finally asked the young man to become his partner. The young man went on to huge financial success and cutting-edge technological advances. His name was Edwin C. Barnes. And the mentor who owned the business? Thomas Edison. You've heard of him, right?

Two Kinds of Mentors

There are two kinds of mentors. The first is someone with which you are in close proximity. You live in the same geographical location. You have access to their Greatness and learn from them directly. The second are those you admire from afar. You read their books or books about them. You research their career and listen to interviews they've given. These mentors can be almost as influential as those with which you have a personal relationship. Either way, find mentors for every area of your life, and learn, imitate, emulate, and become *The Greatness Revolution*!

What Matters

From this chapter remember:

1. A mentor-apprentice relationship is more rare today but is essential to learning to practice desire, determination, and especially discipline because, as Confucius says, "Knowledge without practice is useless. Practice without knowledge is dangerous."

2. A mentor helps the apprentice establish built-in controls so that the apprentice uses his or her skills responsibly and morally.

3. Intentionally seek mentors in the Six F's of a Great Life.

4. Develop long-distance mentors by studying their lives, writings, and videos, and develop mentors in close proximity for the interpersonal dynamic and accountability.

Your Turn

Step One: List five potential mentors who embody either success in the field you want to enter, the Dream or

	calling you have, or one of the *Six F's of a Great Life* you would like to improve upon.
Step Two:	Next to their names, write down your plan for moving into a relationship with them. Part of this plan involves talking with them directly about how much you admire them and you'd like them to be your mentor.
Step Three:	Consider what you may have to give to become an apprentice. How much are you willing to give up? How much do you want your apprenticeship and your Dream? Remember, *give and it will be given to you.* Edwin C. Barnes chose to move to West Orange, New Jersey just to be near his mentor, Thomas Edison.
	Make a list of what you are willing to give up. You may never have to give all that is on this list, but you need to plan what you will give so when the time comes you are prepared.
Step Four:	List five people you consider long distance mentors. These are people you will not currently have a personal relationship with, but want to learn from them through books, online videos, and various social-media outlets. You may even be able to establish an e-mail correspondence with them. Next to each name write down a strategy to accomplish your goals. For example, you might write down, "Purchase the latest biography on this person and read ten pages per day."
Step Five:	Execute your plans and adjust them as necessary.

STOP! DO NOT READ ON UNTIL YOU'VE COMPLETED THE *YOUR TURN* SECTION OF THIS CHAPTER.

18

A Journey

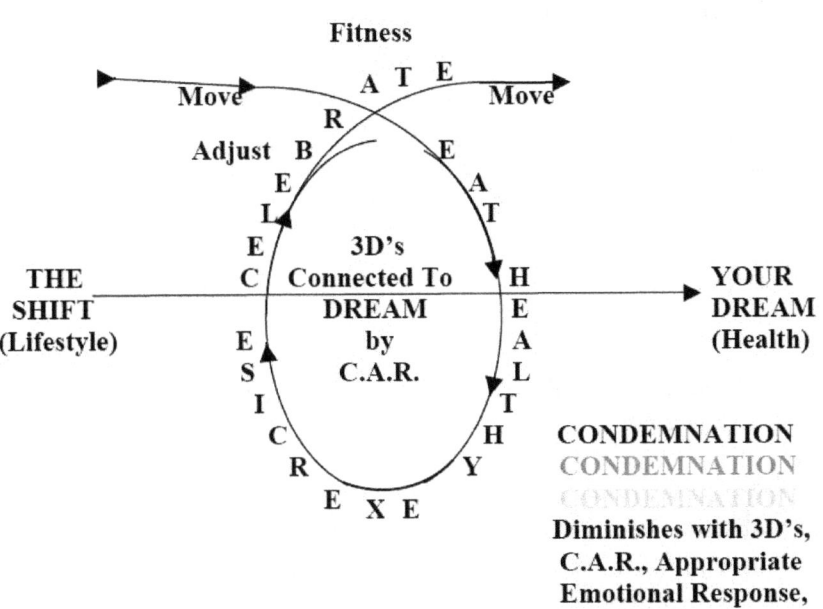

Caterpillar in the Cave

I was the heaviest I had ever been. I would get up in the morning, back aching, and look at my reflection in the mirror. I didn't like what I saw. I could see in the eyes of that man hopelessness and longing. He was hopeless about his future. He longed for purpose, so he used food to try to fill the emotional void.

No matter how much pizza, Chinese takeout, or burgers he ate, he couldn't fill that void. He was trying to escape his pain using food. He realized this was a behavior he had grown up with. It had been modeled to him as a child, and it really did not affect him externally until his metabolism had slowed down at the age of forty-two. But forty-two years of an unhealthy story had begun to show itself in his waistline.

I can remember saying to Margaret, my wife, "I am so fat!" and her lack of any response. The silence was full of the two greatest teachers: love and pain. It was perhaps one of the greatest things my wife ever "spoke" to me. When your life partner loves you enough to avoid saying anything excusing your unhealthy behavior, be it physical, emotional, or spiritual, you know you are facing a pivotal moment, an opportunity for The Shift. My physical health had affected my attitude toward my teaching, my Faith, my Family and Friends, my Fitness, my Foundation, my Finances and my world. I didn't like who I was or who I was becoming. These were two of the toxic stories I had attached to the events in my life:

- I am fat, and I'll always be fat. There's nothing I can do. It's too late to change.

- I should change my diet, so I'll just have one bowl of cereal instead of two, and this high fat, low fiber, processed Chinese food once a week won't kill me. Neither will the pizza, or burgers…

But I knew:

- If I ask what's wrong, I won't ask for very long. I need to ask, "Are these stories serving me?"

- Weak people look outward and blame others. Strong people look inward and make adjustments.

- Most people would rather be right than be successful.

- Forgiveness is protection. It keeps you from being poisoned and paralyzed.

- "Without vision, people perish." Without a calling, you have no hope.

- A calling is only a wish until you attach *desire, discipline*, and *determination* and live them daily.

- *Connection, association,* and *reflection* are the vehicles to help you attach the *Three D's* to your Dream.

- I choose to be either the subject or object in the sentences of my life. I can act or be acted upon?

One day I made The Shift, though I did not really see any results for a while. It takes a thousand miles before the tsunami becomes a powerful force.
I asked myself:
How much more weight do you need to gain to show you aren't on the list of the important people in your life?

How much more weight do you need to gain to show yourself you don't love yourself?

What do you have to lose if you continue down this path? Your health? Your mobility? Your freedom? Your family? Your life?

Every burger and pizza you eat, moves you down the path of heart problems that run in your family. You have a choice: You can change your lifestyle and maybe your health will improve, or you can keep doing what you are doing and know exactly where it is going to lead. You can remain comfortable and grow more uncomfortable as your life moves on, or you can become uncomfortable and move toward being more comfortable.

Take off your shackles, turn around, stop believing the shadows on the wall, see the light at the cave's mouth, and walk toward truth and life.

I told Margaret, "I am changing my lifestyle. I will be making my own meals. I will exercise six days a week." I used the fitness product line of the business in which my wife and I work. I had a shake for breakfast and lunch. I made a salad with some chicken or fish for dinner.

Knitting the Cocoon

I remember my first run. It was two miles. I thought I was going to die. I remember my first road bike ride. It was 12 miles on flat roads. I thought I was going to die.

I ran three days a week. I rode three days a week. I weighed myself on the first day. I was two hundred fifty-two pounds. I did not weigh myself again for four and a half months, because, for me, it was about a lifestyle change, not weight. I struggled through choosing to eat differently, sore muscles, and early morning runs and bike rides.

For the first few weeks I really didn't see much of a difference in my body or condition. I decided I would celebrate every day I ate healthy and exercised, but if I didn't, I would not beat myself up. I attached the proper emotion to any event. I let go of condemnation, forgave myself, learned, and moved on. I chose this story: *I'm not trying to lose weight. I am changing my lifestyle. I am becoming who I am called to be.*

Butterfly Emerging

Four and a half months later at church, a friend of mine came up to me and said, "Wow! Are you ok?"

"Ya! Great! Why?" I replied. Frankly, she sort of scared me.

"You are so skinny!" she said. "You have lost so much weight! Are you ill?"

I hadn't seen this person for quite some time, so I figured my weight loss seemed sudden to her. That's how it is with people who are not aware of the commitment and work involved in following a goal. They aren't aware of how much time, effort, and practice, how much *desire, determination,* and *discipline* it takes on a daily basis. Four and a half months was not sudden to me. Honestly, though I knew I had lost some weight, I hadn't given weight loss a thought. I was just eating healthy and exercising regularly, and I felt great!

"No, I'm not ill," I told my friend. "I've changed my eating habits and I'm exercising regularly, and I feel great!"

After our encounter I thought, "Well, maybe I should weigh myself."

I stepped on the scale: two hundred pounds! In four and a half months I had lost fifty-two pounds.

I had a calling: to be healthy, happy, and whole. I attached *desire, determination,* and *discipline* to that calling. When I looked in the mirror every day, I *connected* all I was doing. I *associated* the appropriate emotion to the events and food in my life, and I *associated* with like-minded people wanting wholeness. I reflected on where I'd been, where I was, and where I was going by *listening, reflecting, learning,* and *making adjustments* as I moved on in the spirals of my life.

It's easy to get the impression that those four and a half months flew by and were easy. My story does not do justice to how difficult it was at times to exercise when I didn't feel like it, or to avoid eating something I knew was not good for me. I embraced a lot of *obstacle-opportunities* during that time, just as I do every day in any of the *Six F's of a Great Life*, and I walked hand in hand with my best friend, Discomfort, who told me what I needed to hear.

I had a burning *desire* to be healthy and whole so I could do things with my children and, hopefully, my grandchildren, as I grew older. My *desire* was so strong I practiced good eating and exercising habits with *determination* and *discipline*. I *connected* all moments on the journey, *associated* with those who were also exercising and eating healthy, and *reflected* on how to improve my practices to accomplish my *calling*.

Momentum built, and I found myself running half-marathons and marathons, biking forty to sixty miles, and competing in triathlons, all to the rhythm of my one billion heartbeats. I planted, cultivated, and harvested. The Shift led first to activity, and the activity changed my mind to believe and achieve. My mind made the longest journey of all: the thirteen-inch journey from the head to the heart, and once my heart changed, I knew anything I put my mind, body, and soul to I could complete.

Fitness has been one of the greatest teachers I've ever had. The experience showed me that Greatness lies in every one of us, and that with a goal, The Shift, *desire, determination, discipline, connection, association,* and *reflection,* "impossible" can turn into "I'm possible."

My wellness experience changed my physical, emotional, and spiritual life for the better. It helped me love myself so I could love and serve others more. It revolutionized my mind, body, and soul, *cerebral, visceral,* and *the heart* of man, pointing me toward *wholeness* and *excellence.* It was a pivotal moment in my Greatness Revolution!

Butterflies Before Me

John Maxwell writes, "Nothing of significance was ever achieved by an individual acting alone . . .'behind an able [person] there are always other able [people].'"[123] My *Fitness* journey was not a solo endeavor, nor does it continue to be. Back when I began, my good friend, Bob, took me under his wing, supplied a bike to ride, showing me how to road bike. My wife, Margaret, said almost daily, "You are Brad Thomas, you can do anything when you decide to do it." It was positive and empowering, and helped me climb out of bed for an early morning run or ride.

And there were many more people on my team. I was reading their books, listening to their trainings, and reading their articles. Yes, I ultimately had to decide, commit, and attach activity. I was the number one person who had to commit and follow through, but I was not alone in my endeavor. I was part of a team of like-minded people who were headed in the same direction with the same goals in mind.

Butterflies After Me

I once saw an illustration. A butterfly emerges from its cocoon and flies above the heads of some people who have just been watching its emergence, filled with awe. The butterfly sees the wonder on their faces and thinks, "They're amazed at what I have done. But I only get to do this once. They can do this every day if they want!"

Sometimes I ask students to write down the one sentence they want others to say about them when their time on this earth is over. This proves to be difficult for many. For whatever the reason, most of us are not comfortable with our legacy. Most people let life happen instead of deciding what their life will be. Just like the choice to either act or be acted upon in the sentences of life, we choose the one sentence others will say of our life on this planet. We choose by living who we are!

Here's my sentence: *He empowered others, one person at a time, to intentionally live the transformed life of their callings so they would bring who they were uniquely designed to be to their community and world.*

We are here on this "pale blue dot"[124] for a brief time in the scheme of the cosmos. Every day is a gift to discover and grow so we can become who we truly are, and leave a legacy. Legacies do not live on through things. A name on a building is nice, but it's not a legacy. Legacies live on exponentially through the people we love and influence. Think of the butterflies to be, the ones who will come after you. What will you bring to them? How will you serve them? Who will you choose to live your legacy? Live today with eyes for the future.

What Matters

From this chapter remember:

1. You are the primary influence in the way you live your journey through life.

2. Practice the techniques in this book daily with intention, and you will transform.

3. It takes a team of like-minded people to empower and help you on your journey if you are going to succeed in your chosen Dream.

4. Life is brief, so live with intention the legacy you want to leave that will bless exponentially generations to come.

Your Turn

Step One: **Caterpillar in the Cave.** When it came to my fitness, I believed a lot of illusions. They were shadows on the cave wall. What are the shadows on your wall? What illusions are you holding onto, keeping you from pursuing your Dream? What stories are not serving you? Write them down on a piece of paper.

Step Two: **Change the Stories.** On a different piece of paper, write down alternative stories that will serve you. Burn or throw away the old stories. Adopt, learn, memorize, and repeat the new stories daily.

Step Three: **Knit your own Cocoon.** Attach a daily, *disciplined* activity to each new story. Write down one thing you will do to live each new story you have written. Carry out this new activity daily.

Step Four: **Butterfly Emerging.** Measure your growth and improvement in the areas of the new stories. When you achieve something after a time, when you see improvement in the area you are pursuing, when others complement you in these areas or say something you know relates to The Shift you have made and the new stories you are writing, record this and remember it as encouragement to continue when you feel like giving up.

Step Five: **Butterflies Before Me.** Identify three people who can help you accomplish the activities you have written down to achieve the new stories you have written. These are accountability partners. These are people who can encourage you in the midst of Obstacle-Opportunities. These are like-minded people pointed in the same direction as you. These are people you admire and are comfortable asking for advice, help, or encouragement.

Step Six: **Butterflies After Me.** Write the one sentence you want people to say to describe your life here on this planet. What legacy do you want to leave? It probably has something to do with the new stories you have written.

STOP! DO NOT READ ON UNTIL YOU'VE COMPLETED THE *YOUR TURN* SECTION OF THIS CHAPTER.

19

Time: Your Best Friend or Your Worst Enemy?

Scenario 1
----- = Consequences

Greatness

D I S C I P L I N E

The Ever-Expanding Spiral
Into Your Greatness

3D's, C.A.R., and Grace Over Time............. ⟶ Calling

Scenario 2
----- = Consequences

Greatness
Your Calling

U N D I S C I P L I N E D

The Downward Spiral
Away From Your Greatness

Quiet
Inconsistency in 3D's, C.A.R., and Grace Over Time... ⟶ Desperation

Time is Constant

"Time is a monster that cannot be reasoned with."[127] We can't make a deal with time. We can't argue with time. We can only co-exist with time. Like David Byrne says, "Time isn't holding us. Time isn't after us."[128] Time goes on. And according to Einstein's General Theory of Relativity, Space, Matter, and Time coexist and came into existence together. They simply are, and they continue to move on, even if they are winding down. No, Time won't slow down for us. Time won't speed up for us. *Or will it?*

Sometimes Time Speeds Up

Have you ever looked at the clock and said, "Where did the time go?" Maybe it's playing an instrument, singing, writing, spending time with friends, or serving others. This may be a sign of your Greatness and your calling. When you lose track of time, some aspect of that activity relates to your Greatness.

When you lose track of time in an activity, reflect on the activity and ask why. By pinpointing what made the activity so fulfilling, you pinpoint aspects of your calling and Greatness.

Sometimes Time Slows Down

When I trail run, I'm amazed when I return to my car and I've only been gone for forty-five minutes. In the process of my run I've been meditating, having visions, hearing lines of writing, taking in the natural beauty, listening to my breathing, feeling the rhythm of my mind, body, heart, and soul.

For me, trail running is a spiritual experience; so much transpires in that forty-five minute period. It seems I've been on the trail for hours. Trail running engages my mind, body, and soul to focus on Faith, Foundation, Finances, Friends, Family, and Fitness all at once, which is why time slows down. Trail running allows me to practice four of my top five strengths: intellection, ideation, connectedness, and belief, all while I focus on Fitness. It's fulfilling. When time slows down, reflect on the activity and examine why. By pinpointing what made the activity so fulfilling, you pinpoint aspects of your strengths, your calling, and your Greatness.

Time Speeds Up and Slows Down in a Bad Way

Have you experienced an activity where time just stopped, and you think, "Will this ever end?" Or have you been so busy it seems there isn't enough time, and your anxiety increases until you think you might burst? When we experience time in this way, we must reflect on the activity and examine why. By pinpointing what made the activity so unfulfilling, we pinpoint aspects of the areas in us pointing away from our strengths, calling and Greatness.

The moments when time speeds up or slows down in a negative way may not be negative to others. Your fulfilling activities may not be fulfilling to others, and activities draining you may actually fulfill others. Appreciate differences. Realize everyone is significant with a unique set of strengths to give to this world.

What you may see in yourself as inconsequential or insignificant may be extremely integral to our community and world. Stay humble. Withhold judgment. Focus on building your strengths, and leave others to build their strengths. Stop trying to be right and look good. Focus on being successful, on being the very best version of you possible! At some point on your journey, you will need the strengths of the very people you might have discounted had you not focused on building your own character and strengths.

Trailblazing

I just didn't feel like running up "the hill." I was on a five-mile trail I'd run many times before, and on this day, I wasn't firing on all cylinders. It was just one of those days, days we all experience at times. Time was slowing down, in a bad way! In the middle of the run is "the hill," a three quarter mile climb with four specific and dramatic inclines, each incline growing steeper. I just wasn't "feeling it." I was reminded of a pop song: *It's not a hill; it's a mountain as you start out the climb.*[129] In fact, I may have been listening to it on my mp3 player at the time.

I'd run "the hill" many times before, so I knew I could do it. Then I remembered what a friend said to me one time before my first triathlon. She said, "When it gets tough, just smile."

So, I smiled, and my smiling face made me feel empowered. Sometimes when we find ourselves in one of those days, we have to change our minds through a simple action in order to get through. I recommend laughter or a smile. They change things! My body told my head and my head told my heart, "You can do this!" And in that moment I was one in mind, body, and soul, and it was spectacular! It was excellence! It was the only way I was going to conquer "the hill" before me! Time picked up its pace, and so did I!

Sometimes we face moments we must go through when time speeds up or slows down in a bad way. These moments have nothing to do with whether they play to my strengths or not. These are character-building moments. We can learn in every moment, and these moments often hold the best lessons. Moments like this come along, and we must choose to go through them to grow through them.

Moments of struggle are obstacle-opportunities. During these moments we feel like giving up, but we know we can overcome them. What can we do to push through these moments? Smile! As that grin crosses your face, think, "This moment is making something great of me. I am telling my head and my head is telling my heart, 'You can do this!' My body, mind, and heart are lining up, and I am a whole person in this moment, growing stronger within, becoming more of who I am!" If repeated often enough your obstacle-opportunity just turns into an opportunity, and your positive, determined mind-set becomes a habit.

The Penny

One day the Master approached his apprentice. "I have an opportunity for you. I am going to give you a choice. Though I do not speak of it much, I possess great wealth. I have learned money is not the most important thing in life, but it is right up there with oxygen! It is a tool worth having because it helps create opportunities to give and do more. Here is your choice. I will give you one million dollars right now to do what you will. Or I will give you this penny I hold here in my hand, and for the next thirty days I will double the amount. You have five minutes to give me your answer." The Master went away.

The apprentice furrowed his brow and began to ponder what kind of test his Master was giving. "Is he trying to teach me the dangers of greed and the love of money?" he thought. "I could do so much with one million dollars. My family is poor. We have debts to pay, and a million dollars would more than cover them. I could purchase a modest home, make investments, and live a comfortable existence for the rest of my life and for the rest of my children's lives as well." He continued to think through both options until his five minutes was up. He then returned to his Master.

"Have you come to a decision?" his Master inquired.

"I have," said the apprentice.

"What is your choice?"

"Master, I will take the penny doubled every day for the next thirty days. It's clear to me one million dollars today would cover all of my debt and place me on a path of comfort, but if I took the penny compounded over thirty days no matter what the amount, I would have time to contemplate the best way to make the money work for me and those I serve. I would practice patience and continue my apprenticeship, learning how to handle the money because I took the time to think things through. Finally, I realized if I were to take the penny in your hand and it doubled every day for thirty days, by the end of the thirty days I would have well over five million dollars. Patience and perseverance pays handsomely indeed. I have also learned 'a little bit every day is far more powerful than a lot all at once,' and that is a principle I can use in every area of my life. When one grows a little bit every day, he is prepared by the time the little bit is a lot, and how he is with the small things of life is how he will be with the big moments of life. His growth is exponential, but his practices remain the same. I choose the penny, Master."

The Master looked into the eyes of his apprentice, a smile crossing his face. "You have chosen wisely."

Time Has No Teeth

Time is neither a monster nor an angel. Time is a constant. We are the variables. How we manage and use the flow of time determines whether time works for us or against us. Before The Shift regarding my health and wellness, time simply carried out the instructions I gave my *mind*, *body*, and *heart*. After The Shift I accessed my *desire* and practiced *determination,* and daily *discipline,* and time plodded along, my mind carrying out my instructions. My patience and perseverance *paid handsomely indeed!*

We overestimate what we can accomplish in a year, and we underestimate what we can accomplish in five years. Why? Because of our view of time and how we use it.

Yann Martel writes, "Time is only an illusion that makes us pant."[130] In other words, time is not real. Yet we give it incredible power, relinquishing to time our power over our lives. It's amazing how little we actually have to do to keep this from happening, yet time and again (literally) we allow time to direct us. Why? Because the daily easy-to-do activities to transform our lives are just as easy not to do.

Time is not real because the truth is there is no past and no future. There is only now. Yes, lessons from the past exist, but the past is gone. Yet, astonishingly, most of us live as if the past actually exists. What exists are the stories we tell ourselves regarding past events. Some of them serve us, but many of them paralyze us. They keep us from today. They blur our vision, so we fail to see that what we do now affects tomorrow. Today is tomorrow! Tomorrow is our next now!

The stories we tell are not supposed to be about the past. They're supposed to help us live now. They apply to today. Yet most of us allow our past stories to enter into today and keep us from living now. This is the illusion many choose to believe, the shadows on the cave wall.

The same is true of the future. Many people "pant," filled with anxiety about the future. They worry so much about the future they forget that today determines tomorrow. Tomorrow never shows up. It always becomes today.

Because they live in a non-existent future, people fail to act today. They are paralyzed by the future. They become objects instead of subjects in the sentences of life, acted upon instead of acting. They don't realize that they are the variable. They cease to exist.

The greatest existential statement of all time is, "I am," not, "I was," or "I will be." It's even the name of God in three of the world's most prominent religions: "I AM, yesterday, today, and tomorrow." Yesterday, today and tomorrow is all one thing: now.

Ironically, we live in a society plagued by two words: right now! While most are trapped in the past or the future, failing to live daily, simple *disciplines*, which teach us to live now, we still fall into the trap of instant gratification. We want it now!

- We want the winning lottery ticket now!
- We want the big paycheck now!
- We want the new house now!
- We want the promotion now!

We are trapped in the stories of our past or our future, yet we want it all now!

- We want the million dollars instead of the penny!
- We want to live the "great life" without any of the living or even any of the Greatness!

Your calling is right now, doing today and every day what will get you there. On my fitness journey, my weight gain and hopelessness were not instantaneous. They happened over time. My weight loss and health and wellness were not instantaneous. They happened over time.

I went from reactive to proactive, from victim to victor, from object to subject in my life sentences! I developed daily, *disciplined* actions, like healthy food choices and exercise. I stopped undisciplined actions. I took responsibility for my choices, and let time work for me by deciding to act daily with healthy habits.

In a day and age where technology allows us to instantaneously access just about anything, many forget the way we accomplish anything of Greatness involves *discipline, determination,* and *desire,* applied daily over a period of time.

- It's the rhythm of humanity: plant, cultivate, harvest.
- It's the penny compounding every day!

The people we most admire realized and practiced this. Gandhi changed India forever as the driving force behind Indian independence from Britain. Most of us admire Gandhi and recognize his Greatness, but we forget that Gandhi didn't really begin anything in India until he was over forty years old, that he spent at least seven years of his life in jail, and that he was beaten several times. We forget that Gandhi's twenty-eight years in South Africa were all a part of his success in India because he was using *desire, determination,* and *discipline* to accomplish his calling: the unity and dignity of all humans expressed through Indian Independence. His daily disciplined practices and his entire life experience empowered Gandhi to accomplish his calling.

Indian Independence began the moment Gandhi decided in South Africa to live daily a life valuing justice, peace, and non-violent resistance. We tend to only see and celebrate Gandhi's accomplishments, not realizing The Greatness Revolution was not an overnight event but a process, a steady, daily, *disciplined,* and *determined* practice of the principles Gandhi espoused. The Greatness Revolution is a way of life.

Two Frogs

Two frogs grew tired of the swamp and decided to set out one day on a grand journey. Eventually, they happened upon a farm. The frogs hopped into the barn and saw a bucket filled with cream. Not ever having cream, they both decided to try it. So, they hopped into the bucket.

They were filled with delight. Both swam around the bucket, drinking in the cream. Finally, after they had their fill, one frog said to the other, "I am full! I'm ready to go."

"Me too!" the other frog responded.

They began to climb the walls of the bucket, but the bucket walls were so slippery from the cream the frogs couldn't get a good footing.

"We're trapped! What are we going to do?" the first frog screamed to the second frog.

"We have to keep kicking!" the second frog shouted back.

For hours the two frogs swam and swam, kicked and kicked, trying to free themselves from the bucket of cream. After several hours the first frog, out of breath and overwhelmed with grief, said to the second frog, "It's hopeless. There is no way we are ever going to escape this bucket. Why did I ever leave the swamp? If I was there right now, I would be safe and sound on a lily pad, basking in the sun. Now, I will never see my home again. This journey was a mistake. I should have stayed where I was safe and secure!"

"We've got to keep trying!" said the second frog. "No matter how difficult, we can't just resign ourselves to our fate! We must keep kicking! Don't give up!"

"It's pointless!" whimpered the first frog. "We are doomed. We'll never get out of this bucket! I am done for!" And with those last words, the first frog stopped kicking and let himself sink to the bottom of the bucket of cream where he drowned.

The second frog, distraught from the loss of his friend, and now completely alone, felt himself wanting to give up. But from deep within himself he heard a voice: "Keep kicking! Keep swimming! You were meant for more!"

The second frog began to kick and swim with all his might. "I will not give up! I will overcome this or die trying!" he thought. For hours he continued to kick until he felt something curious. Beneath his feet was something solid. He was able to stand on solid ground. Through all his kicking the cream had now become butter, and the frog in one giant leap, hopped out of the bucket and continued on his amazing adventure.

Keep Kicking

It's the same for you and me. We start with a penny. But if we walk our path to our Greatness long enough, using *desire, discipline, determination, connection, association,* and *reflection* over time, we will walk in our Greatness and into our calling. We just have to keep kicking. At first we'll see no results, but eventually positive results will appear, and others will notice. Most will see the change as an overnight, sudden breakthrough. But we'll know better.

Lao Tzu writes, "A journey of a thousand miles begins with a single step."[131] It may feel like a "leap of faith" into darkness, hoping the light will rush in. It may feel like the slippery walls of a bucket, and we may want to kick the bucket rather than keep kicking. It may feel like we have no solid ground upon which to stand. But feelings, while real, often do not align with truth. We trust that time is a key to our calling. We think differently than most about time. We live our callings today! We realize time is neither our best friend nor our worst enemy. We are either our best friend or our worst enemy. It's our choice. We take the first step today. Then, we take another step . . . today. Always today! We repeat the process until we feel solid ground under our feet. Soon we will have traveled a thousand miles, like a Tsunami, gathering momentum.

Your calling is not in the past, nor the future. Your calling is today, lived out in the small moments showing exponential results over time. Using *The Listen and Learn Technique* over time, understanding life is a series of spirals, applying *desire, discipline* and *determination* to your daily life, another spiral begins to form.

While your activity and approach remains constant and consistent and healthy, the spiral of consequences grows larger and stronger and more powerful. You begin to see how your faithful approach to every moment of your life impacts and influences your friends, family, business colleagues, community, and world.

You find your *discipline* and *determination* give you great influence in the circles you inhabit which are ever expanding. You have more money, time, friends, and wisdom all because you pursued your calling with the 3D's, practicing listening and learning, spending time connecting, associating, and reflecting, attaching stories that serve you to events, moving you forward on your transformational journey toward your calling. You are The Greatness Revolution!

What Matters

From this chapter remember:

1. Time is constant. You are the variable. What you do with the time you have determines whether you live the transformed life of your Dream or not.

2. Patient, daily protocols and practices produce exponential results.

3. The journey is messy and may seem hopeless, but with faith and determination, you must keep kicking to see your Dream manifest.

4. Most people are instant-gratification driven people. You are a patient, daily practitioner of your calling and Dream.

Your Turn

Step One: List six actions, one for each of the *Six F's of a Great Life* (*Faith, Foundation, Family, Friends, Fitness, and Finance*) you are doing or will do daily to make Time work for you and not against you.

Step Two: Next to each action explain *how* you think these six small, simple actions compounded daily over time will improve each of the *Six F's* in your life.

Step Three: As you practice these six actions, use *The Listen and Learn Technique* (*Chapter Ten: Spirals: The Listen and Learn Technique*) to Course Correct them. As you evaluate the results, they may need minor adjustments.

STOP! DO NOT READ ON UNTIL YOU'VE COMPLETED THE *YOUR TURN* SECTION OF THIS CHAPTER.

20

Transformation, A Review

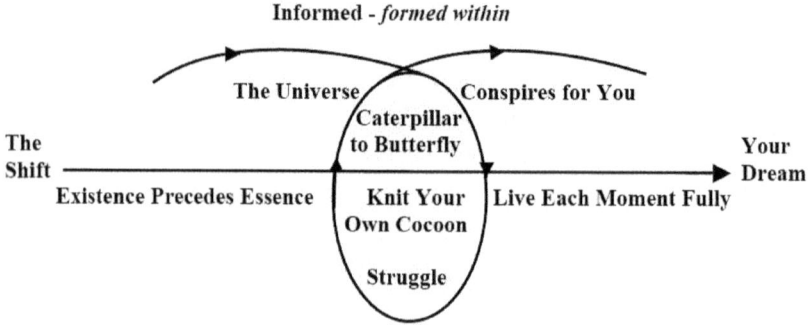

Review

Way back in chapter one we discussed this incredible phenomena: **metamorphosis** - a complete change of form, structure, or substance; a profound change in form from one stage to the next. It's **transformation** - change in form, appearance, nature, or character. The metamorphosis of the caterpillar to butterfly holds several insights for The Greatness Revolution.

Also in chapter one, remember the New Zealand study of children that led researchers to determine people don't change? They found that people become more fully who they are already. If you recall, I took the same personality profile I had taken in high school, and the results were exactly the same. This idea that we do not change but become more of who we are shocks some people, I think, because some people don't know who they really are. Many people sell themselves short about all the strengths within them because they never try to discover all that is within them. And in fact, many people may be trying to be someone else. They listen to and adopt the stories others have written about them, trying to live stories that don't serve who they truly are.

Who Am I?

I grew up and loved playing basketball. I was not the most athletic kid or even the most talented, but I had a strong work ethic, good fundamentals, and I studied the game. I eventually played some junior college ball and won several honors throughout my high school and collegiate career. My father had played basketball in college and had coached college ball as well. Basketball was something we could share. I chose to coach high school ball early in my teaching career. I was a good coach, with several successful seasons. In fact, I am still a coach, just not on the basketball floor anymore. It took me about twelve years of coaching to realize I really didn't fully enjoy coaching basketball. I enjoyed playing the game and being a team captain and leader, but I didn't enjoy being on the sideline.

Why had I spent countless hours doing something I wasn't keen on? I had either written or adopted stories that did not serve me. Although I was a good coach, coaching basketball really wasn't my passion or my calling. I thought it was at the time, and it actually utilized many of my strengths. But I realized this truth:

Just because you are good at something doesn't mean it is your calling.

Something about the activity does point to your strengths and your calling, but sometimes we do things for all sorts of reasons having little or nothing to do with who we are, who we are becoming more fully, and our calling. Here are some of the unhealthy stories I was writing:

- Basketball is who I am, not just a game and a teacher.

- I must be a basketball coach because I receive praise, accolades, and encouragement from others for it.

- I please my father when I coach.

- If you stop coaching, you'll be a quitter.

I was consumed with one of the stories most of us live by: looking good. I was practicing something to look good. I was living my life based on the voices of others instead of listening to my own voice. I let the voices outside override the voice inside.

Another aspect to my coaching was an insatiable desire to win. Being competitive can be a strength when used appropriately. I was and still am very competitive. But I grew so competitive at times I sacrificed my integrity. If I won, I could feed the looking-good beast. I reached a place where the winning never felt as good as the losing felt bad. I had written the wrong story to one of my strengths: competitiveness. My competitive strength was built on a poor Foundation: looking good.

When I finally realized I was coaching and it wasn't my calling, I stopped coaching. Don't get me wrong. I still love basketball. I am grateful for my time coaching. It was one of my greatest teachers in life, and I would not trade my experiences coaching for anything. I got to be with great kids having a lot of fun as well as heartache, growing and learning together. I admire those who coach. I still look back on coaching with fond memories, and I am grateful for the relationships I formed. But I also *listened, reflected, learned, adjusted,* and *moved on.* I was missing my own children's growing-up-years. I enjoyed coaching, but the time, struggle, and politics were greater than my passion for coaching. My passion for my children and my wife were much greater than the passion to coach. I may coach again some day. But if I do, it'll be for the right reasons: to enjoy the game, enjoy the relationships, grow, and have fun.

Who Are You?

Many of us try to be someone else. Humanity doesn't need someone else. We need you! We don't need another Thomas Edison, Bill Gates, or Steve Jobs. We need you! Humanity is like the human body, each part of the body unique, performing a significant function in order for the body to thrive. Humanity is not just supposed to survive. We are meant to thrive! A finger, an elbow, an ankle, a nose are all interconnected and one thing: a human being. The less noticeable parts are actually more essential.

If I lose an arm, I can survive. Amputees speak of phantom pains. Even though a limb is missing, they still feel the limb and the feeling is often quite painful. The missing part of the body is painfully missed. If I don't have a liver, I won't live for long. Without a heart, the body cannot live. When you do not function in your Greatness, using your unique combination of strengths to live your calling, you deprive this body we call Humanity of an integral part, and Humanity cannot thrive. Humanity's Greatness diminishes, and we suffer the pain of an unfulfilled life, community, and world.

If what you have just read is causing you anxiety, I'd like to ease your tension by telling you this:

Who you are is more important than what you do.

Sometimes people mix up who they are with what they do. When people ask me what I do, I respond, "I empower people to become who they truly are so they can bring that to their community and world." Yes, they head tilt. Then I explain that I do that when I teach, speak, coach, or write, all different professions that allow me to be who I am.

Your vocation, calling, and Dream can be accomplished in multiple professions. A profession is not a vocation. So ease up on yourself. Be who you are, and do what you love. Your place in humanity will become apparent to you and others as you authentically pursue your life path with imagination, curiosity, joy, and love. Rejoice in the moment, and live that joy.

You Matter!

No matter how insignificant you may think you are, let me just encourage you to change your story. Every one of us possesses a unique set of strengths we are meant to bring to humanity and the world. Without you, humanity may survive, but without you humanity cannot thrive! If you've written your own story of insignificance, remember, the hidden parts of the human body have greater significance. A beautiful physique means nothing without a heart, without a stomach, and without some guts. You matter! So change your story, and live your calling!

The Metamorphosis

The caterpillar must knit its own cocoon. Its cocoon comes from within itself and its own activity. The caterpillar undergoes a process over time, preparing for its transformation.

The caterpillar must struggle. It must struggle against weather, predators, and for food. When it is ready to emerge from the cocoon, the butterfly must struggle. If it doesn't, its wings will be misshaped, and it will not be able to fly. It can't do what it was meant to do. It must emerge on its own through struggle. Struggle is actually a blessing. Struggle is the Universe's way of conspiring for the butterfly. Discomfort is its best friend.

Every moment of life prepares the caterpillar for transformation. The caterpillar is entirely responsible for that preparation. The moment the caterpillar is born it begins knitting its cocoon. The caterpillar undergoes a complete **Shift** in the cocoon. Inside the caterpillar is a butterfly preparing to emerge. The caterpillar's entire life is designed to become what it truly is: a butterfly. Its existence precedes its essence. When we look at a caterpillar, we actually see a butterfly.

If the caterpillar could look at himself in the mirror, would he see just a caterpillar, or would he see who he really is: a butterfly? What about you? When you look in the mirror, when you reflect on your life, do you see who you are or who you are becoming? Do you see your existence or your essence? Do you have vision?

Mirror, Mirror on the Wall

When we look in the mirror, when we reflect on the moments of our lives, do we see who we were and remain trapped in our past? Do we see who we are and remain satisfied with surviving? Or do we see who we are becoming: one who thrives, and do we press on toward our transformation?

The caterpillar does not stop. If he does, he walks away from his Greatness (becoming a butterfly) because existence is never static. We either walk into our Greatness or walk away from it. *Being is non-being. Being is becoming.*[133] In other words, if we remain the same, we do not exist. The fulfilling life is a constant movement toward growth and becoming.

In his book *The 15 Invaluable Laws of Growth*, John Maxwell writes, "Whenever people stop actively learning and growing, the clock has started ticking down to a time when they will no longer have anything left to give. . .Instead of playing to win, [people] start playing not to lose."[134] In the name of safety and security, so many try to simply hold on to what they have, keep doing just enough to get by, failing to realize this static existence moves them closer to what Henry David Thoreau called *quiet desperation*. They practice *non-being*. Though they have a pulse and respiratory rate, they stop existing.

Change is inevitable, but growth is optional. Those who opt out of growth stop existing. The caterpillar continues to walk in his Greatness. Like the frog that keeps "kicking," the caterpillar walks on because he is the butterfly, living his calling every day, even before the butterfly manifests.

When you look in the mirror do you see the true you? Does your existence precede your essence? Are you making The Shift, changing your mind, changing your ways, adjusting and moving forward daily? Do you *connect, associate,* and *reflect* on your *desire, determination,* and *discipline* every moment, living your calling daily?

We must Shift our minds to see and hear differently if we are going to change the world for the better by living our callings, and taking our significant and integral place in this body we call Humanity. *Do not conform to the **illusions** of this world. Be transformed by the **shifting** of your mind.*[135] Don't settle for being shackled, exactly like everyone else, chained, facing the same direction, doing the same thing, living an illusion, content to remain in the box, in the frame, ignoring the bigger picture and the greater context, the larger vision of true life, your calling and your Greatness!

What Matters

From this chapter remember:

1. Just because you are good at something doesn't necessarily mean it is your calling or Dream.

2. Doing something solely to look good in the eyes of others is not your calling or your Dream.

3. Humanity needs you to be who you are, not try to be someone else.

4. Who you are and what you do are NOT the same thing.

5. Without you humanity will survive, but with you humanity will thrive!

6. If you stop growing, you stop existing. Transformation *is* existing. The status quo is death. Living is never static. It is dynamic. You either walk toward your Greatness and your Dream or away from it.

Your Turn

Step One: List five people you admire and who you trust to give you an honest assessment of what they see regarding you, who you are. These are people you have a relationship with, perhaps family, friends, a church friend, a workout buddy, a teacher or coach.

Step Two: Ask these five people the following question: What would you say are the top five gifts or strengths I possess? Record their answers.

Step Three: Analyze the data you have collected from your friends. Look for trends. Did the same strength or gift come up on several lists? Are there certain answers that relate to one specific trait?

Step Four: Write a conclusion. What does this information tell you about how people view you? What was surprising about their answers? Were these surprises accurate do you think? What information can serve you? What are you learning about who you are?

Step Five: How will this information inform your choices about what you do and what you avoid doing? How will it help you play to your *Greatness*?

Suggestion: I recommend you take a personality profile, so you know your strengths. It changes the way you see and treat yourself and others, and it changes the way you deal with yourself and others. It empowers you to use your strengths and manage your weaknesses. Here are some well-known ones: Strengthsfinder[136]; DISC Style[137]; The Myers-Briggs Type Indicator[138]

STOP! DO NOT READ ON UNTIL YOU'VE COMPLETED THE *YOUR TURN* SECTION OF THIS CHAPTER.

21
Faith

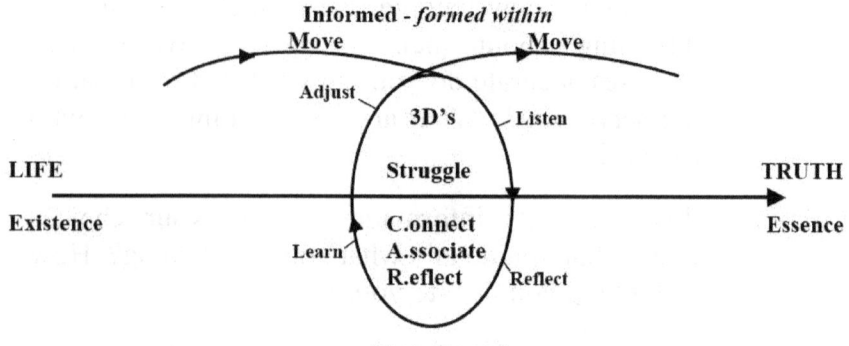

The Two Yellow Lines

Today at some point I will enter my Honda Civic, strap on my seatbelt and head down a two-lane road at sixty miles per hour, heading straight toward other vehicles which are heading straight towards me at sixty miles per hour. We will barrel down on each other, and we will narrowly avoid a head-on collision. . .by inches. Why will we do this?

The two yellow lines painted in the center of the road.

I want to go somewhere, do something, accomplish something, so I choose to get in a fifteen hundred pound bullet and drive directly towards other fifteen hundred pound bullets at high speeds, putting all of my trust in the two yellow lines painted in the center of the road.

Every person on that two lane highway places their trust in those two yellow lines of paint, as if those two yellow lines of paint actually create a powerful, invisible, yet very real barrier rising to the heavens between the side of the road I am traveling down at sixty miles per hour and the other side of the road the oncoming traffic is barreling down at sixty miles per hour.

I trust all the drivers coming toward me are not fooling around with their radio or cell phones, drowsy or intoxicated, and actually have a legitimate driver's license. I probably do not know any of those people personally or their driving or psychological history. Yet, I trust these complete strangers will stay on their side of the road. Why? The two yellow lines painted down the center of the road. Sounds crazy, doesn't it?

Well, that's Faith.

Trust and Risk

It's been said "trust" or "risk" are other words for Faith. Soren Kierkegaard writes about "the leap of faith." Regardless of how small a step it takes to trust or risk, it still feels like a leap because it involves uncertainty and insecurity. It involves our best friend, Discomfort. We all have Faith. We all "trust" in someone or something:

- God
- gods
- The absence of God or gods
- Materialism
- Metaphysics
- Mysticism
- Love
- The Universe
- Spiritus Mundi
- Reason
- Humanity
- Country
- Science
- Nature
- Work
- Money
- Yourself
- Others
- Technology
- Ancient Aliens

- Two Yellow Lines of Paint in the Middle of the Road

The list goes on and on. . .

Whether we admit it or not, we all live by Faith. In fact, it is safe to say practically everything we do in life is either a *leap* of Faith or an *expression* of Faith. The level of Faith we possess involves our own personal risk to payoff ratio assessment in every choice we make and action we take. All choices involve risk and trust. We determine our own level of Faith! Perhaps some have greater Faith than others. A quick perusal of history suggests those with greater Faith influenced their community and world for the better as they walked in their Greatness daily. This is why Faith is one of *The Six F's of a Great Life*.

Out of This World

Have you ever seen Jupiter? Some of us have looked at it through a telescope. Some have seen pictures of it in books taken by the Hubble Telescope. . .or so we've been told. Some of us may have never seen it, but we "trust" it's there because others have told us so. In every instance, there is a level of trust we have determined is appropriate for us to believe in the existence of Jupiter. For some of us, we need to be told by people who have a lot of initials after their names, signifying they are educated and so are trustworthy. For others, our dad who has a telescope is enough. This fact remains: We choose our own level of Faith and the criterion necessary for us to believe something or someone.

When most people hear the word Faith they tend to think of religion. Of course, religion can imply Faith, but just about anything can become a religion. The word religion doesn't just apply to worldviews like Christianity, Islam, or Hinduism. People can be religious about all sorts of things. We create rituals around sports. Just take a look across the U.S. on Sunday afternoons in Fall and Winter. We create rituals around countries and political leaders. The Romans worshiped Caesar as a god, and so many people hope their President will "save" the country. We create rituals around education, wearing black robes and ridiculous looking flat board hats with tassels on our heads at the end of every school year. We create rituals around celebrities, seeking life advice from someone simply because they are famous from television or film. Faith differs from religion, though Faith may or may not be an aspect of religion. And this, of course, leads us to bananas! Yes, bananas!

Bananas

I love bananas. They may be my favorite fruit. One of the things I love about bananas is that when you look at a banana, you know exactly what you're going to get. If the banana is green, you know the meat inside the banana is going to taste bitter and probably give you a stomach ache. If the banana is brown and bruised, you know the meat is going to be a bit syrupy, slimy, and sickeningly sweet. But if the banana is yellow, you know the meat is going to taste fabulous. What's on the inside of the banana matches what the outside of the banana looks like.

This is what I love about the natural world. With almost all of nature what you see is what you get. You know that a Bengal tiger is probably going to attack and eat you. You know a rhino may charge you if you enter its territory. In most of nature you know what you're going to get. The banana, the tiger, and the rhino all have integrity. What you see is what you get. There is really only one major exception in nature to this rule, and we all know it from personal experience. It's humanity. Often with humans what you see is far from what you get.

My advice? Go bananas! Be the same on the inside as you are on the outside. In Harper Lee's award winning novel *To Kill A Mockingbird*, Scout tells Miss Maudie that her father, Atticus Finch, is the same at home as he is on the street corner or in a court of law. Miss Maudie responds that Scout doesn't really know how rare and admirable of a man is Atticus. When what you believe in your heart, think in your mind, and do with your body line up, you are a banana! You have integrity!

Faith Takes Practice

Many people see Faith as "what one believes," and while belief may be a part of Faith, there's more to Faith than just belief. Soren Kierkegaard writes, "[I must] find a truth which is true for me . . . the idea for which I can live and die." The *idea* is the belief part of Faith, but Faith contains another vital component. It's that part about *living and dying* for the idea. Faith takes practice. Faith is living (and dying for) what you believe.

Maurice Blondel writes, "If you really want to understand what a man believes, don't listen to what he says, but watch what he does."[140] It's not just what we say that constitutes Faith. It's also how we live and what we do, and both of those are connected to our why. A person of Faith is a whole person. Cerebral, Visceral, and the Heart of man, his mind, body, and soul all work together. His why, how and what all work together, moving in the same direction. What he believes, what he says, and what he does all work together. He has integrity. Like the banana, what you see is what you get.

It's possible to believe something yet not possess Faith. I can believe lying is wrong and telling the truth is right, but if I am a chronic liar, I don't really possess Faith, or at best my Faith is weak. If Martin Luther King Jr. believed in civil rights but did not march, speak, and organize then undergo beatings, arrest, and imprisonment for speaking and practicing civil disobedience, he would not have possessed Faith.

In *A Prayer for Owen Meany,* John Irving writes, "Never confuse faith or belief - of any kind –with something even remotely intellectual."[141] Belief *is* in the head and is part of Faith, but Faith is also in the heart and the body. It's physical, emotional, and intellectual. Faith is cerebral man (intellectual), visceral man (physical), and the heart of man (emotional) moving in one accord. Faith is the head, the body, and the heart aligning. It is a way of life. All of us are going to practice Faith. How we live and who or what we trust shows it. The question is: Who or what am I willing to trust? Am I willing to grow in my Faith? Will I listen, reflect, learn, and adjust?

Jesus of Nazareth said, "Ask and it will be given. Seek and you will find. Knock and the door will be opened."[142] Those who pursue the kind of truth Kierkegaard was writing about with *desire, determination,* and *discipline* find it. Those who make The Shift and ask, open themselves to find truth. Those who knock on the doors of possibility and walk through those doors, live daily their callings, their Greatness, and their Dreams.

Everyone must find "an idea for which he is willing to live and die." That idea is tied up in our Dream, and that Dream always has something to do with serving others. If it doesn't, then that's no Dream. It's a nightmare!

If you have an idea you are willing to live and die for, you will risk. You will trust. You will *listen, reflect, learn,* and *adjust* at every moment. You will let every moment inform you, form you within, moving you toward your truth and your Dream. You will remain open to hear and see what each moment is teaching you about your relationship with others in your life. You will grow. You will be transformed by your Faith, which is the way you live. And who or what you believe in may change as well because just because you believe in Truth, doesn't mean you fully possess it. That's what the journey is for. So you can grow in your Faith, your Dream, and your Calling. So your life will be The Greatness Revolution.

Vision and Faith

What you see is what you get! *Now wait a second, Brad. You said way back in the chapter one that 'believing is seeing.'* Yes, I did, and I still hold to that. But I am not talking about seeing with your eyes here. I'm talking about seeing with your heart. It seems to me that much of our lives we see, but we don't perceive what's really going on. We hear, but we're not really listening. And it seems to me that if we would see and listen with our hearts (the ancients used the word mind), we would see our Dreams and our callings come to pass in our lives.

What I'm talking about here is Vision. Vision and Faith are connected. Way back in *chapter one* you walked through the

Cave. All of those people chained in the bottom of the Cave were using their physical eyes and ears, and what did they see and hear? Shadows and echoes of what was real. They saw shadows of real things. They heard echoes of real voices and sounds. And they believed the shadows and echoes were all that existed. This is where Faith connects to Vision.

Plato said that there exists an ideal realm. This realm of ideas is the true realm, and this world we inhabit is a poor reflection of that ideal realm. For some this is hard to swallow, but when you think about it we can understand this with simple examples.

For instance, almost every artist, whether a painter, sculptor, or musician, will tell you that when they create a work, more often than not the work they create doesn't exactly match the idea of the work in their mind. They simply can't duplicate that portrait, carving, or song exactly the way they conceived it in their heads. The idea is expressed imperfectly. The idea manifests itself, and while it might be really beautiful, really good, it just doesn't quite live up to the artist's original concept.

Superman. He's cool. Are you a Superman or Superwoman? I mean, Superman can leap tall buildings with a single bound, right? Can we leap tall buildings with a single bound? Of course we can! We just have to get a helicopter, turn it on, and fly it over the building (after you receive helicopter pilot training of course). The idea of leaping a tall building in a single bound is manifested poorly by flying a helicopter over the building. The ideal and the real don't quite match. The real is a poor reflection of the ideal.

By the same token, when I look at me, I see Brad Thomas. But according to Plato and Yoda, this crude matter is not the true Brad Thomas. It is merely a poor reflection of the ideal Brad Thomas (Thank goodness!) that exists in the ideal realm, just as this book is not perfectly expressing the ideas in my mind (I know, you're saying, 'You got that right!'). According to Plato the real world is a dirty, smudged window to the ideal world. This is called idealism. And this brings us to Vision.

Abraham

When you think about your Dream, your Calling, what do you see in your mind? As I mentioned in chapter sixteen, Faith is "confidence in what you hope for and certainty of what you cannot physically see."[143] That, my friends, is the definition of Vision. It's Plato's story of the Cave from chapter one. It's the story of Wilbur and Orville Wright in chapter five. It's the story of Thomas Edison in chapter nine. It's the story of Mahatma Gandhi in chapter fifteen. It's the story of Nelson Mandela in chapter fourteen. And it's the story of you and me. Do you believe it?

There was this guy named Abraham who lived thousands of years ago. God told him (Ya, God talked to him. I know, I know. Just think of it as The Advocate from chapter two) that he was going to be the father of many nations, that his inheritance would be so many people that it would be like the sand on the beach or the stars in the sky! In other words: a lot!

And Abraham believed this! In fact, the story goes that he actually *saw* it, not with his eyes but with his heart. He made a lot of mistakes along the way in his life. He wasn't perfect by any stretch of the imagination, but he traveled in Faith to distant countries, trusting, believing he would be the father of many nations. He got off course many times and had to Course Correct. His family was a mess at times, and his finances were up in the air on occasion, and he was tested to the point where he was going to have to give up his son to death, but he continued to believe the voice within, the Advocate. In fact, because he believed before he saw any results, it was "credited to him as righteousness." In other words, it was a done deal long before it came to pass. And. . .it came to pass!

Vision and Faith. Seeing it in your mind with certainty before anyone sees it materially, that's Vision. Acting on what you see in your mind, living out your Vision, doing the practices daily that move you closer to your Dream or your calling with desire, discipline, and determination, that's Faith.

I'm going to be really honest with you now (rest assured, I've tried to be honest with you throughout this entire book). Without Vision and Faith achieving your Dream or calling is virtually impossible. It can't be done. No one will believe as much in your Dream as you. Not parents, siblings, spouse, or friends. No one! They aren't going to see and hear what you see and hear. You cannot rely on others to give you your Vision and Faith. You're going to have to figure those out on your own and with your God. What do you want? What has God placed in your heart (your *desidere*? Your desire?)? See it! Then go get it! Hear it! And go get it!

The Opposite of Faith

What's the opposite of faith? Most people would say doubt. Others might say fear. But really, when you get to the core of faith, the opposite is not what we might expect. The opposite of faith is certitude. Certainty. Reductionism. Think about it.

Go with your gut! Follow your heart! We like those sayings. Deep inside those are the kinds of sayings we long to follow. But in reality, most of us never go with our gut or follow our heart in the big things. Sure, the choice between a Big Mac or a Whopper, no problem, I'll go with my gut! Red or White with dinner, I'll go with my gut. This shirt or that shirt, I love that one more! I'll go with my gut. But what about my Dream that promises little security, money, and a lot of hardship versus my nine to five job that promises a steady paycheck, predictable outcomes, and a comfortable existence. I'm going with my gu. . . .I'm following my hear. . .uh. . .Well, I'm going with my head. Cerebral man is going to win this one nine and a half times out of ten statistically because that's what your head is programmed to do.

To dream the impossible dream
To fight the unbeatable foe
To bear with unbearable sorrow
To run where the brave dare not go
To right the un-rightable wrong
To love pure and chaste from afar

> *To strive when you're way-worn and weary*
> *To reach the unreachable star.*
>
> *This is my quest: to follow that star*
> *No matter how hopeless*
> *No matter how far*
> *To fight for the right without question or pause*
> *To be willing to march into hell for a heavenly cause*
> *And I know if I'll only be true to this glorious quest*
> *That my heart will lie peaceful and calm when I'm laid to my rest.*
>
> *And the world will be better for this,*
> *That one man scorned and covered with scars*
> *Still strove with his last ounce of courage*
> *To reach the unreachable star.*[144]

"Oh ya. I love that song! So inspiring! It's from that musical. What was it called? Oh ya, *Man of La Mancha*, based on Cervantes' *Don Quixote*. Great show! It was about an old, eccentric man who thought he was a knight. He fought windmills and treated a whore like a princess, and he fought a bunch of less-than-admirable men. I love the words to that song. They are something to remember. Always dream the impossible. See the best outcome in every situation. Strive to do the impossible. See what's really going on in the heart. Bring hope and love to people. Fight for a just cause even if it costs you your reputation, even if it costs you everything because you can't lose your soul if you do that. Well, back to the daily grind. It's a nice story, but you can't live that way. There's no guarantee it's going to turn out to your advantage. Nothing is certain in that kind of life. Now, let's see, Big Mac or Whopper?"

My daughter is a software engineer. She loves what she does. And I am so proud of her and happy for her. She makes really good money doing what she loves. That makes it easy for a parent, right? My son recently graduated from University with an Animation and Film degree, and he wants to create his own animation series and produce and direct it. He loves animation.

And I am so proud of him and happy for him. But animation does not pay real well, like a software engineer, and if I am being honest, there's a part of me as a father that says, "You know, son, this path of animation is going to be pretty tough financially." And there's the rub, right? My parents were the same way with my sisters and I growing up. "You could do that, Brad, but it's going to be tough to make a living doing that. What's your back up plan?"

Can a Dream have a back up plan? Unless your Dream is solely about being wealthy, money cannot be the sole determining factor. If security is an illusion, then pursuing your Dream, is no worse a decision than "playing it safe." I decided as a Father to support my kids in their Dreams. If my children are happy pursuing their callings, whether they make a lot or a little money, whether the road is easy or difficult, whether they need our assistance from time to time, I fully support their decision. Why? Because when your kids are happy, you are happy! When your kids are fulfilled, you are happy. When your kids have the faith to pursue what they love and believe in, you are happy. And whenever you pursue what you believe in, what you really believe in is yourself, the person God made you to be, your uniquely created self with specific gifts and passions. If faith is a payoff to risk ratio, then what is a better risk, believing in yourself or putting your faith in what some other person says you are? That's a no-brainer! Listen to the Advocate within!

What *The Impossible Dream* makes abundantly clear is that anything other than living your Dream is an illusion. Living anything other than your Dream is a shadow on a cave wall. As Plato made abundantly clear in the *Allegory of the Cave,* the idea placed in your heart is your truth to live or die for. The idea placed in your heart is the only truly real thing in your life. What you are called to live, the idea that makes you come alive, the vocation that ignites your passion, the joy you experience when you follow the true desires of your heart, written in the stars, placed there by God Himself, even with all its uncertainty, even when there is no guarantee it is going to work out the way you'd like or the way you expected, even when hardship, obstacles, and disappointments come, you choose to do what you believe to be true, good, and right for your life path. You choose to bless others by living your calling.

I found an article that shared the top five regrets of those who were on their death-beds. Here were the top five themes of regrets as recorded by the nurse who wrote the article:

1. I wish I'd had the courage to live a life true to myself, not the life others expected of me.

2. I wish I didn't work so hard.

3. I wish I'd had the courage to express my feelings.

4. I wish I had stayed in touch with my friends.

5. I wish I had let myself be happier.

In every one of these five themes, certitude is not a value that is expressed. Rather, risk and vulnerability are the values expressed. Courage, *to tell the story of who you are with all of your heart,*[145] to be true to yourself, to be happy, to do what you love rather than "work" or what's expected, to say what you feel rather than hold back tears, hurt, anger, joy, and gratitude were most important in the hearts and minds of those looking back on life. So, being authentic, transparent, whole, and being who you truly are was four of the five top themes from those facing death.

Relationships or staying connected to friends was the second value expressed. Just a quick analysis of these five most mentioned themes shows a four to one ratio. Four of the five themes deal mostly with the individual, and one, staying connected to friends, expresses the importance of relationships to those looking back. To those asked, it seems that how they related to themselves and to others was what mattered most looking back but what mattered least at the time.

Alfred Tennyson writes, "Tis better to have loved and lost than never to have loved at all." Better to have loved yourself and loved others than to remain safe, certain, and in control. And how do you love yourself? By being true to who you are. By following your calling. By bringing your gifts to your community and world. And how do you love others? By doing the same exact thing. Loving others and loving yourself call for the same response: be *who* you are *where* you are *when* you are.

In the holiday classic *It's a Wonderful Life*, George Bailey is a young man who, in his words, has dreamed all his life of "shaking the dust off" the "crummy old town" of Bedford Falls where he's grown up. His father owns The Bailey Building and Loan, a two-penny business that thwarts the evil schemes of a greedy banking tycoon named Potter by giving regular working-class people the opportunity to live their Dream of owning a home and raising a family. Time and again George tries to leave Bedford Falls only to see his departure thwarted because he is the only man who can keep The Bailey Building and Loan going after the sudden, tragic death of his father. George's dream to travel the world, then go to college, then become an architect and build skyscrapers in big cities around the country, living a life of adventure, all dissipate, it seems, when his uncle loses The Building and Loan cash, actually found by Potter who does not return it, but tries to put George and The Building and Loan out of business because of this misfortune.

It's at this point that George loses himself, telling God he wishes he'd never been born. God grants him his wish. Clarence, an angel, leads George into a Bedford Falls without George Bailey ever having existed, and George sees that his mother is a miserable boarding house owner after her husband's death because Geroge wasn't there to keep The Building and Loan running. George sees that Harry, his brother, died as a little boy after falling through broken ice at the local lake, never becoming a World War II hero because George wasn't there to save Harry. He sees that Mary, his wife is a lonely single woman working as a librarian, and their children do not exist because George wasn't there to fall in love with Mary and marry her. George sees numerous townspeople he helped homeless, penniless, and broken because he wasn't there to bless the lives of others with his gift of compassion and economic genius. In short, George sees that without his life, thousands of people in Bedford Falls and around the world would have lost their lives and would not have lived their dreams if not for George. George realizes his Dream was not travel, college, or architecture. His true Dream was building the foundations for thousand of people across the world so that they could all live their Dreams. His life is SIGN-ificant because saving Harry, allowed Harry to save thousands of lives, just one of many exponential results because George Bailey lived a life he thought was worthless and insignificant only to find out that his true Dream, though seemingly meaningless, insignificant, and small was vastly significant and impacting. George's life-calling, his Dream, was to be a Dream-giver. He chose to fight for Shakespeare's King Grace and against King Rude-will in the clearing of his heart.[146] Despite what he thought his Dream was, George grows where he is planted, using his gifts for those in Bedford Falls. Even unwittingly, George is *who* he is, *where* he is, *when* he is, and thousands of lives are transformed, even as he is transformed by the end of the film because of the relationships in his life, the interconnectedness of all the people of Bedford Falls, like a body with many parts, each doing what he or she was designed to do, significant and essential to the community thriving. And George plays his significant part as well. If you haven't seen *It's a Wonderful Life*, see it. . .and make sure you have some tissue.

Like George Bailey, your Dream and listening to your heart definitely doesn't guarantee a life of ease, but settling for certainty, ease, and comfort doesn't guarantee that either. The truth is that life is uncertain at all times. Security is an illusion. Just ask millions of people who lost much of their retirement in the 2008 U.S. economic collapse. What you can be certain of is your heart and your character. If you trust in your Dream and the calling in your heart no matter the outcome, no matter the money attached to it, no matter how easy or hard the journey, you still have your heart and your character, and when you lay your head on your pillow each evening, you can rest knowing who you are and that you have been true to your self. When you examine your heart at the end of the day, it's authentic. Think about it. At least, please, just think about it.

Funky Glasses

Abraham had vision. You need some Vision Glasses. Remember those huge, silly sunglasses people used to wear several years ago. You need some of those for your Vision Glasses. They need to be ridiculously big, and not only that! You need to hang all kinds of things related to your Vision off of them: pictures of places your Dream will take you, symbols that represent integral parts of your Dream, pictures, tinsel, colorful strings, glitter all representing the joy and celebration of your Vision and Dream and what it means to pursue it.

Here's why: When you share your Vision with people, even those closest to you, they are going to think you are crazy! They won't see it. You might as well be wearing some really funky Vision Glasses while they jeer, mock, ridicule, insult, and laugh at you. You see, it's going to be just like the Cave after having seen the true realm beyond the Cave and then being thrust into the bottom of the Cave stumbling around, trying to tell the others the truth about their existence and what you've seen, only to have them mock, ridicule, jeer, insult, and laugh at you as a crazy madman or madwoman!

So get some funky Vision Glasses. Decorate them. Wear them. And be confident in what you hope for and certain of what you cannot physically see. Then go do it. Because in your mind's eye, in your heart, you've seen and heard your Dream, your calling, and pursuing that with anything less than desire, discipline, and determination is a joyless ride to the bottom of a cave!

What Matters

From this chapter remember:

1. Faith is trust and risk.

2. Everything you do in life is either a leap or expression of faith.

3. Your faith involves your own personal risk to payoff ratio in every choice you make. You want a hamburger, so you will get into a car and travel head on toward another vehicle down a highway because you've deemed the payoff of a burger relative to the risk of a head-on collision is worth it.

4. You determine your own level of faith.

5. Faith is more than just belief. Faith is the head, heart, and body aligning. Faith is a way of life.

6. Plato said, "The world we live in is a dim reflection of the true realm, the ideal realm."

7. The opposite of faith is reductionism, basing life only on what is material, tangible, measureable, based solely on the five senses.

8. Faith is confidence in what you hope for and certainty of what you cannot physically see.

9. Vision is seeing it in your mind with certainty before anyone sees it materially.

10. Without Vision and Faith achieving your Dream is virtually impossible. Like Abraham, no one can give you vision or faith, except God.

11. If you are going to take a risk, risk being who you are, living your Dream, rather than being who others say you should be.

Your Turn

Step One: In who or what do you choose to put your faith? Write a one sentence statement of faith?

Step Two: List three ways, three daily actions, you will employ to live what you believe.

Step Three: What will you do when you don't feel like practicing your faith? List three ways you will overcome those moments you don't feel like living what you believe. (Hint: These solutions probably have something to do with either *doing* something (visceral man) or relying on what you *know* (cerebral man) and telling yourself this daily.

Step Four: Practice the three actions daily.

STOP! DO NOT READ ON UNTIL YOU'VE COMPLETED THE *YOUR TURN* SECTION OF THIS CHAPTER.

22

The Greatness Revolution

Revolution...

a radical, pervasive, sudden, complete, or marked change; from the Latin root word volvere, meaning "to turn around."

We see it on the evening news. We read about it online or in the newspapers. Another dictator toppled by a massive demonstration in the streets or a violent military coup. One day the world was one way, and the next day everything changes: the American Revolution, the French Revolution, the Arab Spring, Indian Independence, the Bolshevik Revolution. Our perceptions of what we thought we knew about the world are overthrown overnight.

Were we to slow down and examine any of these revolutions, we would see the momentary upheaval had been building and growing for years. The Russian Revolution was a result of hundreds of years of aristocratic oppression. The American Revolution was a result of years of, among other things, taxation without representation. The French Revolution was a result of years of corruption and oppression. The reasons for every one of these seemingly sudden, radical changes did not occur overnight, but had been building through the years, until the people affected by the oppression realized waiting would not change anything, only action would.

Revolution also occurs in individuals. Gandhi, Martin Luther King Jr., and Nelson Mandela all experienced a revolution, but the fruit of their personal revolutions were not immediate. In personal revolutions the consequences or the effects often manifest slowly in the world. There is a delay between the cause and effect. Gandhi's epiphany in South Africa came in a moment, and he spent over sixty years of steady work before India's home rule. The Civil Rights Act came years after King and others began to speak, demonstrate, and practice civil disobedience, and the work still continues in the United States. Nelson Mandela spent twenty-seven years in prison yet revolutionized South Africa by adopting a policy of forgiveness, though South Africa still has a long journey ahead in race relations even today.

These people's personal revolutions were seeds of growth not just in them, but in the world around them. They were sowing seeds even as they themselves continued to practice their Faith and grow in their Greatness. Seeds have to germinate, be watered and tended over time before any fruit is harvested. It's the ancient rhythm deep within us: Plant. Cultivate. Harvest. Any results of these figures' personal revolutions show this truth:

Revolution occurs when practices over time build momentum.

So, let's break down the definition and see what revolution is and why we need *The Greatness Revolution* to sweep across our world:

Revolution is. . .

Radical
going to the root or origin;
forming a basis or foundation;
existing inherently in a thing or person; having roots;
in medicine, aimed at removing the source of the disease.

The Greatness Revolution is radical. To become Great, I must get to the root or origin then plant it in fertile soil. The greatest mind-changers in history called the root "metanoia," a Greek word translated "repentance." This word, repentance, has been misinterpreted. We tend to think of the word as a religious term, but its Greek root word, "metanoia," simply means " a changed mind," making a decision to turn around, to face a new direction, to see the world and yourself in a new way, a different way, a transformed way, not in the way most people see it. In other words, you make The Shift. The root or origin begins with The Shift in my mind. You see, the root, "metanoia," exists in me already, and when I make The Shift, a renewing of my mind, I uncover the root so that it can be replanted in the fertile soil of my changed heart. I water it daily with positive affirmations and life-giving practices. Then, the root begins to branch out, forming a strong system. That root system consists of the healthy stories I attach to the events in my life, promoting my healthy personal growth.

Very quickly I begin to see and hear differently. The Shift and the stories I've exchanged for the stories that have not served me remove the source of my "Dis-Ease." My life of quiet desperation ceases. I am born again. The shackles are off. I turn one hundred eighty degrees, my back to the cave wall, filled with shadows, pointed toward the light of true life beyond the cave. I've seen it with a clear and specific vision.

As the roots grow, I awaken to what exists within, my Desires and Dreams beginning to blossom over time, my desire for love and belonging and in turn my desire to love and accept others, to be one in spirit and in life. To most of the world, all of these dramatic changes within go unnoticed. The root system of a tree is typically three times larger than the plant above the surface and remains unseen. It is the same for the radical Shift into my Greatness. My growth within is exponential before the world takes notice. No visible, perceptible change in the consequences of my daily life shows, but the radical Shift within has created the ripple in a sea that over time and distance will become a positive tsunami of impact.

Revolution is...

Pervasive
spread throughout; from pervade –
to spread through, especially subtly or gradually.

The Greatness Revolution is pervasive. Once the root has been planted and I awaken to the Dream within, a desire "from the stars," placed in me by my Creator, takes hold of my imagination, and a vision of my Dream rises before me. It begins to spread throughout all the areas of my life subtly and gradually, as I begin to practice *discipline* and *determination* in the *Six F's of a Great Life*: Faith, Foundation, Family, Friends, Fitness, and Finances.

I connect every activity in the *Six F's*, realizing how I am in one area is how I will be in any other area. I associate with other like-minded individuals influencing me positively on my transformational journey through life as I pursue my Dream. Using *The Listen and Learn Technique,* I reflect on what every moment has to teach me about who I am and who I am becoming and what I can learn and apply to living my Dream and walking in my Greatness.

The Greatness Revolution has already occurred with The Shift. Now all that is left is the manifestation of my Greatness into the material world, like the caterpillar to butterfly. The material change is subtle and gradual, but the ripple at sea has grown to a wave. I know over time, with *desire, determination,* and *discipline*, my Greatness Revolution will reach the shore with massive, positive impact.

Revolution is. . .

Sudden?
happening, coming, made or done quickly, without warning or unexpectedly; occurring without transition from the previous state; abrupt.

The Greatness Revolution seems sudden. The Wright brothers did not decide to develop manned flight and the next day do it. Thomas Edison did not decide to invent the light bulb and then make it the following day. Henry Ford did not decide to make the automobile affordable and then open the perfect assembly line that evening. The revolutions we see on the nightly news did not occur in one day.

Any revolution seems sudden, but it takes time to manifest my Dream into material existence. When the plane first flew, or the light bulb filament first glowed, or the first affordable cars rolled off the assembly line and into the driveways of thousands, it seemed like a breakthrough and a sudden change in the way of the world, but The Wright brothers, Edison, and Ford actually spent their entire lives preparing daily for those moments.

The best time to plant a tree is thirty years ago. The second best time is today. The Wrights, Edison, and Ford did not wait. They tried something daily and adjusted daily. They kept acting on what they knew and what they had. They knew their ideas would never come to pass unless they planted it and tended to it "today," realizing that "today is tomorrow."

Even though the tsunami is one hundred feet high, moving at six hundred miles per hour across the ocean, the four-inch shift in the crust of the earth that caused it, and the small bump in the ocean's surface often go unnoticed by those along the shore, until suddenly a giant wall of water comes crashing.

The unnoticed, daily activities I practice in my Faith, Foundation, Family, Friends, Fitness, and Finances over time create exponential growth and momentum until those around me notice my success and often respond with amazement and shock. What most fail to realize is my Greatness and my Dream have always been present as I practiced the small, daily disciplines, so when the magnitude of my success is finally witnessed by others, to me it's no surprise. I've been practicing these disciplines for years because they are my way of life.

Revolution is...

Complete
having all parts or elements;
lacking nothing; whole; entire; full;
finished; ended; concluded;

The Greatness Revolution is complete. When I walk into my Greatness I apply *desire, discipline,* and *determination* to my daily activities in all areas of your life: Faith, Foundation, Family, Friends, Fitness, and Finances.

Martin Luther King Jr. writes, "For some strange reason I can never be what I ought to be until you are what you ought to be. And you can never be what you ought to be until I am what I ought to be."[147] King's assertion holds true for my relationships with others, but it also holds true for me individually. If I am not what I am meant to be in every area of my own life, my Greatness has no chance to manifest. It's what my family, community, and world needs from me, the very best version of myself possible, lacking nothing, striving to be whole, entire, and full!

I'm not talking about perfection here. I'm talking about progression. I'm talking about wholeness: Cerebral Man, Visceral Man, and the Heart of Man all one, moving in concert together. I practice "arête," the ancient Greek idea of excellence, of moral virtue, of fulfilling my calling or Dream, of living up to my full potential because I am whole. I live by the adage, "God knows I'm not who I want to be, but thank God I'm not who I used to be."

Of course, I may never be completely finished becoming who I am meant to be, and my Dream may not be finished in my lifetime as was the case with Martin Luther King Jr., but that is no reason to stop living the Dream daily because, in large measure, my Dream is not just about me. It's about serving and adding value to others, my community, and my world.

And what if I do accomplish my Dream in this lifetime? What if I do see it come to fruition? There will be another Dream to fill my heart, perhaps the Dream I am really called to pursue and complete. What I thought was my Dream may actually be the stepping-stone to the real thing. I am always progressing. Sometimes I have to complete what I thought was my Dream in order to move beyond it and experience transformation.

Accomplishment is not a result. It is a principle, a way of life that values process, progress, wholeness, excellence, and fulfilled potential.

Revolution is. . .

A Marked Change
strikingly noticeable transformation;
strikingly different from what it is
or from what it would be if left alone;
strikingly noticeable change or an exchange;
strikingly noticeable act of passing

from one state or phase to another.

The Greatness Revolution is marked change. It is the caterpillar to butterfly, two seemingly different creatures, the latter actually already residing in the former. When I begin The Greatness Revolution, I begin a *strikingly noticeable transformation*. I become *strikingly different* from who I was and whom I would be if I left my personal growth into my Greatness to chance with no intention to live my Dream and Greatness. I make a strikingly noticeable exchange. I Shift my thinking that then manifests in my behaviors and practices as I use *desire, determination,* and *discipline* to live my Dream.

Like the caterpillar to butterfly, my transformation goes unnoticed to others, but as I attach activity to my Dream, I personally experience the strikingly noticeable passage from unintentional and reactive to intentional and proactive. Only when the butterfly emerges from the cocoon does anyone really see the caterpillar's transformation. So too, only when my Dream manifests do others see the transformation of who I was into who I have been becoming over time with *desire, discipline*, and *determination.* To most the change seems sudden, but I know the change occurs every day over time, and I live daily with peace and patience The Greatness Revolution, a radical, pervasive, not-so-sudden, complete, or marked change.

Revolution is...

Evolution
a process of gradual, peaceful, progressive change or development.

Embedded in the word revolution is evolution. When people espouse revolution, they tend to speak with passion about immediate and sudden change, but anyone who studies revolutions knows steady oppressive practices, stewing discontent and poor economic and living conditions precede "sudden" political changes.

If you have read this book to this point, you recognize there is more to your life than you are currently experiencing. You want more. It may be that you are not unhappy with your current life, but you long to grow more in your relationships, your career, and your aspirations. In other words, your Dream. You want more than your current conditions, which may seem to be stifling, unfulfilling, or even oppressive at times. You've come up against one of the greatest enemies to Dreamers: comfort.

The Caesar's of the Roman Empire adopted the practice of *Bread and Circuses*. This was a strategy to keep the people of Rome *comfortable* by supplying just enough *Bread* to keep bellies full and satisfied, and *Circuses*, entertainment in the form of the violent games of the Coliseum. Caesar wanted people with full bellies and entertainment that diverted attention from what might be wrong with his rule. This would keep Caesar's Empire intact. And this strategy worked for a time. The problem was that people do want to have food and be comfortable, but they also want real adventure and significance. Comfort in the form of *Bread and Circuses* will never satisfy the longing in us for significance.

Success and significance are two important words to those who want to live Greatness. Success is about my personal goals, accomplishments, and milestones, all of which are good. But it is significance that is the game-changer in life. In the word significance is the word *sign*. A sign always points to something. On the highway, a sign points to the upcoming exit, a gas station, or a restaurant. It gives me directions and points to something beyond where I am.

Living a life of significance is living a *sign-life*. A life of significance always points to something bigger than oneself. It is a life not just about the Big Me. It is about Humanity and how who I am and what I do points to the something greater. A life of Greatness is not *Bread and Circuses*. A life of Greatness is not even about getting more bread or being more entertained. It's not about two, three, or four loaves of bread or three, four, or five vacations a year.

Greatness is about significance, fulfilling the calling on my life for something bigger than myself. For me, personally, that is God. My faith is why I wrote this book, why I want every person to become who God intended them to be, to know His Grace, be Grace-full, and extend Grace to others. I am called to empower others to become who they are more fully so they can bring that to their community and world. I know that comes through surrender to what God has placed in me to be and do. I want my life to point to God's unconditional love and grace.

Here's the question: What is a life of significance for you? To what does your life point? If all we ever experience is success, well, that will be good. But when we experience our significance, well, that is Great! Greatness!

Karl Marx writes, "Religion is the opiate of the masses."[148] But a new opiate has reared its drab and mediocre head. It's an insidious monster because it doesn't really seem like a monster. It's not much to look at, and it doesn't seem to have any teeth. It seems to ingest its victims slowly and mundanely. What is it?

More and more in the Western industrial world, *oppression*, *discontent*, and a *poor quality of life* rise because of the one true opiate to living the Greatness Revolution: comfort. In our Western world today life is defined as longevity. Mediocrity is the new religion, and today *comfort, safety* and *security* are the opiates of the masses. Having just enough to survive has replaced the human *desire* to thrive! Henry David Thoreau's statement, "most men lead lives of quiet desperation in the form of resignation,"[149] rings truer today than ever.

Most people go to a job, doing something having nothing to do with their strengths or Dreams. They work to pay the bills and live for weekends. They work for money instead of making money work for them. Most Americans view five hours of television daily, watching other people live their Dreams, replacing their own Dreams with mere wishes, escaping their work for the day, deadening their senses with sensory overload. It is Aldous Huxley's *Brave New World*[150].

We need to wake up and Dream! I have signed my emails "Revolution!" now for many years. I have always meant a revolution of the soul, my soul in particular, and hopefully the souls of others with whom I am in relationship. I decided it was time for me to take the next step, and that is why this book exists. I want to get the word out, and here's the word you need to know and say every day to experience your Greatness:

I Am Amazing! I Have a Calling! I Have Today!

I Have a Dream Inside of Me!

I Must Live My Dream
Because It Will Make the World Better!

I Can Apply the Tools in This Book to Help Me Live My Dream!

No One Cares About My Dream as Much as I Do,
So I Will to Live My Dream With Desire, Determination, and Discipline
Regardless of the Voices Around Me!

I Wake Up and Dream!

I Make The Shift!

I Am a Different Tsunami Washing Over Others
With Peace, Compassion, and Empowerment,
Removing Their Dirt, Dust, Doubt, and Despair,
Leaving Only Their Dream.

If I Ask What's Wrong, I Won't Ask for Very Long.
I Ask, "Are The Stories I'm Writing
About the Events in My Life Serving Me?"

I Exchange the Stories Not Serving Me
for Stories That Serve Me!

I Know My Why, My How and My What,
and I Let My Why Drive Me.

If I Don't Know Why,
I'll Never Really Try.

I Make My Why, My Vision, Specific.
Clarity brings Focus
And Focus brings Directed Action
And Directed Action Brings Positive and Productive Results.

If I Don't Know Where I'm Going
Any Road Will Take Me There.

I Plan, Commit, and Pace Myself!

Steady Finishes the Race.

When It comes to My Plan,
"Ready. Fire! Aim."

I Attach Significance to the Activity, Not the Outcome.

I Attach Desire, Determination and Discipline to My Dream!

I Give and It Will Be Given to Me.

I Recognize that Life Moves in Spirals;
I Don't Get Stuck in a Moment, Paralyzed.
I Let Go of the Negative Emotions and Keep the Lesson of the Moment!

As a Successful Person, I Do Daily
What Unsuccessful People Do Occasionally!

I Employ the Listen and Learn Technique
in Every Spiral of My Life:
I Listen to the Moment.
I Reflect on the Moment.
I Learn from the Moment.
I Adjust My Choices and Plans
Based on What I've Learned,
And Move into the Next Moment,
Better Prepared for My Transformational Journey!

*I Avoid the Three R's of Self-Destruction:
Resentment, Resistance, and Revenge!*

*I Practice the One R of Self-Preservation:
Respect!*

I Forgive.

*I Combat the 3R's of Self-Destruction and Every Adversity in
My Life with Forgiveness!*

I Forgive Myself So I Can Forgive Others.

I Love Myself So I Can Love Others.

*I Am a Grace-Driven Person,
Not a Guilt-Driven Person.*

*I Make Sure I'm on the List of Important People in My Life
And I Make Sure I'm Not the Only One on that List!*

*Comfort is Everyone's Friend.
He'll Whisper Sweet Nothings in My Ear.
He'll Tell Me What I Want to Hear.*

*But Discomfort is My Best Friend.
He'll Tell Me What I Need to Hear
If I'm Willing to Listen and Learn.*

*When I Find Myself in Discomfort,
All Heaven Breaks Loose.
It Just Feels Like Hell for a While!*

*Discomfort and Struggle
Are the Universe Conspiring for Me!*

*My Struggles Don't Define Me.
My Struggles Refine Me.*

*When Time Speeds up or Slows Down in a Good Way
I Pay Attention to What I Love About What I Am Doing*

*In Those Moments.
It's pointing out Something about My Greatness!*

*When Time Speeds Up or Slows Down in a Bad Way,
Or When I Find Myself in Moments of Struggles
Facing Obstacle-Opportunities, I Smile!
I Know "These Moments Are Making Something Great of Me!"*

*I Recognize I Am Subject to Everything in My Life
And I Choose How to Respond!*

*Life is Like a Series of Sentences,
So I Spend the Majority of My Time
Being the Subject in the Sentence and Not the Object!
I Choose to Act and Not Be Acted Upon!*

I Am Proactive, Not Reactive!

*Choices Matter,
and Choices Over Time Either Move Me Toward My Greatness
or Away From My Greatness.
So I Choose Wisely!*

Wisdom is Vision!

*I Associate the Proper Emotional Response to An Event:
I Learn from It, and Move On,
Retaining the Lesson
and Letting Go of the Negative Emotions.*

*Success Lies on the Other Side of Failure,
So I Go Through Failure and Succeed!
I Go Through It, and Grow Through It!*

*I Celebrate Moments of Success and Excellence,
and I Remember Them!*

*I Surround Myself with Positive, Responsible,
Self-Reflective, Empowering, Like-Minded People
With Forward-Looking Eyes.*

*Every Day I Connect, Associate, and Reflect
On Each Moment of My Life,
And I Use C.A.R. to Attach
Desire, Determination, and Discipline to My Dream!*

*I Find Mentors for the Six F's of a Great Life:
Faith, Foundation,
Family, Friends,
Fitness, and Finances.*

*I Remember Time is Neither
My Worst Enemy Nor My Best Friend.
Time is Constant.
I Am the Variable!*

*I Partner With Time to Live My Dream
And Walk in My Greatness by
Practicing Discipline in the Six F's of a Great Life!*

*I Play to My Strengths
and I Manage My Weaknesses!*

*I Do What I Want with My Life.
I Listen to the Voice Within.*

I Don't Let the Voices Outside Override the Voice Inside!

I Turn My "Maybe" Into "Will Be!"

I Have Faith!

Trust and Risk are Just Other Words for Faith!

*Faith Takes Practice!
The More I Practice the Greater My Faith!*

*Faith is Essential to Living My Dream
and The Greatness Revolution!*

I Seek Truth and I Will Find It!

A Balanced Life and a Life With Rhythm

in Faith, Foundation, Family, Friends,
Fitness, and Finances
Will Move Me Toward My Dream
and My Greatness!

I Don't Work for Money.
I Make Money Work for Me!

Those Who Make Money Work for Them
Live Off Their Assets and Pocket Their Paychecks.
Those Who Work for Money
Live Off Their Paychecks and Have Empty Pockets.

How I Am in One Area of My Life
Is How I Will Be In Other Areas.

I Am Mindful of All Areas of My Life,
And I Practice a Non-negiotiable in Each Area.

God Knows I'm Not Who I Want to Be,
but Thank God I'm Not Who I Used to Be.

Every Day I Plan, Listen, Learn, Adjust
and Practice Time Flow.

I Plant. I Cultivate. I Harvest.

These are just some of the practices in this book. Write these down and post them around your house, in your car, at your workplace, and anywhere you can keep them before you at all times. Read them again and again, and see yourself living them through all you do and say. Thoughts are things! What you think about, you bring about. What you focus on grows. Over time you will become what you seek: Greatness!

Revolution is. . .

Greatness
unusual or considerable in degree,
power, and intensity.

The application of these tools will not make you Great. You are already "considerable in degree, power, and intensity." Your Greatness resides within you. You've always been Great. The application of these tools will help you *unlock* your Greatness and empower you to live The Greatness Revolution. And just think, if everyone was living The Greatness Revolution, what an amazing community and world we would inhabit!

No, there is nothing sudden about The Greatness Revolution, except, perhaps, The Shift. Other than that, The Greatness Revolution has nothing to do with anything sudden. The Greatness Revolution has everything to do with a process of gradual, peaceful, progressive, change or development over time, using the tools and techniques described in this book. When your Greatness Revolution begins to manifest in the material world, it will seem sudden to many because they may not understand the tools in this book you have been practicing. But you will know better.

You will find when you apply these techniques, "the universe will conspire for you," and signs, ideas, and so-called "coincidences" will pop up before you, helping you walk in your Greatness and into your Dream. I believe the full implementation of the tools in these pages will move you in your Greatness.

But it doesn't matter what I believe.
It matters what you believe.
It's your choice.
Your life is in your hands.
What will you do?

I hope you will make The Shift.
I hope you will choose to Dream.
I hope you will Plan.
I hope you will Act on that Plan, Adjust,
And Move into Each Moment,
A Little More Transformed than the Previous One.

I hope you will attach your

Desire, Determination, and Discipline to your Dream.

*I hope you will
Connect To, Associate With, and Reflect On
Your Dream, Activity, Yourself, and
Your Relationships.*

*I hope you will
Listen,
Reflect,
Learn, and
Adjust.
I hope you will choose your Greatness.*

*I hope you will begin
The Greatness Revolution!*

Your Turn

Step One: Take The Greatness Revolution Pledge. Write out the following on another sheet of paper. Sign it and post it in your home. Read it every morning and evening and in-between.

My Greatness Revolution

I, _____, commit to my Dream to
_____
_____
_____.

- I will practice the Three D's of my Dream: Desire, Discipline, and Determination.

- I remember my Desire is from the stars, written in my heart, placed in me by God, a part of my destiny, of who I AM.

- I remember Discipline involves doing the little things daily over time, and successful people do daily what unsuccessful people do occasionally.

- I remember Determination is the one key all successful people possess, and I never, never, never give up until my Greatness and my Dream manifest in my life!

- I remember, like the caterpillar's transformation, I "knit my own cocoon," taking responsibility for my life.

- I remember "everything making the caterpillar a butterfly already exists in the caterpillar," understanding my Greatness already exists within me and my existence precedes my essence. It is simply a matter of time before my Greatness and Dream manifest in my life as long as I keep walking in my Greatness.

- I remember "the caterpillar must struggle," embracing Obstacle-Opportunities as moments to listen, reflect, learn, adjust, and move on to the next moment better prepared and stronger for the struggle.

- I have a Vision for my life, remembering wisdom is vision, learning from my past, planning for my future, and living right now, convicted that today is tomorrow!

- I let go of the negative emotions of my past or the anxieties of my future, and I focus on what I can do where I am right now to serve myself and others as I live my Dream.

- I love myself so I can love others.

- I forgive myself so I can forgive others.

- I connect moments I experience, understanding everything is actually one thing.

- I associate the appropriate emotional response to both Obstacle-Opportunities and moments of excellence.

- I understand that success lies on the other side of failure, so I go through failure and into success, learning from failure.

- I associate with like-minded individuals who are positive, empowering, and make me better in all Six F's of a Balanced Life: Faith, Foundation, Family, Friends, Fitness, and Finance.

- I Reflect on the moments of my life, asking the questions making me a whole person, using cerebral man, my head, visceral man, my gut, and the heart of man, finding a balance by listening to my heart.

- I practice C.A.R. to attach the Three D's to my Dream.

- I practice Forgiveness toward myself and others.

- I show Mercy to those who have wronged me.

- I accept the Grace of God in my heart and give that same Grace to others, seeing who I am and who they are in their transformed state. I see my and others Greatness in every moment.

- All these things are part of Greatness, and I choose to walk in them daily. I am walking in my Greatness today! I am the Greatness Revolution!

Signed   Date

Step Two: Live it every day! And feel the blessings shower down upon you while you shower blessings upon others!

START! YOU ARE DONE READING THIS BOOK. YOU'VE COMPLETED THE *YOUR TURN* SECTIONS OF THE CHAPTERS. NOW USE THIS DEEP INTERNAL WORK AND THE PRACTICES IN THIS BOOK TO LIVE YOUR DREAM. YOU CAN DO THIS. I KNOW IT!

LIVE THE GREATNESS REVOLUTION!

Chapter Notes

Foreword

[1] Schlatter, John Wayne "Jack." *Gifts by the Side of the Road.* 2nd ed. New Junction, New Hampshire: Heart Productions and Publishing, 2011. Print.
[2] Schlatter, John Wayne "Jack." *I Am a Teacher.* Grand Junction, Colorado: Our Town Press, 2004. Print.
[3] Schlatter, John Wayne "Jack." *I Am a Teacher. Chicken Soup for the Soul Reader's Choice.* Ed. Jack Canfield, Mark Victor Hansen, and Amy Newmark. Cos Cob, Connecticut: Chicken Soup for the Soul Publishing, 2013. Print.

Chapter 1: The Problem
[4] Coehlo, Paulo. *The Alchemist.* Trans. Alan R. Clarke. New York: Harper Collins, 1993. Prologue Translation, 1998.

Chapter 2: Believing is Seeing

[5] *Talmud Berakhot*, 55b.
[6] The Cave illustration adapted from Plato's *The Allegory of the Cave.* Plato. *The Allegory of the Cave. 50 Essays: A Portable Anthology. Third Edition.* Ed. Samuel Cohen. Boston: Bedford/St. Martin's, 2011. 292-299. Print.
[7] The Dunedin Multidisciplinary Health and Development Study. Dunedin, New Zealand. http://dunedinstudy.otago.ac.nz/studies/
[8] The Myers and Briggs Foundation. http://www.myersbriggs.org.
[9] Donne, John. *John Donne's Poetry.* Ed. Donald R. Dickson. London: W.W. Norton & Company, 2007. Print.
[10] *1 Corinthians 12:10*

Chapter 3: The Shift

[11] The arrow just below the chapter heading represents your life from start to finish. But really, when does life begin? What does it truly mean "to live"? Is it simply breathing in and breathing out? Having a pulse? To paraphrase the existentialist Paul Tillich,

"Being is non-being. Being is becoming." Truly existing, truly living is about transformation, the caterpillar to butterfly. Simply going through the motions is not living. Until you know *WHY* you are, can you truly live?

[12] A Greek *life-death-rebirth* deity. Transformation....boom! There it is!

[13] For a revealing look at just how amazing you are check out Rob Bell's video: *Everything is Spiritual.* Rob Bell. Zondervan, 2002. DVD.

[14] Soren Kierkegaard, the Danish Existentialist asserted that the real problem of life is to discover what is one's true talent, secret gift, or authentic vocation.

[15] Johnson, Spencer. *The Precious Present.* New York: Doubleday, 1992. Print.

[16] *Psalm 118:24*

Chapter 4: The Stories We Tell

[17] One's lifeline is determined in large measure by the stories he tells himself. As Henry Ford is reported to have said, "Whether you think you can or you think you can't, you're right!" Whatever one's perception and mindset regarding any circumstance, that is exactly what he will get. Most people think "seeing is believing," but a wise person knows that "believing is seeing." When one opens his mind to possibilities, he always sees more of them. When one opens her heart to experience, she always grows more. When one tells herself stories that serve about the events in her life, she becomes. When one listens to the head trash of negativity and stories that do not serve him about events in his life, he stops growing. He stops knitting his cocoon and slowly wastes away. One must Shift her mind and then let that renewed mind travel to her heart. Then she is ready for the greatest adventure of all: true existence!

[18] Thoreau, Henry David. *Walden* and *Civil Disobedience.*

[19] Jung, C.J. *Memories, Dreams, Reflections.* Vintage; Reissue edition (April 23, 1989).

[20] Thoreau, Henry David. *Walden.* First published in 1854. Thoreau writes, *"The mass of men lead lives of quiet desperation. What is called resignation is confirmed desperation."*

[21] To get started check out these interesting articles: Stephen S. Hall. "Repairing Bad Memories." *MIT Technology Review.* Web. 17 June 2013. Emily Singer. "Manipulating Memory." *MIT Technology Review.* Web. 21 April 2009.

[22] Helmstetter, Shad. The Power of Neuroplasticity. Kindle Edition. Park Avenue Press. First Edition. 20 Jan. 2014.

Chapter 5: The Why is Your Dream

[23] The illustration at the beginning of the chapter shows that true life begins when one makes The Shift. She replaces the negative stories, what I call the "head trash," that keeps one asking, "What's wrong with me?" and, instead, she begins telling herself stories that serve her to become who she truly is, to be transformed by this renewing of her mind, to walk in her Greatness. When one makes this Shift, he is free to begin exploring his Why, his Dream, his reason for living, his Calling, or the Purpose for his life. And though this exploration, this journey, sometimes takes a little while (sometimes a long while), as long as one remains aware of his passion, he will be able to clarify and create laser focus on that "Significant Something" he is called to bring to humanity. The Shift is the spark of enlightenment, and his Why is the fuel that turns that spark into an all-consuming fire of passion.

[24] Sinek, Simon. *Start with Why: How Great Leaders Inspire Everyone to Take Action.* Penguin (USA), 2011. Print.

[25] *Proverbs* 29:18

[26] See Friederich Nietzsche's essay *Beyond Good and Evil.* First published in 1886.

[27] Schopenhauer, Arthur. *The World As Will.* Dover. 1996.

[28] Camus, Albert. *The Outsider.* Penguin Modern Classics. Penguin. 2006

[29] Cummings, E. E. *E.E. Cummings: A Miscellany*. Ed. George J. Firmage. Harcourt Brace Jovanovich Inc. *No longer in print, though available for free at* http://www.muebooks.com/ee-cummings-a-miscellany-PDF-4793986/.

Chapter 6: The First Step Toward Your Dream

[30] Your Why is what I call your Dream. The truth is that most people go through life asleep. Every so often someone comes along who actually wakes up! He or she is an awakened one. In fact that is what the word Buddha means, "Awakened One." Jesus of Nazareth (who is in a unique category unto himself), Joan of Arc, Siddhartha Gotama, Gandhi, Julian of Norwich, and Saint Francis of Assisi are just some of those "awakened ones" on my short list. They understood this paradox: Wake up and Dream! Manifest the Why inside you! It is placed in you for a reason, so bring it by doing whatever it takes to bless humanity with your "Significant Something." Once you make The Shift and you know Your Dream, your life has purpose and meaning that serves as the driving force toward your transformation as you knit your own cocoon and *go* through and *grow* through struggle.

[31] Jefferson, Thomas. *Selected Writings*. Vol. 6. Ed. Harvey C. Mansfield, Jr. AHM Publishing. 1979. Print.

[32] *Luke 6:38*

[33] *Acts 20:35*

[34] For this idea and an accessible compendium on many of Kierkegaard's ideas I recommend the following collection: Kierkegaard, Soren. *Provocations: Spiritual Writings of Kierkegaard.* Ed. Charles E. Moore. Maryknoll, New York: Orbis Books, 2007. Print.

[35] For all things Zig Ziglar go to the following website: http://www.ziglar.com.

[36] The Declaration of Independence: *We hold these truths to be self evident. That all men are created equal. That they are endowed by their Creator with certain unalienable rights. That among these are life, liberty, and the pursuit of happiness.*

Chapter 7: The How is Your Plan

[37] You make The Shift. You know and grow your Dream within. To manifest your Dream you need a Plan for your lifeline. You don't need a great plan. You don't even need a good plan. If you have a great or good plan that is terrific! But really, the only plan you need is the plan that gets you going. Plans always change. They should! They must be adjusted as life throws us curves! But without a Plan, you experience the only true failure in our existence: you never start. When we write down a Plan, when we speak out a Plan, even if it is a flawed Plan after implementation, we are more likely to manifest and accomplish our Dream because we are not only aware of our Dream, we have now moved our Dream from our subconscious mind to our conscious mind, and we see events in our lives through the lens of our Dream. We will make choices, decisions, and steps toward our Dream because it is upmost in our consciousness. A Dream rests in the heart, but a Plan allows it to occupy our minds and calculate actions for our body. The Plan is an essential component to aligning the head, the body, and the heart.

[38] *Romans 12:2*

[39] *Psalm 37:4. The Old Testament.*

[40] Rumi. Quoted from Phillips, Jan. *Marry Your Muse: Making a Lasting Commitment to Your Creativity.* p. 75. Wheaton: Quest Books. 1997. Print.

[41] *Matthew 5:37* and *James 5:12*

[42] *1 Corinthians 9:25*

[43] Roosevelt, Teddy. Speech given April 23, 1910 at The Sorbonne in Paris, France.

[44] Hill, Napoleon. *Think and Grow Rich.* Fortune Publishing Group, 2013. Print.

[45] Tim Redmond helps all kinds of organizations and businesses with "transformational growth." To explore Tim's ideas go to http://redmondleadership.com.

[46] Olson, Jeff. *The Slight Edge: Turning Simple Disciplines into Massive Success.* Success Books, 2011. Print.

[47] Maxwell, John. *Becoming a Person of Influence.* Thomas Nelson. 2006. Print.

Chapter 8: Goals

[48] Your lifeline is always supported by the 3D's of your Dream: Desire, Determination, and Discipline. Your commitment is all about the heart and the destiny placed there. Commitment is underpinned by Desire. Your pace is driven by Discipline, daily small activities that bring exponential growth over time. Your Plan is empowered by your Determination. It is the written expression of your "fixed direction toward a goal."
[49] *Mark 10:17-31*

Chapter 9: The What

[50] The Spiral. Most people believe that every day is pretty much the same. Most people find themselves "living the circle" of life. But life is not a circle. Life is a Spiral. The Spiral represents a series of moments: a lifetime, a decade, a year, a month, a day, an hour, a minute, or moments within a moment. While most people are going through the motions of the same day again and again, those practicing the Greatness Revolution recognize that while every day may be similar, each day and moment is unique and has something new to offer, a lesson to learn about oneself, one's Dream, and the world he or she chooses to create and live in. The "circle" of life is static, reactive, and even regressive. The Spiral of life is dynamic, progressive and transformative, and only a renewed mind that has made The Shift, only the one who continually seeks and refines his or her Dream lives the Spiral. Each Spiral is an event or series of events, and those who have made The Shift attach stories to those events that serve. These stories determine your What, what you do in the moments of life, the Spirals of life. Until one sees life as a Spiral, his lifeline remains a flatline. No crash cart can resuscitate this flatline. One must choose to truly live. Spirals begin when one wakes up and Dreams, finds his or her calling, purpose, or vocation. Life is not

events, one after another. Life is a process of transformation. Life is a Spiral.

[51] *Proverbs 29:18*

[52] Though many interpretations exist, the myth of Sisyphus primarily conveys the idea that overwhelming pride, or hubris, will lead to one's downfall, and it is pride that often gets in the way of accomplishing our dream. This pride in Sisyphus came from his belief he was cleverer than Zeus, or he was simply very clever. Being too clever can lead to one's demise. In *Chapter 12: C.A.R. The Vehicle to Your Dream*, I explore the Greek view of humanity. One might say that one of Sisyphus' biggest problems is he dwells in cleverness, in cerebral man, the mind, and he ignores the visceral aspects and the heart of man (see Chapter twelve). Sisyphus' actions signify how most of us stay busy with what we believe are important activities, but they all come to nothing because they are only a partial use of one's gifts or talents. Sisyphus' actions end up being useless and unendingly frustrating because he does not use all of himself, cerebral, visceral, and the heart of man, to be a whole being. This is the story of many people. They use only part of their gifts or all of their gifts but for the wrong purpose. They do not give all of themselves to their Dream. They try to control their life, living in fear, instead of taking "the leap of faith" with their hearts, using their heads to plan and problem-solve, and their gut (or actions) to accomplish their meaningful and significant Dream.

[53] Kierkegaard, Soren. *Fear and Trembling.* Penguin Classics, 1986. Print

[54] Coehlo, Paulo. *The Alchemist.* Harper Collins, 2006. Print.

[55] Irving, John. *A Prayer For Owen Meany.* Reprint Edition. Harper, 2012. Print.

[56] Hill, Napoleon. *Think and Grow Rich.* Fortune Publishing Group, 2013. Print.

Chapter 10: Spirals: The Listen and Learn Technique

[57] When one employs the 3D's of a Dream in every Spiral, every moment, it doesn't seem that his Dream is any closer to

manifesting. It is easy to believe that what one does in a moment is insignificant. However, those who make The Shift, know their Dream, and understand that life is a process, that every moment is a unique opportunity to learn and grow in one's Greatness, employing the 3D's in each moment over Time, thus creating Momentum (3D's/T = M). An awakened one knows, "Successful people do daily what unsuccessful people do occasionally." Doing the small daily tasks over time creates exponential growth, moving one closer to his or her Dream.

[58] Zimmer, Hans. Various Artists. *The Lion King: Special Edition.* Walt Disney Records, 2003. CD.
[59] *Groundhog Day.* Dir. Harold Ramis. Perf. Bill Murray, Andie MacDowell, Chris Elliot, and Stephen Tobolowsky. Columbia Pictures, 1993. DVD.
[60] *Matthew 13: 14-15; Isaiah 6:9*

Chapter 11: Choice

[61] Choice is the greatest gift we've been given. We are free to choose in any given Spiral of life whether to accept, reject, ignore, respond, or avoid the forces pressing upon us from within and without in the current Spiral of life. Most people reject the freedom to choose in the guise of victimization. Some well-known examples of this are things like, "I have to go to work." No you don't. You choose. "I have to pay the bills." No you don't. You choose. "I have to mow the lawn." No you don't. You choose. "I have to buy that for my wife." Well, yes, you probably have to do that. Just kidding!

    Whatever a moment might throw at us, the fact still remains that we choose what to do in every moment. No matter what one chooses in each Spiral, he must take full responsibility for his choice. If he does not, he is an object not a subject. He gives away his power, and, even more so, himself. By using *The Listen and Learn Technique*, choosing, and taking full responsibility for the choice wherever it leads, one grows into his Greatness and closer to his Dream. Even if the outcome of one's choice has an adverse or negative affect, he must accept the consequences, listen, reflect, learn, and adjust for the next time he confronts the same or a similar Spiral. In this way every Spiral of life serves in his transformation.

[62] Tim Redmond helps all kinds of organizations and businesses with "transformational growth." To explore Tim's ideas go to https://redmondgrowth.com.

[63] Emerson, Ralph Waldo. *Essays*. Westvaco, 1978. Print.

[64] Bradbury, Ray. *A Sound of Thunder and Other Stories*. William Morrow Paperbacks, 2005. Print.

Chapter 12: C.A.R.: The Vehicle to Your Dream

[65] Connection. If you are sitting in a room right now reading this, and I asked you how many walls were in the room, what would your answer be? The correct answer is one. It's just that this one wall takes various angles. Everything is connected. It's all one thing. One of the differences between those who live their Dream and those who don't is that those who live their Dream understand that even the most seemingly disparate things are connected. Think about one of the most profound teachers in history, Jesus of Nazareth, who said things like *if you want to be first, you must be last* or *if you want to lead, you must be a servant*, or *if you want to live, you must die*. These paradoxes, these seemingly disparate ideas are connected. Those who see the connections live their Dream. This reckons back to the illusion most people believe, that *life is a circle.* But life is a Spiral, and every Spiral is different yet teaches similar lessons if one is awake and listening. In Herman Hesse's novel *Siddhartha*, the protagonist, Siddhartha, was a child, a young man, a son, a Brahmin, a Samana, a merchant, a ferryman, and a father at different stages of his life, yet in every one of those Spirals he was still Siddhartha. The butterfly is also the caterpillar. They are one. When one begins to see each moment of his life as connected, he realizes *who he is, where he is,* and *when he is* is precious because he will always be *who he is, where he is, when he is*, even though he undergoes transformation. As he undergoes each moment, aware of its relationship to other moments, he is informed, *formed within*; he is transformed, changed into his true

form, even in death and especially after death, for death is simply the knitting of another cocoon. Connect the Spirals, see the relationships, and unlock the eternal truths every moment shares.

[66] *Proverbs 29:18*

[67] Johnson, Spencer. *The Precious Present.* New York: Doubleday, 1992. Print.

[68] *For a brief explanation of Haystacks by Monet visit* http://www.metmuseum.org/collections/search-the-collections/437122.

[69] Kierkegaard, Soren. *Journals and Papers.* Ed. and Trans. Howard V. Hong and Edna H. Hong, 4 vols. Bloomington: Indiana University Press, 1967-75. Print.

[70] *The Lion King.* Dir. Rob Minkoff and Roger Allers. Perf. Matthew Broderick, Jeremy Irons, James Earl Jones, Whoopi Goldberg, Niketa Calame. Walt Disney Studios Home Entertainment, 2011. DVD.

[71] *C.S. Lewis spends extensive time discussing the Greek view of humanity in "Chapter 2 Men Without Chests" in The Abolition of Man.* Lewis, C.S. *The Abolition of Man.* Harper One, 2009. Print.

[72] Alighieri, Dante. *Inferno.* Trans. John Ciardi. Signet Classics, 2009. Print.

[73] Lewis, C.S. *The Abolition of Man.* Harper One, 2009. Print.

[74] Olson, Jeff. *The Slight Edge: Turning Simple Disciplines into Massive Success.* Success Books, 2011. Print.

[75] *Proverbs 27:17. The Old Testament.*

[76] Carl Jung.

[77] For more information on Keith Kochner and Mentorship Mastery visit http://mentorfish.com.

Chapter 13: Time Flow

[78] Life has rhythm and balance. When one balances the Six F's, Faith, Foundation, Family, Friends, Finances, and Fitness, he experiences wholeness. He lives with his head, his body, and his heart, dancing together as one. It is not that he is perfect. He is whole because the inclusion of all the Six F's and the head, heart, and body brings love, peace, and joy. Over Time he lives the

manifesting fulfillment of his Dream all the while living the Dream Daily. We all have a certain number of heartbeats. None of us knows that exact number. What we do know is that the key to a life well-lived is to make each heartbeat count!

[79] Tzu, Lao. *Tao Te Ching. Chapter 8.*
[80] *Matthew 9:37, Luke 10:2*

Chapter 14: The Three R's of Self-Destruction

[81] Every Spiral in life is an opportunity to practice *The Listen and Learn Technique*. The more mindful one is of *The Listen and Learn Technique*, the more she will practice it and the greater the depth of growth she experiences. Those who practice this technique regularly are like the caterpillar that knits its own cocoon and embraces struggles. This struggle makes the caterpillar stronger and better equipped for the transformative process to become what it is intended to become, a butterfly. The difference between those who achieve their Dream and those who do not rests in practicing daily *The Listen and Learn Technique* in the many unsexy, often mundane, every-day Spirals of life.

[82] *Ecclesiastes 4:1-2*
[83] *Ecclesiastes 4:8-12*
[84] Caesar was murdered on March 15, 44 B.C.E. by more than sixty people according to Eutropius.
[85] *To Kill A Mockingbird: 50th Anniversary Edition.* Dir. Robert Mulligan. Perf. Gregory Peck, Mary Badham, Phillip Alford, John Megna, and Frank Overton. Universal Studios, 2012. DVD.
[86] Gyatso,Tenzin, The Fourteenth Dalai Lama. *Compassion and the Individual.* http://www.dalailama.com/messages/compassion.
[87] Fischer, Louis. *The Life of Mahatma Gandhi.* Harper and Row, 1983. Print. While the quote is widely attributed to Gandhi, no citation directly places this exact wording occurring anywhere in Gandhi's writings, though he may have spoken it at some time. Fischer writes in his biography of Gandhi a variation of the idea, and because of this, I cite his comprehensive work on the Mahatma's life. I highly recommend this biography and the film

upon which it is based, directed by Sir Richard Attenborough and starring Ben Kingsley.
[88] *Romans 12:18*
[89] *Matthew 7:12*
[90] Tzu, Lao. *Tao Te Ching. Chapter 8.*
[91] Assayas, Michka. *Bono in Conversation with Michka Assayas.* Riverhead Books. Penguin. New York. 2005-2006. Print.
[92] *2 Corithians 4:17*
[93] *Matthew 7:5*

Chapter 15: Forgiveness

[94] Forgiveness. Sometimes one tells himself stories regarding others that are just not true. He sees others and their actions from his limited perspective, and he does not take into account all of the forces the other person is subject to in life. When this happens, he enters into a Spiral, a moment, with a preconceived view of a person and that person's actions toward him. In that moment one often believes the person who has acted unjustly, cruelly, or thoughtlessly does this solely in relation to him. When this occurs, it becomes easy for one to harbor resentment, resist, and seek revenge. Often these Three R's of Self-Destruction follow one from one moment to every moment he encounters in relation to the person who has offended. Far worse, one can transfer The Three R's from this experience into Spirals with other people and in other circumstances. In fact, it is safe to say that being offended in one area or relationship in life, if left unaddressed, will lead to offense in other areas of life. This is when the Spiral becomes a circle because every moment is likened to every other moment.

The way one keeps from carrying The Three R's into more moments is quite simple, yet, for most, difficult to do, just like anything that will lead one to walk in his Greatness, living his Dream. First, one must admit he is what I call "a mixed bag of tricks." One accepts he has light and darkness inside him. One accepts his imperfections, embraces the beauty within, and focuses on being a whole person, a person whose mind, body, and heart dance in perfect rhythm with one another. One knows he is not perfect but progressing. Once one admits he is a "mixed bag of tricks," he possesses the humility to understand he is no different from others who are a "mixed bags of tricks" too. One sees all are on the same journey, just at different places in progress and transformation, and this gives one the same love he has for himself for others. He can forgive others the same offenses he has perpetrated, and he can even forgive offenses he has never committed because "there but for the grace of God go I." He realizes, even if his wrong actions are different from the actions of others, the core of the offense is the same because he recognizes when it comes to being human, we're all in the same boat.

    With this in mind he lets go of The 3R's and forgives the one who has wronged him, giving that person the benefit of the doubt. He writes a new story that serves him to move into the next moment of life free because he loves himself and others equally.

[95] *Matthew 18*

[96] Maugham, W. Somerset. *The Summing Up.* Penguin Classics, 1992. Print. The quote contained in The Greatness Revolution is widely circulated on the web on various quotation websites. The actual quotation is "For my part I do not think I am any better or any worse than most people, but I know that if I set down every action in my life and every thought that has crossed my mind the world would consider me a monster of depravity."

[97] Nin, Anais. *Seduction of the Minotaur.* Swallow Press. 1961. Print. *Nin attributes this quote to The Talmud.*

[98] Dostoevsky, Fyodor. *Crime and Punishment.* Trans. Constance Garnett. Dover Thrift Edition. Dover Publications. August, 2001. In his Epilogue, Dostoyevsky has the protagonist Raskolnikov come to grips with the disease that infects humanity, namely it is the virus of unforgiveness, typically in the form of pride, the absence of the Heart of Man and a preponderance of Cerebral Man. Dostoevsky describes it as an illness. Raskolnikov, himself, fights this disease throughout the entire novel until he finally changes his mind and sees his ever constant companion, Sonya (a nickname for Sophia, meaning divine wisdom which is the love of God, for God is love) who unconditionally loves Raskolnikov despite the cruelty and hardships he places on her, along with the hardships of her life

as well. It is her unconditional and faithful love for Raskolnikov, despite his cruelty and hard heart, that prompts Raskolnikov to accept grace, forgiveness, and mercy, the love of God, an attribute, as Shakespeare puts it in *The Merchant of Venice*, that is the very essence of God.

[99] *Matthew 22:39*

[100] *1 Corinthians 13:1-3*

[101] I actually attended a leadership conference where Marcus Buckingham spoke, and he said the quote I mention. He has done extensive research on playing to your strengths and managing your weaknesses in his previous work with the Gallup organization and now on his own in several endeavors including The Marcus Buckingham Company, leading the "strengths revolution." *For more go to http://www.tmbc.com.*

[102] *Lamentations 3:22-23*

[103] *John 9:3*

[104] *Isaiah 61:3*

[105] *Isaiah 61:1-3*

Chapter 16: The Six F's of a Great Life

[106] Every Spiral of one's life consists of The Six F's of a Great Life. Of course, sometimes it feels like that is not true at all. Moments of financial struggle make one myopic, and he forgets about Faith, Foundation, Family, Friends and Fitness. A Faith crisis can cloud one's vision of gratitude for the other F's in her life. The point is that whether one sees them or not, all of the F's pervade every moment. When one loses sight of some of them, he tends to live out of balance and unhealthily. Are there moments where one will focus more on one of The Six F's? Yes. Each person will experience seasons, like a family member with failing health becomes a large part of one's daily life, or one spends more time than normal with a friend in crisis. However, maintaining a vision of all Six F's and continuing to practice activities in every area, even in the midst of moments of crisis, in the long run will help a person maintain a positive perspective. Crises in one of The Six F's seems devastating until one remembers and expresses

gratitude for the other F's of life. Furthermore, when one practices balance in these areas, when a crisis does come, he is more prepared for the crisis. For example, with financial balance (no debt and available cash flow) an unexpected family illness is much easier to go through because the financial burden is lessened, and one can focus on what really matters. No matter how balanced one is in The Six F's of a Great Life, sometimes life is going to throw him curves. If he maintains balance in these areas, those curves will be easier to proactively address.

[107] Irving, John. *A Prayer For Owen Meany*. Reprint Edition. Harper, 2012. Print.

[108] Martel, Yann. *Life of Pi*. New York: Houghton, Mifflin, Harcourt, 2003.

[109] *Hebrews 11:1*

[110] *1 Corinthians 10:23.*

[111] *Matthew 7:24-27*

[112] See Brene Brown's *Daring Greatly*. Gotham. 2012. Print. This is a great book about vulnerability and how to find a sense of love and belonging. I highly recommend this book.

[113] *Forks Over Knives.* Dir. Lee Fulkerson. Perf. T. Colin Campbell, Caldwell B. Esselstyn Jr., Neal Barnard, Junshi Chen and Connie B. Diekman. Virgil Films and Entertainment, 2011. DVD.

[114] Evans, Mike. *23 ½ Hours: What is the Single Best Thing We Can Do for Our Health.* http://www.youtube.com/watch?v=aUaInS6HIGo.

[115] Kiyosaki, Richard. *Rich Dad Poor Dad: What the Rich Teach Their Kids About Money That the Poor and Middle Class Do Not.* Plata Publishing, 2011. Print.

[116] Kiyosaki, Robert. *Rich Dad, Poor Dad: What the Rich Teach Their Kids About Money That the Poor and Middle Class Do Not.* Plata Publishing. 2011. Print.

[117] *Matthew 7:7*

[118] *Acts 20:35; Luke 12:48*

Chapter 17: Mentors

[119] The Mentor-Apprentice Relationship. If you want to grow in an area of life, finding a mentor is a must. Although you can practice meta-cognition (stepping outside of yourself and analyzing what you believe, think and do to improve), a person who has tasted and seen success in an area in which you want to be successful will move you into your Greatness much more efficiently because of that mentor's experience. A mentor knows the paths and pitfalls along the way to Greatness and provides a vision and a roadmap for you to follow. A mentor trains you in the necessary skills. A mentor guides the you through *The Listen and Learn Technique* by asking questions and sharing experiences helping you Connect, Associate, and Reflect on your own experiences, questions, and every Spiral of life in order to live your Dream.

[120] Confucius. *The Analects*. Simon and Brown, 2012. Print.

[121] Crichton, Michael. *Jurassic Park*. Ballantine. *While injured, Ian Malcolm talks about the lack of discipline in the scientific community and how it just takes the next step without learning anything about the thing it is trying to take the next step with, in this case, dinosaurs. Malcolm makes clear the lack of discipline cerebral and visceral man practices when he fails to pay attention to his heart, the moral and emotional center of what it means to be truly human.*

Chapter 18: A Journey

[122] Fitness. When it comes to fitness, each Spiral, each moment in life, plays a role, whether it is eating healthy, whole foods (nutrition is 80% of good health), exercise (10% of good health), or an awareness of one's genetics (10% of good health). When you attach Desire (your heart), Determination (cerebral man – your mind), and Discipline (visceral man – your gut), using Connection, Association, and Reflection, you begin to see your Greatness in your fitness journey. Understanding it is not about perfection but progression, transformation, and being a whole person, you celebrate your daily choices toward healthy living, and when you

do not practice healthy choices in food or exercise, you do not condemn yourself and get stuck in a Spiral now turned circle, playing over and over, again and again, your downfall until you are paralyzed in an unhealthy story. Instead, you use *The Listen and Learn Technique*, letting go of the head trash and emotional baggage that does not serve you. You hold on to the lessons learned that serve you, and you continue on into the next Spiral. This is a particularly difficult practice for many.

For example, you decide on an exercise regimen, say going to the gym four times per week. When you miss four days in a row at the gym, sometimes you stop going because in your mind you've blown it. What has really happened is your momentum has been lost, but that is all that has been lost. The only way to re-establish momentum is to begin going to the gym again. Instead of condemning yourself for missing four days in a row, you understand that success in large measure is about doing the activity consistently in order to maintain momentum and see exponential results over time. You let go of the negative emotions threatening to paralyze you, and you hold on to the lessons regarding consistency that serve you.

[123] Maxwell, John. *Go for the Gold: Inspiration to Increase Your Leadership Impact.* Thomas Nelson, Int. Edition. 2008.
[124] This phrase comes from the writings of Carl Sagan. A YouTube video captures the essence of what I see as Sagan's grasp of our need for humility, purpose, compassion, and significance as specks on a speck in the Universe.

Chapter 19: Time: Your Best Friend or Your Worst Enemy?

[125] Disciplined action over time is the key to your Dream. You do not have to do more disciplined work. You continue to do small, disciplined actions in every Spiral, every moment of life, and something curious happens, at first imperceptibly, but, as time passes, exponentially. The growth and results of the small disciplined actions grow more and more massive. The Spiral of results is ever expanding while the small, disciplined actions

remain simple and consistent. This Discipline bolstered by Desire and Determination, as well as Connection, Association, and Reflection over Time leads to the fulfillment of your Dream.

[126] By contrast undisciplined actions in any area of life also leads to consequences, but these consequences grow exponentially in a negative direction. A simple example is health and wellness practices. One cheeseburger will not kill you, but a cheeseburger every day over thirty years will! Heart disease, diabetes, high blood pressure, some forms of cancer are directly linked to the nutritional choices and level of activity one chooses every day. A cheeseburger is a small action, but compounded over time, that small action leads to huge negative consequences, like open-heart surgery or insulin dependence. Inconsistently practicing the 3D's and C.A.R. leads to the Downward Spiral into a life of quiet desperation away from your Dream.

[127] *Simon Birch.* Dir. Mark Steven Johnson. Perf. Joseph Mazzello, Oliver Platt, David Strathairn, Dana Ivey and Ian Michael Smith. Hollywood Pictures Home Entertainment, 1999. DVD.

[128] "Once in a Lifetime." Talking Heads.

[129] U2. "I'll Go Crazy if I Don't Go Crazy Tonight." *No Line on the Horizon.* Interscope, 2009. CD.

[130] Martel, Yann. *Life of Pi.* New York: Houghton, Mifflin, Harcourt, 2003.

[131] Tzu, Lao. *Tao Te Ching. Chapter 64.*

Chapter 20: Transformation

[132] Transformation. When The Shift occurs, you begin to live the Spirals of life, moving toward the Truth you are willing to live or die for, your Dream. No longer caught in a "flat-lined" existence or a "circle" of life mentality, you live with intention, letting every moment inform you, form you within, to become who you truly are. Your very Essence begins to take shape. You live each Spiral, each moment fully, and you are fully present. Like the caterpillar, you knit your own cocoon, taking responsibility for your own actions, realizing that the consequences for your actions

(or lack of actions) rest entirely on your own shoulders. You believe, "If it is going to be, it's up to me." Like the caterpillar, you embrace struggles, knowing that struggle is how you learn, and it serves to make you stronger for the journey to Greatness that lies ahead. As an "Awakened One" who has made the Shift and moved your Dream from your subconscious to your consciousness, your eyes and ears are opened, and you now see and hear the universe conspiring for you to live your Dream and walk in your Greatness.

[133] Tillich, Paul. *The Courage to Be.* New Haven: Yale University Press, 2000. Print.
[134] Maxwell, John. *The 15 Invaluable Laws of Growth.* New York: Center Street: Hachette Book Group, 2012. Print.
[135] *Romans 12:2*
[136] Clifton Strengthsfinder https://www.gallupstrengthscenter.com/
[137] DISC Personality Test http://www.thediscpersonalitytest.com/
[138] The Myers-Brigg Type Indicator http://www.myersbriggs.org

Chapter 21: Faith

[139] Besides love, an equally essential component to living one's Dream and walking in one's Greatness is Faith. All humans put their faith in something. For me, I put my faith in Jesus Christ, the God Man, when God entered into the Universe and became human and when Grace entered into the Universe of Karma and fulfilled Absolute Truth once and for all. All I teach comes from His Word, the Old and New Testament, and from His Holy Spirit that lives in me because of Christ's life, death on a cross where God took all my sins upon him receiving the death I deserved even though he did not deserve it but chose to lay His life down, and His resurrection when he chose to pick up his life again because He was innocent and sinless and has all authority in heaven and on earth and beyond the Universe to do so, thus conquering death once and for all. If you want to know more about Him, I'd love to talk (discoveringyourgreatness@gmail.com). We all practice faith in some way. Soren Kierkegaard writes that one must at some point take *the leap of faith*. One must step into the darkness and

hope the light rushes in. To most people, your *leap of faith* seems absurd because your Truth, your Dream, and your Essence, who you truly are and the values resting in your heart, may not line up with most people surrounding you who are content to remain shackled in the cave, staring at the shadows of existence, living the "circle" of life, but you have "tasted and seen" your Dream, and you believe in your Truth or your Dream, which is to say you believe in you, who you are, who you were meant to be, and who you are becoming. You realize that Life is Truth. You realize that your Existence precedes your Essence, so you take the leap of faith daily in every Spiral of life, living the adventure, the inward journey through outward forms. You see that all of our outward journeys are really interior journeys. You see that the further up one goes, the farther in one goes. This brings fulfillment in every moment. You are fully filled because you are listening to the voice inside, directing your path, the trail of the true human being.

[140] In his work *L'Action,* Blondel argues one confronts the meaning of life through his actions. How he acts or lives determines the meaning of one's life. Action is necessary. Not acting is still acting, but in that case others determine one's meaning. When one acts he is subject to what he does and he is responsible for the "meaning" of his life. For Blondel, life is constant decision-making and acting.

[141] Irving, John. *A Prayer For Owen Meany.* Reprint Edition. Harper, 2012. Print.

[142] *Matthew 7:7*

[143] *Hebrews 11:1*

[144] Lyrics from the musical *Man of La Mancha,* based on Don Miguel De Cervantes' classic novel *Don Quixote.*

[145] Brene Brown discusses this in one of her many profound *Ted Talks.*

Chapter 22: The Greatness Revolution

[146] Shakespeare, William. Romeo and Juliet. *Friar Laurence speaks to Romeo about the struggle of the heart between grace,*

love, and rude will, selfishness and how if the latter wins, then death soon follows.

[147] King Jr., Martin Luther. *"Remaining Awake Through a Great Revolution," Address at Morehouse College Commencement,* 2 June 1959. Print.

[148] This appeared in the introduction to Marx's unpublished work *A Contribution to the Critique of Hegel's Philosophy of Right.* However, the introduction was published in 1844.

[149] Thoreau, Henry David. *Walden.* First published in 1854. Thoreau writes, "The mass of men lead lives of quiet desperation. What is called resignation is confirmed desperation."

[150] Huxley, Aldous. *Brave New World.* Harper Perennial Modern Classics, 2006. Print.

www.ingramcontent.com/pod-product-compliance
Lightning Source LLC
Chambersburg PA
CBHW050102170426
43198CB00014B/2432